World-wide Shakespeares

World-wide Shakespeares brings together an international team of leading scholars in order to explore the appropriation of Shakespeare's plays in film and performance around the world. In particular, the book considers the ways in which adapters and directors have put Shakespeare into dialogue with local traditions and contexts.

The contributors look in turn at 'local' Shakespeares for local, national and international audiences, covering a range of English and foreign appropriations that challenge geographical and cultural oppositions between 'centre' and 'periphery', big-time' and 'small-time' Shakespeares. Their specialist knowledge of local cultures and traditions make the range of appropriations newly accessible to world-wide readers. Drawing upon debates about the global/local dimensions of cultural production and on Pierre Bourdieu's notion of the 'cultural field', the contributors together demonstrate significant new approaches to intercultural appropriations of Shakespeare.

Responding to a surge of critical interest in the poetics and politics of appropriation, *World-wide Shakespeares* represents a valuable resource for those interested in the afterlife of Shakespeare in film and performance, within and beyond Anglophone cultural centres.

Sonia Massai is a Lecturer at King's College London. She has published on Shakespeare and adaptation and is editor of *Titus Andronicus* for the New Penguin Shakespeare series and of Thomas Heywood's *The Wise Woman of Hoxton* in the Globe Quartos.

World-wide Shakespeares

Local appropriations in film
and performance

Edited by Sonia Massai

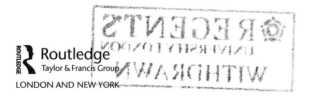

R Routledge
Taylor & Francis Group

LONDON AND NEW YORK

First published 2005 by Routledge
2 Park Square, Milton Park, Abingdon, Oxon OX14 4RN

Simultaneously published in the USA and Canada by Routledge
270 Madison Ave, New York, NY 10016

Routledge is an imprint of the Taylor & Francis Group

© 2005 Edited by Sonia Massai

Typeset in Baskerville by Keyword Group

Printed and bound in Great Britain by MPG Books Ltd, Bodmin, Cornwall

British Library Cataloguing in Publication Data

A catalogue record for this book is available from the British Library

Library of Congress Cataloging in Publication Data

World-wide Shakespeares: local appropriations in film and performance/edited by Sonia Massai.
    p.cm.
1. Shakespeare, William, 1564-1616—Adaptations—History and criticism. 2. Shakespeare, William, 1564-1616—Film and video adaptations. 3. Shakespeare, William, 1564-1616—Stage history—Foreign countries. 4. Shakespeare, William, 1564-1616—Appreciation—Foreign countries. I. Massai, Sonia.

PR2880.A1W67 2005

822.3'3—dc22

                                                2004028867

ISBN 0-415-324556 (hbk)
ISBN 0 115 32156 1 (pbk)

For Jill

Contents

Part Three: Local Shakespeares for international audiences

Contributors

Saviour Catania is a Senior Lecturer in Film Studies at the Centre for Communication Technology at the University of Malta. His post-doctoral research includes screen adaptations of Victorian and Gothic fiction, Shakespearean drama and ancient Greek theatre. He has published in *Literature/Film Quarterly*, *Entertext* and *Studia Filmoznawcze*. Forthcoming publications include articles on Arthurian legend and classical myth on film. He is currently researching foreign film versions of *Wuthering Heights* and *King Lear*.

Tobias Döring is Professor of English at the University of Munich. His research fields are early modern and post-colonial studies. He has published on Shakespearean drama and on African and Caribbean literature. Most recent is his book on *Caribbean–English Passages* and a collection of essays which he co-edited, *Performances of the Sacred in Medieval and Early Modern England*. He is review editor of the yearbook of the German Shakespeare Association.

Lukas Erne, Professor of English Literature at the University of Geneva, Switzerland, is the author of *Shakespeare as Literary Dramatist* (Cambridge University Press, 2003) and *Beyond 'The Spanish Tragedy': A Study of the Works of Thomas Kyd* (Manchester University Press, 2001), and the editor, with M. J. Kidnie, of *Textual Performances: The Modern Reproduction of Shakespeare's Drama* (Cambridge University Press, 2004). He is currently editing the first quarto of *Romeo and Juliet* for the New Cambridge Shakespeare.

Suzanne Gossett is Professor of English at Loyola University, Chicago. She is a general editor of Arden Early Modern Drama and has most recently edited *Pericles* for the Arden Shakespeare, third series (Thomson Learning, 2004) and *Eastward Ho!* for the *Cambridge Works of Ben Jonson* (forthcoming). Her other editions include Ben Jonson's *Bartholomew Fair*, the Second Part of Lady Mary Wroth's *Urania*, Thomas Middleton's *A Fair Quarrel*, *Jacobean Academic Plays* and *Plays from the English College, Rome*. She has published many articles on early modern drama, on topics as varied as feminist editing, masques, collaboration, and family structure in Shakespeare's romances.

Barbara Hodgdon, Adjunct Professor of English at the University of Michigan, is the author of *The End Crowns All: Closure and Contradiction in Shakespeare's History* (Princeton, 1991), *The First Part of King Henry the Fourth: Texts and Contexts* (Bedford-St. Martin's, 1997) and *The Shakespeare Trade: Performances and Appropriations* (University of Pennsylvania Press, 1998). She was guest editor for a special issue of *Shakespeare*

Quarterly (Summer 2002) on Shakespeare films and is currently editing *The Taming of the Shrew* for the Arden Shakespeare, third series, and co-editing, with William B. Worthen, *The Blackwell Companion to Shakespeare and Performance*.

Ton Hoenselaars is Associate Professor in the English Department of Utrecht University. He is the author of *Images of Englishmen and Foreigners in the Drama of Shakespeare and His Contemporaries* (Fairleigh Dickinson UP, 1992). He has edited *Shakespeare's Italy* (Manchester UP, 1993, rev. 1997), *Reclamations of Shakespeare* (Rodopi, 1994), *The Italian World of English Renaissance Drama* (Delaware UP, 1997), *Jeanne d'Arc entre les nations* (Rodopi, 1997), *English Literature and the Other Languages* (Rodopi, 1999), *The Author as Character* (Fairleigh Dickinson UP, 1999) and *Travelling Theory* (Fairleigh Dickinson UP, 1999). Other recent projects include *400 Years of Shakespeare in Europe*, edited with Angel-Luis Pujante (Delaware UP, 2003), and *Shakespeare and the Language of Translation* in the Arden Shakespeare Companion Series (2004). He has also written on Emily Brontë, James Joyce and Joseph Conrad. He is the founding Chairman of the Shakespeare Society of the Low Countries and managing editor of its journal *Folio*. He is currently writing a monograph on *Shakespeare and Richard Wagner*.

Mark Houlahan is a Senior Lecturer in English at the University of Waikato, Hamilton, New Zealand. His essay is part of an on-going study on the diffusion of Shakespeare in post-colonial settler societies, on which subject he has published widely. When possible, he takes part in 'local' Shakespeare productions and festivals.

Maria Jones is Senior Lecturer in English at the University of Wolverhampton. She has published articles on Shakespeare in performance on stage and screen. She is author of *Shakespeare's Culture in Modern Performance* (2003) and is currently working on a project concerning dowries in Renaissance drama.

Margaret Jane Kidnie, Associate Professor of English at the University of Western Ontario, Canada, is the editor of *Ben Jonson: The Devil is an Ass and Other Plays*, and Philip Stubbes's *The Anatomie of Abuses*. She has co-edited with Lukas Erne *Textual Performances: The Modern Reproduction of Shakespeare's Drama*, and published articles on bibliography, textual theory and performance. She is currently editing *A Woman Killed with Kindness* for the Arden Early Modern Drama series and writing a book on late-twentieth century performance and adaptation.

Elizabeth Klein is a fiction writer, poet and essayist who speaks and writes widely on Jewish American literature. She has recently served as editor of a special edition of *Shofar* (Fall 2002), the quarterly publication of the Midwest Jewish Studies Association, on Jewish American poetry. A retired instructor from the University of Illinois English department, her work includes the novel *Reconciliations* and *Approaches*, a chap-book of poetry. Her work has appeared in many journals including *The New York Times Magazine, Redbook, Prairie Schooner* and *Another Chicago Magazine*.

Marcela Kostihová is an Assistant Professor of English at Hamline University. She has recently completed her doctoral dissertation on *Shakespeare Ltd.: Political Bardolatry in Post-Socialist Czech Republic*. Her research interests include gender and sexuality in Renaissance literature, politics of translation of canonical literature, and interpretative practices of canonical literary and artistic works in relation to current socio-political contexts.

Ruru Li has published widely in the area of intercultural appropriations of Shakespeare in China as well as of the traditional and modern Chinese theatres. Her book *Shashibiya: Staging Shakespeare in China* was published by Hong Kong University Press in 2003. She has also contributed to international journals including *Shakespeare Survey*, *Shakespeare Quarterly*, *The Drama Review*, *Theatre Research International* and *Asian Theatre Journal*. She co-edited with John Gillies a CD-ROM on *Shakespeare on the Chinese Stage 1980–1990*, which is now hosted by *Shakespeare in Asia* on the Stanford University website. She is currently working on *Tradition and Innovation: Performance and Performer in Contemporary Peking Opera* and area editing for Greenwood's *The Encyclopaedia of Asian Theatre*.

Sonia Massai, Lecturer in English Studies at King's College London, has edited *Titus Andronicus* for the New Penguin Shakespeare series and Thomas Heywood's *The Wise Woman of Hoxton* for the Globe Quartos series, and is now editing John Ford *'Tis Pity She's a Whore* for the Arden Early Modern Drama series. She has published articles on Shakespearean adaptations in *Shakespeare Survey*, *New Theatre Quarterly* and *Studies in English Literature*, and is currently completing a book on *Shakespeare and the Rise of English Drama in Print* and co-editing with Thomas L. Berger a new critical edition of *The Paratext in English Printed Drama to the Restoration*.

Alfredo Michel Modenessi is Professor of English and Comparative Literature at the National University of Mexico. His work on the appropriation of Shakespeare in Mexico has recently appeared in *Shakespeare Survey*. He contributed to Michael Dobson's and Stanley Wells' *Oxford Companion to Shakespeare* and to Ton Hoenselaars' *Shakespeare and the Language of Translation* (the Arden Shakespeare Companion Series). His translations of Shakespeare and Renaissance Drama include *Love's Labour's Lost*, *Edward II* and *Arden of Faversham*.

Sabine Schülting is Professor of English Literature and Cultural Studies at the Free University of Berlin. She is the co-editor of the German *Shakespeare Jahrbuch* and her publications include a book on the intersections of race and gender in sixteenth and seventeenth century travelogues (*Wilde Frauen, fremde Welten: Kolonisierungsgeschichten aus Amerika*, 1997), as well as articles on Shakespeare and the early modern age, Victorian literature, gender studies and film. She is currently working on a book-length study on Victorian representations of urban poverty.

Michael Shapiro teaches at the University of Illinois, where he is both Professor of English and Director of the Program for Jewish Culture and Society. He has also held visiting positions at Michigan State University, Cornell University, Reading University (UK) and Tamkang University (Taiwan). He is the author of *Children of the Revels: The Boy Companies of Shakespeare's Time and Their Plays* (Columbia UP, 1976) and *Gender in Play on the Shakespearean Stage: Boy Heroines and Female Pages* (Michigan UP, 1964, reprinted 1994), as well as articles, notes and reviews in English Renaissance drama and modern Jewish literature. He is currently studying radical revisions of *The Merchant of Venice*.

Robert Shaughnessy is Professor of Theatre at the University of Kent. He has published articles on early modern and contemporary theatre; his books include *Representing Shakespeare: England, History and the Royal Shakespeare Company* (Harvester Wheatsheaf, 1994) and *The Shakespeare Effect: A History of Twentieth-Century Performance* (Palgrave, 2002). He has also edited two collections of essays on *Shakespeare in Performance* (Macmillan, 2000) and *Shakespeare on Film* (Macmillan, 1998), and an anthology, *Four Renaissance Comedies* (Palgrave, 2004). He is currently writing a volume on Shakespeare for the Routledge Critical Guides series and editing *The Cambridge Companion to Shakespeare and Popular Culture.*

Boika Sokolova is Research Fellow at Birkbeck College, University of London, and teaches for the London Programmes of the Universities of California and Notre Dame. She has published widely on Shakespeare, Marlowe, performance, and the reception of Shakespeare in Europe. She is the author of *Shakespeare's Romances as Interrogative Texts* (Edwin Mellen, 1992), the co-editor with Michael Hattaway of *Shakespeare in the New Europe* (Sheffield Academic Press, 1994) and the co-author with Alexander Shurbanov of *Painting Shakespeare Red: An East-European Appropriation* (Delaware UP, 2001).

Poonam Trivedi is a Reader in English at Indraprastha College, University of Delhi, India. She has published widely on the topic of Shakespeare in India. Her recent publications include: 'Reading Other Shakespeares', in *Remaking Shakespeare Across Media, Genres and Cultures* (2003); '"Play[ing]'s the Thing"': Hamlet on the Indian Stage' in *Hamlet Studies* 24 (2002); 'Shakespeare on the Indian Stage', in *A Cambridge Companion to Shakespeare on Stage* (2002); and 'Interculturalism and Indigenisation: Shakespeare East and West', in *Shakespeare and his Contemporaries* (2000). She has authored a CD-ROM on '*King Lear* in India' (2004) and co-edited a collection of essays, *India's Shakespeare: Translation, Interpretation and Performance* (2005). Her current project is a cultural history of the performance of Shakespeare in India.

Acknowledgements

This collection grew out of a seminar on 'Critical and Creative Appropriations of Shakespeare' held at the International Shakespeare Association Congress in Valencia in April 2001. I therefore wish to express my gratitude to the organizers of that conference, to Barbara Sebek, who co-chaired the seminar discussion with me, to all the contributors to this volume, who have been tremendously supportive and great fun to work with, and to Barbara Hodgdon, for all her generous support and encouragement.

I would also like to thank the British Academy for their award of an Overseas Conference Grant to travel to the Thirtieth Congress of the Shakespeare Association of America (Minneapolis, 2002), where my essay 'Subjection and Redemption in Pasolini's *Othello*' was first presented, and Thomas L. Berger, for supporting my application. Special thanks also to Jill Levenson, chair of the seminar on 'Shakespearean Adaptation: The Latest Word', and to all the seminar members who kindly offered feedback on my essay. I am indebted to Cristina Petri for her comments on this essay, to Douglas Lanier for alerting me to the rise of the Anglo-American tradition of cinematic responses to *Othello*, and to Cosimo Pacciani, who inspired me to work on Pasolini. Several colleagues and friends kindly read the introductory chapter 'Defining Local Shakespeares' in its several incarnations. Their feedback was invaluable. My special thanks to Suzanne Gossett, Robert Shaughnessy, Ton Hoenselaars and to the participants in Christy Desmet's seminar at the Thirty-First International Shakespeare Conference at Stratford-upon-Avon (July 2004).

I would finally like to express my gratitude to Liz Thompson (commissioning editor), who has supported this project from its inception and to all the editorial staff at Routledge and at Keyword Group Ltd, who have patiently held my hand each step of the way. Last, but not least, I wish to thank Cosimo Pacciani, Elda Matteucci and Giulio Massai, for all their help and affection.

Introduction

1   Defining local Shakespeares

Sonia Massai

THESEUS: [A]s imagination bodies forth
The forms of things unknown, the poet's pen
Turns them to shapes, and gives to airy nothing
A local habitation and a name.

(A Midsummer Night's Dream 5.1.14–7)[1]

ACHILLES: Tell me, you heavens, in which part of his body
Shall I destroy him – whether there, or there, or there –
That I may give the local wound a name,
And make distinct the very breach whereout
Hector's great spirit flew? Answer me, heavens!

(Troilus and Cressida 4.5.245)[2]

Local Shakespeares in a global context

The adjective 'local' occurs only twice in the Shakespearean canon. Remarkably, both occurrences are linked to the act of giving a name, first to the airy nothings bodied forth by the poet's imagination, and then to the equally fabulous signs inscribed by the soldier's quill, his sword, onto the enemy's body. Shakespearean usage suggests that the creative potential of writing is realized through the act of siting, or 'making local'. The act of naming and the act of siting share a constitutive feature. As Ferdinand de Saussure established, language signifies *relationally* starting from its smallest signifying unit, the phoneme. Similarly, 'local' means 'pertaining to or concerned with a position in space' (*OED*, A1) and, more specifically, 'pertaining to a particular place in a system' (*OED*, A4) as, for example, in algebra, when the value of a number depends on its 'place' or 'serial position'. Given the relational nature of language one can argue that signification itself depends on giving airy nothings 'a *local* habitation and a name'.

   This collection stems from the realization that if any signifying practice, including Shakespearean appropriation as a mode of (inter)cultural production, is local, then the categories of 'local' and 'global', which are increasingly invoked to define the current stage in the history of the afterlife of Shakespeare's works, need careful reconsideration. Are we often guilty, as Mark Houlahan puts it later on in this volume, of 'tak[ing] the global to be the multinational and the corporate, blandly disseminating sameness throughout the world, and the local to be the heroic, small scale attempts to sustain … difference' (p. 141)? Recent anti-globalist movements and pioneering critical reflections on such movements have indeed alerted us to the risks of the increasing influence of the global – in its ideological, political, cultural and economic manifestations – over the local. One of the major effects of globalization has to do with the relatively new phenomenon of a geographical divide between *local* manufacturers of goods (often in the Third World) and the *universally* recognizable logo or brand name (generally associated with corporations in the First World). In the first chapter of her book *No Logo*, which is suggestively titled 'New Branded World', Naomi Klein argues that 'the astronomical growth in the wealth and cultural influence of multinational corporations over the last fifteen years can arguably be traced back to a single, seemingly innocuous idea developed by management theorists in the mid-1980s: that successful corporations must primarily produce brands, as opposed to products' (Klein 2001: 3).

The steep rise in the number and variety of Shakespearean appropriations and their significant role in mass culture (film, television, best-selling novels), as well as in more traditional sites of cultural production (theatre, secondary and tertiary education, academic debate), suggest that Shakespeare has effectively become a successful logo or brand name. In 'Shakespeare and the Global Spectator', Dennis Kennedy confirms earlier analyses, such as Barbara Hodgdon's *The Shakespeare Trade* (1998) or Michael Bristol's *Big-Time Shakespeare* (1996) and *Shakespeare's America, America's Shakespeare* (1990), which helped us realize that the Shakespeare industry is not immune from shifts in economic and marketing strategies. According to Kennedy, '[g]iant entertainment conglomerates, controllers of film studios, TV companies, the recording industry, and publishing houses create products that operate economically the way Coca-Cola does' (1995: 50). Even the theatre, which according to Kennedy remains 'extraordinarily labor-intensive and local', has contributed to turning Shakespeare into a global phenomenon. As Kennedy points out, 'the touring of theatre companies on a large scale' has brought Shakespeare around the globe and 'the ease of jet travel has simultaneously brought spectators from all over the world to theatrical centers' where Shakespeare is performed (1995: 51).

Has Shakespeare become one of the powerful global icons through which local cultural markets are progressively Westernized? Is the dream (or the threat) of a technologically linked, equalizing, world-wide culture for the global village and of a super-cultural, universally enjoyable and consumable Shakespeare imposing Western values over other cultural traditions and economies? Several studies have analyzed the institutional uses of Shakespeare and the normative influence that the reception of his work has had in the modern age.[3] However, theorists of the global dimensions of cultural production believe that the global should not be understood solely in terms of a progressive cultural impoverishment and erasure of local differences. Fredric Jameson, for example, has argued that:

> It is essentially standardization that effaces the difference between the center and the margins. And although it may be an exaggeration to claim that we are all marginals now, all decentered in the current good senses of those words, certainly many new freedoms have been won in the process whereby globalization has meant a decentering and a proliferation of differences.
>
> (1998: 66)

After positing that current modes of cultural production can be read as an 'immense global urban intercultural festival without a center' (1998: 66), Jameson does warn us that an over-optimistic endorsement of interculturalism does not by itself guarantee a constructive response to issues of cultural (and economic) dominance versus cultural (and economic) marginality. The global/local debate, in other words, which often generates either rash and under-theorized eulogies of – or sceptical responses to – interculturalism, reproduces the same critical impasse which has divided post-colonial critics into supporters and detractors of hybridity as a viable alternative to the hampering oppositions between hegemonic and subaltern cultures. As Ania Loomba and Martin Orkin have put it, hybridity can be taken to denote 'a potentially radical state, one that enables [colonial and post-colonial] subjects to elude, or even subvert the binaries, oppositions and rigid demarcations imposed by colonial discourses', or 'a condition that marks the alienation of subordinated people from their own cultures' (1998: 66). Even Homi Bhabha's notion of mimicry obsessively reinforces the binary structure of signification under colonial and post-colonial circumstances:

> Mimicry is … the sign of a *double* articulation; a complex strategy of reform, regulation and discipline, which 'appropriates' the Other as it visualizes power. Mimicry is also the sign of the inappropriate, however, a difference of recalcitrance which coheres the dominant strategic function of colonial power, intensifies surveillance, and poses an immanent threat to both 'normalized' knowledges and disciplinary powers.
>
> (1989: 235, my emphasis)

Mimicry is always double. Even when at its most radical, distorting and subversive, mimicry implies the omnipresent image of the dominant other as its ultimate point of origin. 'Almost the same but not quite'; 'almost the same but not white' (1989: 238). Mimicry does not overcome but rather implies the ghostly presence of an original authenticating binary.[4] Mimicry is a 'form of colonial discourse that is uttered *inter dicta*' (1989: 239), that is, between pre-existing discourses. Bhabha's emphasis on discursive formations and his suggestion that mimicry 'coheres' while it 'subverts' ' "normalized" knowledges' reveal the unmistakable influence of Foucauldian theories on how (colonial) power is supposed to operate.

The terms of the debate in both fields of post-colonial and global/local studies have inevitably affected how we currently think about Shakespearean appropriations. Denis Salter, for example, has strongly denied Shakespearean appropriation any radical function: 'instead of radically reconstituting Shakespearean textuality, resitings merely seek to extend its authority in seemingly "natural" ways' (1996: 127). At the other end of the spectrum, Kate Chedgzoy, among others, sees 'Shakespeare as an empowering resource which has allowed other voices to make themselves heard, to stake a claim to cultural centrality' (1995: 2).

When I first started planning this collection I consciously decided that *World-wide Shakespeares* would not only provide an overview of recent world-wide appropriations of Shakespeare but that it would also encourage contributors to think about the politics of appropriations anew, outside the Foucauldian box, as it were. As Jameson reminds us, 'the categories …, the models and forms of thought in which we inescapably have to think things through, … have a logic of their own to which we ourselves fall victim if we are unaware of their existence and their in-forming influence on us' (1998: 75). The fact that a substantial number of contributors focus on appropriations that originated in areas which cannot be adequately described as post-colonial highlights the need for a model of cultural appropriation which can effectively account for the variety of localities from which Shakespeare is being appropriated, for the range of textual strategies employed by its adapters, and for the impact world-wide Shakespeares have on their target audiences.

Shakespeare as a global cultural field

World-wide appropriations of Shakespeare stretch, challenge and modify our sense of what 'Shakespeare' is. Pierre Bourdieu's notion that 'the producer of a work of art is not the artist but the field of production as a universe of belief which produces the value of the work of art as a *fetish*' (1995: 229) usefully suggests that Shakespeare can best be understood as the sum of the critical and creative responses elicited by his work. Bourdieu describes the cultural field as

> a veritable social universe ... with its relations of power and its struggles for the preservation or the transformation of the established order, that is the basis for the strategies of producers, for the form of art they defend, for the alliances they form, for the schools they found, in short, for their specific interests.
>
> (1993: 163, 181)

Writing more specifically about the philosophical field, Bourdieu explains that although each field 'imposes itself as a sort of autonomous world', any field is in fact the 'historical product of the labour of successive philosophers [read 'Shakespeareans'] who have defined certain topics as philosophical [read 'relevant'] by forcing them on commentary, discussion, critique and polemic' (1979: 496). The field, in other words, determines what it is possible to say about or do with Shakespeare at any particular moment in time. However, Bourdieu ascribes agency to 'new entrants', to those outsiders who get a feel for the cultural game and become active participants within the field. Bourdieu, like other post-Marxist theorists, believes that subjectivity and cultural production develop from specific relations to objective, material structures, but he also believes that 'one cannot predict position-takings [how an individual agent will position him/herself within the field] from dispositions (*habitus*)' (1995: 270). Furthermore, the fluidity of the field is ensured by the fact that 'the relation ... between the available positions and the position-takings does not entail a mechanistic determination' (1993: 184). Bourdieu therefore provides a useful, alternative model to understand the dynamic interaction between established modes of critical and theatrical production and innovative strategies of appropriation. Although, as Bourdieu explains, 'the probable future of a field is inscribed, at each moment, in the structure of the field, ... each agent makes his own future – thereby helping to make the future of the field' (1995, 272). In fact, according to Bourdieu, out of all the other fields – the philosophical, the political, the ideological – 'the literary or artistic fields are characterized ... by the extreme permeability of their boundaries and the extreme diversity of the definition of the posts they offer' (1995: 226). The range of appropriations analysed in *World-wide Shakespeares* shows that the boundaries of Shakespeare as a cultural field have not only stretched, but moved altogether.

Changes in the structure of the field do not necessarily imply that its power is threatened or diminished. Like Foucault, Bourdieu suggests that subversion can be merely functional to the survival of the field and the power relations or positions within it: 'the most audacious intellectual breaks ... still help to preserve the stock of consecrated texts from becoming dead letters' (1979: 496). It is indeed worth pointing out that Paul Yachnin, one of the few scholars to realize that Bourdieu's 'idea of a relatively autonomous field of cultural production with its own institutional politics is crucial to any account of revisionist and oppositional rewriting of Shakespeare', concludes that those who rework Shakespeare 'are bound within a literary field that is neither of their own creation, nor within their own power to alter' (2001: 37, 49). However, Yachnin adds an interesting disclaimer to his conclusions: 'I should note that neither Bourdieu's model nor my argument is meant to apply to revisionist treatments of Shakespeare by artists outside the cultural field of the developed world' (2001: 53). Several of the essays in *World-wide Shakespeares* suggest that 'revisionist treatments of Shakespeare outside the cultural field of the developed world' would indeed challenge Yachnin's conclusions but not Bourdieu's model. Bourdieu's notion of the cultural field seems in fact to overcome the theoretical strictures imposed by the Foucauldian model of power and discourse on post-colonial theorists. Crucially, Bourdieu specifies that 'one of the most significant properties of the field of cultural production, explaining its extreme dispersion and the conflicts between rival principles of legitimacy, is [that] … the extreme diversity of the "posts" it offers … def[ies] any unilateral hierarchization' (1993: 43). Unlike Foucault, Bourdieu believes that the subject can take up different positions within the cultural (or other) fields, and that the field, which is not only a 'field of forces' but also a 'field of struggles', changes as a result of local contributions within that field:

> every new position, in asserting itself as such, determines a displacement of the whole structure and that, by the logic of action and reaction, … leads to all sorts of changes in the position-takings of the occupants of the other positions.
>
> (1993: 58)

Overall, the range and the quality of appropriations analysed by the contributors to this collection undoubtedly suggest that Shakespeare in the late twentieth and early twenty-first centuries can best be described as a field of forces as well as *genuine* struggles.

By stressing the fluidity of the field, its lack of any unilateral hierarchization and the permeability of its boundaries, Bourdieu provides a powerful model to describe not only the impact which world-wide appropriations of Shakespeare have on their audiences, but also the *raison d'être* of a project like *World-wide Shakespeares*. This collection fulfils one of its main objectives by granting visibility to several unfamiliar appropriations, whose chances of becoming significant positions within the field are too often curtailed by a limited awareness of the 'state of play' in its sub-regions. Writing about the ideological field Bourdieu argues that in order to acquire agency, newcomers have to 'participate in its production, to occupy a position which counts, that is, *which others have to take account of*' (1979: 429, my emphasis). *World-wide Shakespeares* encourages the scholarly community to take account of a wide range of appropriations, some of which have been overlooked because of their cultural and linguistic diversity.

Surveying the field: aims and objectives

World-wide Shakespeares has a genuinely international scope. The majority of contributors focus on appropriations which have had little if any exposure beyond their local target audiences. Thanks to the wide range of localities included in this collection, strategies of appropriations in post-colonial contexts (Döring, Houlahan and Trivedi) can be compared to ways in which Shakespeare's plays are being used in countries where the shift from post-communism to the rise of a new Europe has prompted ambivalent responses to Western culture (Kostihová and Sokolova). Also useful is a comparison between post-colonial localities and countries like post-Cultural Revolution China, where intercultural appropriations, informally referred to as 'Shakespeare in jeans' and bitterly condemned by the Communist regime as a 'form of capitalist decadence' (Li p. 40), are now flourishing. Western Europe itself, which has a long history of critical and creative responses to Shakespeare, is a vibrant 'field of struggles', where the iconic value of Shakespeare's plays is effectively challenged by means of subtle meta-theatrical, meta-cinematic (Massai), and meta-cultural strategies (Schülting).

Another important objective of this collection is to encourage its readers to reflect on how local, partisan and unstable the centre(s) of the field start(s) to appear when appropriations in English, performed in well-established theatrical venues, or widely distributed in cinemas around the world, are discussed alongside foreign or unfamiliar ones. Shakespeare's America, for example, turns out to be an extremely fragmented region of the field, where shifts from urban to rural (Gossett) and from dominant to liminal (Shapiro/Klein) cultural centres often reveal incompatible ways of 'meaning by Shakespeare'. Immediately 'South of the Border' Shakespeare is instead being used by a new breed of Mexican directors as a radical antidote against centralized attempts to impose North American and European values on local institutions (Modenessi). British cultural centres do not seem to be immune from local and global tensions either. Recent productions often 'articulate the ambiguities, and the nervousness, of contemporary "English" Shakespeare, in the cultural and economic context of globalization' (Shaughnessy p. 113), while familiar debates on what constitutes 'authentic' Shakespeare reveal ongoing battles over access to culturally central venues within the ever shifting geopolitical landscape of British theatre (Jones). Dominant critical trends are similarly shown to stem from and defend the interests of specific scholarly communities. Interesting similarities between adaptations and well-established schools of criticism have led some contributors to expose the local nature of dominant critical approaches (Erne, Catania and Hoenselaars) and the strength of cultural traditions which inform and determine how we think about Shakespeare (Kidnie).

The mid-twentieth century was chosen as a starting point in this collection because the concomitant advent of theory, the increasing popularity of Shakespearean appropriations, the theorization of the post-colonial condition, and the rise in theatrical and cinematic internationalism have since then encouraged a progressive critique of the Shakespeare myth. The collection was therefore conceived with both film and performance in mind. Research in the field of Shakespeare on film has come of age, and, as many recent studies have effectively shown, issues of authenticity, canonicity and appropriation are most profitably tackled through an interdisciplinary approach to film, performance and cultural studies.[5] Another determining factor has been the growing awareness not only that younger generations often come to Shakespeare first through its cinematic adaptations, but also that many directors allow their theatrical experience to feed into their experiments with film and vice versa.

The scope of this collection reflects the growing awareness that the field of Shakespeare Studies has been radically transformed by the emergence of significant world-wide localities, within which Shakespeare is made to signify anew. The inclusion of appropriations from familiar localities within the field, such as England and the United States, alongside appropriations from areas which have traditionally been understood as 'liminal', 'peripheral' and, most crucially, 'post-colonial', shows that instability, dissonance and oppositional negotiations over Shakespeare's work are a common phenomenon throughout the field, and not only at its margins. As Stuart Hall has noticed, the 'global [read Westernized] post-modern is not a unitary regime, ... simply unproblematic and uncontradictory' (Hall 1991: 33); similarly, Janet Abu-Lughod and Ulf Hannerz have pointed out that 'we have a globalizing but not necessarily homogeneous culture' (Abu-Lughod 1991: 142) and that 'when studying culture, we now have to think about the flow between places as well as that within them' (Hannerz 1991: 126).

Dealing specifically with the post-colonial condition, Marshall Sahlins condemns a 'certain historiography that is quick to take the agents of imperialism as exclusive players of the only game in town'. This type of historiography, he continues, 'is prepared to assume that history is made by the colonial masters, and all that need be known about the people's own social dispositions, or even their "subjectivities", is the external disciplines imposed upon them'. The familiar conclusion to which this line of reasoning leads is that 'the main historical [or more widely cultural] activity remaining to the underlying people is to misconstrue the effects of such imperialism as their own cultural traditions' (Sahlins 2000: 477). Refreshingly, Sahlins points out that the West derives its sense of cultural superiority from a conscious adaptation (or miscontruction) of an alien tradition. Modernity in the West, Sahlins reminds us, stems from the conscious efforts made by humanist scholars, literary artists and philosophers between the end of the fourteenth and the mid-seventeenth centuries, to appropriate the distant, fundamentally alien culture of the Greeks and the Romans. Shakespeare's contemporaries, Sahlins continues, 'decorated Christian churches with the facades of classical temples, ... wrote history in the style of Livy, verses in a mannered Latin, tragedy according to Seneca, and comedy in the mode of Terence' (2000: 479). Renaissance culture is nevertheless rarely, if ever, dismissed as a mere 'cultural counterfeit'. Taking on board Sahlins's tenet that 'no culture is *sui generis*' (2000: 489), the contributors to this collection 'provincialize'[6] dominant Shakespeares by showing how, far from meaning 'universal', 'global' is in fact the product of specific, historically and culturally determined localities.

Michael Neill rightly points out that such a re-orientation has so far been 'more rhetorical than real' (1998: 184). Dennis Kennedy's *Foreign Shakespeare* (1993), for example, is not exceptional in being still strongly Euro- and Anglo-centric. Christy Desmet and Robert Sawyer's *Shakespeare and Appropriation* (1999) similarly includes only one essay on non-European adaptations in a foreign language. In contrast, *World-wide Shakespeares* has been specifically conceived to devote sustained attention to appropriations from a mixed range of geographical locations. Focusing exclusively on foreign Shakespeares seems equally inappropriate, since such categorization reinforces lingering notions of English Shakespeares as a normative standard from which all other appropriations depart. The juxtaposition of appropriations from familiar and unfamiliar regions of the field is also pragmatically rewarding. Recent appropriations of *The Merchant of Venice*, for example, show that while European directors and adapters are still using the play to 're-member' twentieth-century Jewish history (Jones and Schülting), non-European practitioners add local frames of reference which invite an exploration of the Jewish issue as well as local ethnic politics (Houlahan and Klein/Shapiro).

While more comprehensive and geographically varied than other studies so far devoted to Shakespearean appropriations, *World-wide Shakespeares* cannot possibly be exhaustive, given the range of localities from which Shakespeare has been appropriated since the mid-twentieth century. Contributors themselves occupy a wide range of positions within the field and have used their familiarity with specific sub-regions to provide readers with enough contextualization to make sense of the productions discussed in this volume. The arrangement of the essays into three groups – 'Local Shakespeares for Local Audiences', 'Local Shakespeares for National Audiences' and 'Local Shakespeares for International Audiences' – was partly determined by the target audience or distribution of each appropriation and partly by the growing awareness that due to the increased number of global exchanges of cultural and material commodities and the 'exponential growth of international migration, ... there is no "nationally grounded" theoretical paradigm which can adequately handle the epistemological situation' (King 1991: 6). Theorists of the global dimensions of cultural production agree that the formulation of a 'theory of culture at the level of the international' can only be undertaken starting from 'different social, spatial or cultural locations in the world' (King 1991: 5). Such locations include neighbourhoods, cities, regions and sub-regions, linguistic, religious and political ecumenes, along with national identity and traditions, as equally significant determinants of cultural production. This spatial re-ordering of culture at the levels of the local, regional, national and international suggests that several recent enquiries into the role which Shakespeare has had in the shaping of national cultures and dramatic traditions[7] should be complemented by new investigations into a much wider variety of localities, including specific local, regional, national and super-national 'positions'.

Another significant feature of the appropriations discussed in each group of essays is their increasingly syncretic combination of frames of references which are available to local *and* to international audiences. Local Shakespeares adapted with local audiences in mind and then revived elsewhere often elicit puzzled responses (Trivedi). Conversely, the appropriations analysed in the last group of essays have proved more easily 'exportable' possibly because they defamiliarize Shakespeare through the use of spectacle (Kidnie) or local poetic and visual conventions (Houlahan and Catania), while bringing to the fore recognizable tropes of their reception history in Anglophone localities. Although, as Barbara Hodgdon has usefully pointed out, the terms 'adaptation' and 'appropriation' are 'two extremely slippery labels' (p. 157), there may indeed be different modes of interventions available to Shakespearean practioners, which need further consideration. Rather than a rigid taxonomy, the arrangement of the essays gathered in this volume draws attention to differential strategies of appropriation, ranging from the use of uncompromisingly local, to a blend of local and more widely recognizable, frames of reference.

Making sense of infinite variety: a working methodology

The choice of Bourdieu's model of cultural production for a re-assessment of how Shakespeare signifies within a range of world-wide localities may seem at odds with the collection's attempt to provincialize Europe. Do the critical lenses provided by 'metropolitan' theorists, such as Bourdieu, distort rather than enhance our appreciation of the ideological, cultural and aesthetic specificity of world-wide appropriations of Shakespeare? Does Bourdieu's notion of the cultural field provide a viable model to establish how individual appropriations operate in relation to its beleaguered, unstable and multiple centres? Bourdieu's work is enlightening as it is unnervingly slippery when it comes to providing straightforward definitions of its own terminology and categories. Typical of Bourdieu's methodology is the frequent combination of explicatory passages, where he discusses and qualifies the theoretical principles informing his work, and case studies, which enrich his theoretical discussion while inevitably interrupting the flow of his argument. One cannot help feeling that the interspersion of case studies, the privileged domain of the sociologist, with abstract reasoning, the privileged domain of the philosopher, is meant to prevent readers from thinking that they can easily extract axiomatic (and recyclable) principles from Bourdieu's carefully paced and bewildering detailed analysis of well-defined areas of sociological, literary and cultural inquiry. As mentioned above, Jameson usefully warns us against thinking that theoretical categories are neutral lenses which simply enhance our ability to read the 'raw' material we wish to analyse and understand in all its complexity. In this respect, Bourdieu seems to make a deliberate and conscious effort to formulate his theoretical framework so that it emerges gradually and never univocally from the vast amount of 'raw' material he analyses. Bourdieu's method allows for the fact that the 'raw' material, in our case the messy stuff of literary and theatrical visions, revisions, improvisations, intertextual and intercultural citations, will not 'stand still' as we try to analyse it and classify it. Besides, Bourdieu's constant, often fragmented, reformulation of his definitions suggests how the 'raw material' will inevitably affect our choice and constant adjustment of our theoretical lenses. Jameson, once again, proves helpful as he stresses how 'our problem lies as much with our categories of thought as in the sheer facts of the matter themselves' (1998: 75). I am positively inclined to believe that Bourdieu provides a more viable set of theoretical categories than Foucault for a re-assessment of how Shakespeare has been appropriated within a range of world-wide localities from the middle of the twentieth century to the present. However, it was the 'sheer facts of the matter themselves', that is the extraordinary variety of 'positions' which appropriations examined in *World-wide Shakespeares* turn from mere 'possibles' into actual 'posts' (or 'outposts') in the cultural field, which determined the theoretical framework of this collection, rather than vice versa. Ultimately, it is the 'sheer facts of the matter themselves', and not Bourdieu *per se*, which enable us to see Shakespeare as if '[we] had eyes again'.

Part One

Local Shakespeares for local audiences

2 *A Branch of the Blue Nile*: Derek Walcott and the tropic of Shakespeare

Tobias Döring

The English in the West Indies

The local is a difficult terrain. The very terms and concepts we employ in order to describe the specificities of a locality may be misleading because they are too general for what they are supposed to capture: the here and now often elude common linguistic categories. Language works through opposition and comparison. So if in Shakespeare, as shown in the introduction to this volume, the adjective 'local' is linked to the act of name-giving, this link suggests a promise as much as a problem. How *can* new cultural spaces be aptly named and understood? Does the act of naming indeed function as an act of siting which localizes experience? Or does it rather displace its referent into an unstable signifying system and thereby dislocate it? Historically, such questions have been most powerfully addressed within the context of colonial encounters.

In 1887 the English writer and historian James Anthony Froude went on a tour through the West Indies. To him, these islands represented both the glories of the British Empire with its civilizing mission and the more problematic by-product of nineteenth-century economic liberalism. Once the epic scene of Britain's greatest naval victory, the cradle of the Empire was now simply a sugar manufacturing colony. As long as liberalism ruled in Westminster, Froude feared, the New World colonies would be regarded as a mere economic asset. Froude believed that such a cavalier attitude on the colonizer's part would lead to their regression into unruly primitivism. As he explains at some length in his travelogue *The English in the West Indies, or The Bow of Ulysses*, tropical islands require the continued care and stern authority of their European master, lest they revert to barbarity. For 'there are no people there in the true sense of the word, with a character and a purpose of their own' (Froude 1909: 306). Wherever he goes, Froude looks for evidence of English intervention which has successfully elevated and transformed local customs. Crucially, familiar sights abound: an idyllic mountain village in Jamaica looks to him like 'an exact reproduction of a Warwickshire hamlet'; a small church in Barbados seems just like 'a parish church in England'; and on the island's central square he notes approvingly a statue of Lord Nelson – just like at home in London (1909: 37, 101, 216). This Victorian traveller understands the local only when he can frame it through familiar categories.

The same holds true for a Shakespeare performance he witnessed in Tobago. The local descendants of African slaves asked permission to play for the English governor, and to everyone's surprise they decided to stage *The Merchant of Venice*. According to Froude this ambitious choice deserved respect, but the quality of their performance could only be described by quoting Hippolyta's verdict on the workmen's play as 'sorry stuff'. And yet there was one notable exception: 'Shylock's representative', we read, 'showed real appreciation', and Froude suggests why this should be so: 'With freedom and a peasant proprietary, the money lender is a necessary phenomenon, and the actor's imagination may have been assisted by personal recollections' (1909: 51).

As a matter of fact, Shakespearean drama had long been performed in the West Indies (see Omotoso 1982, Ch. 1). Shakespeare as a world-wide brand name precedes the age of jet travel. Since the eighteenth century, the colonial elites in the plantocracy welcomed English touring companies on their estates. Shakespeare's central presence in the repertoire reinforced their connection to their mother country. However, the local amateur production on Tobago, so dismissively described by Froude, does not fall squarely in with this tradition. We may well wonder what those plantation workers planned to show their colonial administrator through their ill-received performance. For we need not accept Froude's standpoint and see their project as a touching effort towards assimilation, where the Shakespearean text provides the roles for blacks to rehearse their progress towards civilization. We should rather acknowledge the scope of performative engagements which this play offers. The Prince of Morocco's 'Mislike me not for my complexion/The shadowed livery of the burnished sun' (2.1.1–2) acquires topical relevance within the context of this production. Even more so, the famous speeches of the despised Jew pleading for justice and lawful recognition bear powerfully on the local situation. That the black actor, as Froude notes, delivered them 'with real appreciation' might indeed be due to 'personal recollections' – though different from the ones Froude has in mind. Instead of eagerly submitting to European cultural models, the whole performance might have served to stage a plea for political representation – albeit a plea slyly articulated through borrowed masks.

This production shows the cultural and political ambivalence intrinsic to world-wide Shakespeares. On the one hand, the ubiquity of Shakespearean performance has often licensed claims of universalism celebrating the plays for their avowed invention of the human. On the other hand, every performance does not just repeat but also changes a given text and therefore creates the potential for cultural difference. For this reason, Shakespearean appropriations have often been staged to reclaim cultural identity. Caribbean authors have mainly used *The Tempest* in this way (see, for instance, Hulme and Sherman 2000). At least since George Lamming articulated his own position as a post-colonial writer through Caliban in *The Pleasures of Exile* in 1960, this play has frequently been rewritten to explore power relations in the New World and beyond. However, although such projects set out to reject imperial notions such as Froude's, they also work to re-inscribe them, because any rewriting of the Shakespearean text to some extent perpetuates the cultural authority it means to abrogate. When Lamming (1901. 0), for example, claims 'to make use of *The Tempest* as a way of presenting a certain state of feeling which is the heritage of the exiled and colonial writer from the British Caribbean', he is still formulating his critical agenda through a canonical text.[1] What does this mean for contemporary Caribbean writers like Derek Walcott?[2] And what does this suggest for our own engagements with world-wide Shakespeares?

Cleopatra in Trinidad

A hundred years after Froude's voyage, a Trinidadian theatre company plans to stage *Antony and Cleopatra*. Their director, called Harvey St. Just, is a professional from England, but most of the actors are local amateurs, who struggle with the unfamiliar text.

After weeks of troublesome rehearsals, the opening night ends in disaster. The lead actress, called Sheila Harris, resigns so that an understudy must take over. The stage-hand has not been briefed and, at the tragic climax, sets up the wrong prop: during her final soliloquy, Cleopatra finds herself standing opposite a painted banana tree. The audience laugh and the critics write scathing reviews: 'the only indigenous thing onstage last night, in Mr. St. Just's abbreviated, aborted, and abominable mounting of *Antony and Cleopatra*, was a bunch of bananas inadvertently trundled onstage during the farewell speech of Cleopatra, about whom more later. Certain things remain sacred, or else our civilization is threatened...' (Walcott 1986: 269).

The review and protagonists of this production belong to the realm of fiction, because they are themselves part of a stage play, Derek Walcott's *A Branch of the Blue Nile*. And yet, this play suggests several clear parallels with actual cultural projects and can therefore be read as a critical reflection on Caribbean engagements with Shakespeare's legacy. Premiered in Barbados in 1983 with Earl Warner as director,[3] Walcott's drama employs the age-old device of the play-within-the-play in order to establish whether universalist assumptions about Shakespeare can be effectively challenged by localized creative practices. The Barbadian première received enthusiastic reviews across the entire region, perhaps not least because it formed a rare example of what Bruce King (2000: 425) has called an 'international West Indian' project. Produced and sponsored by Stage One, a local non-profit company dedicated to Caribbean drama, the performance included artists and actors from the various island states. Two years later, the play's success continued with a Trinidadian production, also directed by Earl Warner, which turned out to be the last major local performance of a Walcott drama before he won the Nobel Prize in 1992. Outside the region, however, this particular play of his has been less well received. Stage One was planning to take it to New York, but had to cancel under pressure from Equity, the Actors Union, which had to flatter members with the belief that they were protecting American minority actors against West Indians. An Amsterdam production in 1991, in Dutch translation, toured the Netherlands but failed to attract interest in other European countries. Ironically then, while *A Branch of the Blue Nile* explores the fate of European culture in transcultural dislocation, international audiences outside the West Indies rarely got a chance to see it performed. At any rate, the play both commemorates and continues Walcott's own lifelong dedication to Caribbean theatre, especially his pioneering work with the Trinidad Theatre Workshop he founded in 1959 (see King 1995). Here, his idea had long been to set up a space in which the rich diversity of New World cultures could find articulation, i.e. a stage, as he famously put it in 1970, 'where someone can do Shakespeare or sing Calypso with equal conviction' (Walcott 1993b: 46).

However, this confident and programmatic claim has often proved problematic. Performances of 'Shakespeare' and 'Calypso' are not simply indicative of 'the global' and 'the local', but represent conflicting positions in cultural politics, as suggested by the controversies which used to surround Walcott's work. In 1971, for example, Lamming published *Water With Berries*, a *roman à clef* in which an ambitious Caribbean actor named Derek plays Othello before a white English audience. Lamming's novel, itself patterned on *The Tempest*, shows how the Shakespearean canon functions as a controlling script which allocates cultural roles and which, for post-colonial purposes, should resolutely be abandoned. What Lamming therefore castigates as Derek's misguided aspiration – his craving for recognition from metropolitan elites – forms part of the historical background and of the critical material reworked in *A Branch of the Blue Nile*. Against this background, my reading[4] of Walcott's play text aims to show how its metadramatic structure situates Shakespearean performance in a particular locality and, at the same time, redraws its cultural co-ordinates.

Why, then, *Antony and Cleopatra*? The choice and use of this particular play raise several questions. What is Cleopatra to Trinidad? What can a Jacobean Roman history drama about war and passion do or signify in a late-twentieth-century tropical island? Trinidad's heterogeneous and widely urbanized society has long been dedicated to a popular Carnival tradition, but there has never been a permanent playhouse or an established theatre tradition on the island. So how might the literary and the local setting of Walcott's drama meaningfully interrelate? Such issues are, in fact, debated with some vehemence in the play. As Sheila says: 'Trinidad isn't Egypt, except at Carnival,/so the world sniggers when I speak her lines' (Walcott 1986: 285). With this argument, the lead actress explains to the director why she has decided to abandon the project. To her, geographical distance marks insurmountable cultural difference. Director Harvey tries to solve the problem by introducing her to method acting, but fails in the attempt. Instead of making the foreign part her own, Sheila just remarks: 'it's bad method anyway, and maybe it doesn't travel' (1986: 218).

Another member of the company called Chris, who is supposed to play Antony, supports Sheila's views. None of the European classics, he argues in an angry outburst, have anything to say to him or to the local audience: 'I ain't care who the arse is Shakespeare, Racine, Chekhov, nuttin in there had to do with my life, or the life of all them black people out in the hot sun of Frederick Street at twelve o'clock trying to hustle a living' (1986: 246). Chris has written his own play, a typical Trinidadian backyard comedy, set in a recognizable domestic place and drawing on popular traditions. In keeping with Chris's agenda, the play is not written in English blank verse but in Trinidadian Creole, the language of the people, which also marks his own speech (as just quoted) and which, in a famous statement, the poet Kamau Brathwaite (1984: 10) has declared to be the true expression of local experience: 'the hurricane does not roar in pentameter'. Within Walcott's metadrama, rehearsals for Chris's comedy take place as a counterpoint and challenge to Harvey's Shakespearean project. The issues raised *in* the play therefore anticipate the issues raised *by* the play: how do Shakespeare and the Caribbean relate to each other? *A Branch of the Blue Nile* gives voice and face to prominent positions in this long-standing debate in Caribbean literature. This debate has wider implications in relation to world-wide Shakespeares.[5] Staging the spectacular failure of an *Antony and Cleopatra* performance, the play questions assumptions about the viability of cultural translation, thus addressing the controversy associated with intercultural appropriations of Shakespeare in a post-colonial context.

Antony in Egypt

When Walcott's protagonists resent the roles they have been given and resist the established acting method, they effectively remind us of a fundamental point in post-colonial theory. In the words of Michael Neill (1998: 168), this is 'the idea that *reading* is always done *from somewhere*'. The place of reading matters because, as many critics since Said (1983: 4) have argued, meaning is a localized product resulting from a specifically situated act of reading. For this reason it is ironic and rather problematic that, according to some commentators, Walcott features as a so-called cosmopolitan writer, or in a troubling phrase, as an 'espouser of hybridity' (Cartelli 1999: 13), whose work is said to transcend the concerns or constraints of locality. Against such notions, I would like to emphasize how his creative and critical engagements with the Shakespeare canon take place from a position *within* Caribbean culture.

What is at stake here can be illustrated by going back to Froude's account of the West Indies. Comparison is a recurrent rhetorical device. In Jamaica, he notes, the forests are 'as beautiful as the forest at Arden', the nights occur to him 'like the gloaming of a June night in England', the Trinidadian climate is 'hotter during daylight than the hottest forcing house at Kew', and Barbados appears just 'like the Isle of Thanet' (Froude 1909: 58, 102, 218, 232). The Victorian travel text thus constitutes itself by means of similes, demonstrating how the colonial gaze appropriates all unknown places by arranging them into domestic categories. In fact, the rhetoric of comparison is as old as the tradition of European travelogues. Any travel writer trying to describe encounters with radically unfamiliar sights cannot but avail himself of some familiar points of reference. However, such a strategy leads into serious difficulties. When, for example, Herodotus, the Greek historian and ethnographer, sets out to describe the strange creatures living in the Nile, the very act of naming them is haunted by comparisons that mistake, rather than capture, their true nature: the Egyptian hippopotamus is not really a river *horse*, although its given name suggests as much. In the case of another local creature, the puzzling crocodile, Herodotus (1910: 148–9) makes that point himself: 'Of all known animals this is the one which from the smallest size grows to be the greatest: for the egg of the crocodile is but little bigger than that of the goose [...]. It has the eyes of a pig, teeth large and tusk-like [...]. The name of crocodiles was given them by the Ionians, who remarked their resemblance to the lizards, which in Ionia live in the walls'. This passage illustrates the problem noted at the outset: how to find apt linguistic terms by which the local can be named.

Against this background, it is telling what another traveller observes in Egypt and the creatures in the Nile. As soon as Shakespeare's Antony returns to Rome, he is questioned about the foreign country. 'What manner of thing is your crocodile', Lepidus asks him and is told: 'It is shaped, sir, like itself, and it is as broad as it hath breadth. It is just so high as it is, and moves with its own organs. It lives by that which norisheth it, and the elements once out of it, it transmigrates' (2.7.38–42). As John Gillies (1994: 121) has argued, Antony's report can be read on two levels. In some way, it simply parodies the kind of ethnographic rhetoric exemplified by Herodotus, whose similes are invoked only to be ridiculed. Yet in a fundamental way, this parody calls into question the pervasive strategy of representing other territories in terms transferred and wilfully imposed on them. In this sense, Antony's tautologies could be read as marking Rome's inability to come to terms with Egypt. The crocodile, Cleopatra's heraldic beast, here frustrates all imperial desire for naming and subjection; its difference persists. This reading might perhaps suggest why Walcott was so interested in this play. Another source of interest for Walcott may have been the discrepancy between actor and role, person and persona explored in *Antony and Cleopatra*, which Neill (1994: 78–89) describes as a 'dislocation of identity'. Such dislocations lie also at the core of colonial predicaments.

'My body was invaded by that queen./Her gaze made everywhere a desert'. Reversing Cleopatra's historical role, Walcott's Sheila here describes the process of rehearsal as a physical and territorial conquest: 'I found myself walking in pentameter'

(Walcott 1986: 285). Her speech echoes what has been analysed as the discursive power underpinning colonial authority through exerting itself over other bodies. In his classic study *Black Skin, White Masks*, for example, Frantz Fanon (1986: 211) argued that violence in the colonial arena operates precisely by placing the other into such a position of dependency: 'The Negro is comparison. There is the first truth. [...] The Antilleans have no inherent value of their own, they are always contingent on the presence of The Other'. Fanon's diagnosis shows what is at stake in Walcott's metadrama. According to the local actors, the mechanisms Fanon analysed are perpetuated and their bodies made to bear fundamentally alien and alienating masks. Yet again, this might suggest a relevant conjunction of the issues explored through Shakespeare's *as well as* through Walcott's text because the Shakespearean Cleopatra, too, has been analysed as a figure fully contingent on the presence of the 'Other'. As Dympna Callaghan (1996: 53) argues, 'instead of accepting the fiction of Cleopatra's status as a subject of representation, we can analyse her as an object of it – one which tells us nothing about femininity, Egyptian or otherwise, but about the Western masculinity which has fantasized her into existence'. *A Branch of the Blue Nile* is culturally and ideologically significant and, among other appropriations, worth critical attention because it shows what happens when such fantasies come up against the realities of post-colonial experience.

If colonial experience, as we have seen, is shaped by a rhetoric of constant comparison, we can understand the pressures on contemporary writers trying to reshape, or perhaps retrieve, an idiom that acknowledges the cultural specificities in their own sense of place. These pressures are particularly troublesome for Caribbean writers because the official designation of their region, the 'West Indies', derives from a historic fallacy. With each repetition of this given name, Columbus' cartographic error lives on and continues to displace the islands into a wrong and Eurocentric frame of reference. And yet, it is this very frame in which and *on* which Walcott works. Crucially, Walcott's play stages reservations not only against Harvey's Shakespearean project but also against the Trinidadian comedy supposed to replace it. Significantly, this local project fails just as badly because, for all its good intentions, it seems to exhaust itself in folk clichés. What are the implications of these two failed projects for Caribbean theatre and for the proliferation of world-wide Shakespeares?

Shakespeare in the World

It has been noted that the classic world staged in *Antony and Cleopatra* presents itself as a world divided between 'Rome' and 'Egypt', a division which can all too easily be viewed through familiar binary oppositions. But, as Ania Loomba has pointed out (1989: 126), the spatial politics of the play fail to support any stable opposition. Each world is inscribed with cultural difference, so that the sense of place yields to a sense of transition. The same process, I suggest, takes place with and within Walcott's metadrama. In *A Branch of the Blue Nile* both the Shakespearean project and the domestic comedy fall through; both performances must come to nothing as long as they try to confine themselves to one place only, instead of trying to acknowledge and mediate spatial and cultural differences. What this means can be gauged from a scene of on-stage acting in which Cleopatra, preparing for her final departure, encounters the Clown speaking in Trinidadian Creole:

MARYLIN/CLEOPATRA: Hast thou the pretty worm of Nilus there, That kills and pains not?

GAVIN/CLOWN: Madam, I have him, but 'tain't go be me who go ask you handle him, because one nip from this small fellow and Basil is your husband; this little person will make the marriage, in poison and in person, but the brides who go to that bed don't ever get up.

(Walcott 1986: 262)

This scene resituates the traditional script into a carnivalized dialogue which both re-members and dis-members the literary script. To justify this strategy, Walcott's Harvey points to Shakespeare's own practice of adapting classic authorities, confronting them with popular and local idioms: 'I felt since the Bard had swiped a prose hunk off old Plutarch, and since in old Willy's day the clowns spoke dialect, and since our dialect is so Jacobean, I felt quite justified' (1986: 268).

It is crucial, though, not to mistake such scenes as simple evidence of local adaptation nor to misread the transcultural passages they undertake as passages towards a safe haven. As my earlier examples have shown, Walcott's protagonists do not unquestioningly espouse hybridity but voice serious misgivings about imported models. Still, such models turn into raw materials for them to work with. *A Branch of the Blue Nile* exposes the limitations of both uncritical appropriation and absolute rejection of Shakespeare's global legacy. Two performance projects fail; and yet, the double failure opens up new opportunities. At the end of Walcott's play, most members of the company have left the island, but Chris has left behind the script for a new play inspired by their frustrated efforts. Its title is 'A Branch of the Blue Nile' and Chris's script is nothing but the very play the audience have been watching. In this way, Walcott's metadrama ends by leading to a new beginning, taking a self-referential turn towards its own precarious position between claims of the global and the local, between Shakespeare and Calypso, between failure and accomplishment.

In his discussion of the contemporary legacies of world-wide Shakespeares, Neill concludes: 'To cut oneself off from Shakespeare in the name of a decolonizing politics is not to liberate oneself from the tyranny of the past, but to pretend that the past does not exist' (1998: 184). It seems to me that Walcott's work has long challenged spectators and readers to face this very issue: how to address and how to redress a shared past, without pretence and without ready submission to its power. In this respect, the trope of the 'Blue Nile', which he uses as a title for the double performance, suggests a programmatic point. Since Herodotus, the Nile has represented the wonder and enigma of an uncharted world. The very mystery of its sources has long fuelled fantasies about the search for true origins. For many Western travellers, the 'Blue Nile' used to be paradigmatic of their desire to penetrate the interior of the so-called 'Dark Continent'. By contrast, Walcott's emphasis on '*A Branch* of the Blue Nile' implies that the search for authentic origins has yielded to a recognition of the pluralized and branching networks of belonging, and that the claim of sources yields to claims of destination. It is therefore highly significant that Chris is featured as the author of this play because it was Chris, as mentioned earlier, who once insisted on the search for authenticity. As Walcott's play unfolds, an essentialist notion of locality is challenged and transformed. Chris emerges as the acting dramatist, who finally lives up to his name: 'Christopher, or 'Christo-ferus', which already implies a history of transference and cultural transformation.

In Walcott's work, Christopher Columbus is less a figure of European domination than of Eurocentric fallacies and, for all that, of creative and productive dislocations. *A Branch of the Blue Nile* charts transcultural transformations in contemporary Caribbean performances. Thus, unlike Lamming's Derek, Walcott shows how appropriations of Shakespeare, far from providing alien and alienating masks or tropes which shape local productions, allow familiar figures to be tropically inflected and tropologically transformed. Even the rhetoric of comparison need not only signify secure domination. In his Nobel Prize speech, Walcott has cited Froude as an example of colonial condescension and misreading (Walcott 1993a: 8). So when we re-read this Victorian travelogue in the post-colonial perspective here established, Froude's obsessive recourse to domestic categories suggests nothing but his own limitations and his failure to come to terms with a puzzling New World. As with his views on the local production of *Merchant of Venice*, his similes mark less the sameness than a semblance of identity that he strives to conjure. The local Nelson statue, for example, is painted in 'a bright pea-green' and most of the exotic plants, despite their common names, turn out to be essentially different (Froude 1909: 37, 61). Inflected by the tropic, European names and cultural artefacts are indeed more seriously dislocated than it might seem at first sight. But then, the local always is a difficult terrain.

3   Political *Pericles*

Suzanne Gossett

In Washington, the political city, political *Pericles*. In May and June of 1998 the Washington Shakespeare Company presented *Pericles* in a warehouse adapted as a theatre. The production, directed by Joe Banno with Cam McGee as dramaturg, had two main innovations: first, rather than the play moving from place to place while the audience remained fixed, there were seven small stages, and at appropriate moments the tour guide, Gower, led the audience from one to the next. Next, Pericles' 'journey from innocence through disillusionment' was identified with the America of the decades from 1968–98, 'with all its true-or-false idols in place: country living, military might, counter-culturalism, higher learning, Reaganomics, scientific research, God, and of course, sex' (Banno 1998).[1] To assist the audience, a three-page handout listed major political and cultural events in the United States between 1968–70, 1977–81 and 1996–98, beginning with the Tet Offensive under President Johnson and concluding under President Clinton with the Paula Jones sexual harassment suit and a recent school shooting.

Only a year later, in the summer of 1999, in the bucolic outdoor environment of the American Players Theatre in Spring Green, Wisconsin, which Frank Lloyd Wright chose for his home, another production of the play by Julian López-Morillas (a remounting of one he had directed at the Berkeley/California Shakespeare Festival in 1979) took an explicitly 'elemental' view of *Pericles* as 'An Everyman story, marked by all the archetypal events common to each human life: birth and death, love and loss, sin and forgiveness' (López-Morillas 1999). These two productions raise general questions about the critical/political appropriation of Shakespeare and specific questions about the problems facing directors of *Pericles*, who seem regularly to succeed either with the first or the second half of the play.

The Washington production was made possible by its physical space. There were only 117 seats in a very large area. Arranged in a circle around the room, on a floor painted blue to suggest the sea, were six of the seven locations: a small kitchen on a southern army base for Antioch; a porch in middle America for Tyre; a college president's office in New England for Pentapolis; a boat for the scenes at sea; a contemporary emergency room for Ephesus; a bordello for Mytilene. The central stage, slightly larger than the others, represented Tarsus. The production took advantage of the fact that the play returns to Tarsus at various points in the first four acts to show change over time: the location was described by one reviewer as a hippie commune that evolved into a corporate headquarters (Pressley 1998). Pericles, a 'seeker from the sixties', moved through these spaces as America did.

One problem of the Washington production was discerning the precise relation between the political reading and the innovative dramaturgy. The audience travelled physically through space but only metaphorically through time. At Spring Green, in contrast, there was a fixed stage conventionally suggestive of a ship's deck, but three successively older actors played Pericles in a transparent representation of the 'ages of man'. Progression to the successive locations in Washington might be read simultaneously as steps in twentieth-century American development, as stages in Pericles' personal disillusionment, and as the ages of man, but the audience, somewhat distracted by the participatory requirement placed upon them to rise and move at stated intervals, may have grasped the connections only intermittently.

The passage of 'real', American time in the Washington *Pericles* was embodied in parallel developments in large social spheres, especially the drug culture, technology and gender relations. The production established its point of origin in chronological and political time by connecting the opening scene to the Vietnam war (the initial entry on the timeline is the January 1968 Tet Offensive; successive entries detail the march on Washington, the My Lai massacre and President Carter's 1977 pardon of draft evaders). Pericles was in uniform and Antiochus wore multiple medals; Pericles' entry into the contest for Antiochus's daughter was symbolized by his handing over his dogtag. Many small signs suggested that the location was rural Appalachia, from thick southern accents to the very young daughter's jumper and white socks. The drug references began at Tarsus in Act 1; the timeline includes Woodstock in 1969 and the deaths of Jimi Hendrix and Janis Joplin of overdose in 1970. Dionyza and Cleon, wearing long hair and beads, were passing around a joint. They welcomed Pericles with a peace signal, undressed him and hung beads on him, but to represent his unfamiliarity with this world he coughed on the marijuana cigarette they proffered. In Act 2 the Tarsian couple were snorting cocaine; by Act 4 they were mainlining. (California's approval of prescription marijuana is noted in 1996.) Technological developments were intimated by the beeping machinery of the emergency room and by having Leonine and Dionyza conduct their arrangements via telephone. All of 4.1 took place on a beach, and when Dionyza, sunbathing, became uncertain that Leonine would go through with the murder she called on a portable phone to stiffen his resolve ('Remember what I have said' 4.1.45).[2]

Changing gender relations were more elaborately and self-consciously staged. In the text, Antiochus's daughter has only two lines: 'Of all 'ssayd yet, mayst thou prove prosperous;/Of all 'ssayd yet, I wish thee happiness' (1.1.60–1). Depending upon stage action, the significance of her comment may vary from formulaic – the daughter in Spring Green, all icon of incest, was wrapped with her father in a large piece of cloth – to truly desperate, a plea for escape from the situation into which the abused girl has been forced. At the Washington Shakespeare the childish daughter, terrified of her father, eagerly whispered into Pericles' ear until Antiochus pulled her away. In contrast, the next daughter, Thaisa, conducted the tournament for her own hand by playing tennis against each suitor; she beat them all except Pericles. In a further blurring of the line between 'production' and 'appropriation', the dramaturg adopted from the Oxford 'reconstruction' of the text an extra speech for Thaisa at the point of her marriage, believing that otherwise the young woman was 'not active enough' for a scene set in 1980.[3] (The 1977 timeline includes the 'First National Women's Conference to plan feminist future'.) Cerimon was a female surgeon at 'St. Diana's Hospital'; Boult was a female dwarf on crutches who, when the Bawd told him/her to use Marina 'at thy pleasure' (4.5.146), grabbed a dildo and began to threaten Marina with it.

This politicized production encountered two difficulties that may be inevitable in such undertakings. First, as revealed by comparing entries on the handout with the production, there were discrepancies between what the unadapted text could accommodate and what the director might have liked to include. The timeline embodies a vision of America that emphasizes cultural conflicts, such as those between war supporters and protestors, advocates and opponents of civil rights, the National Organization for Women and the Moral Majority. Most of these emerged at least sketchily on the stage. But the timeline also repeatedly notes the country's pervasive violence, listing murder victims from Martin Luther King in 1968 and John Lennon in 1980 to the Menendez parents, Tupac Shakur and Nicole Simpson, the casualties of the Unabomber, and groups of school children killed by their classmates in the late 1990s. These found no place to anchor in the text and thus no visible place in the action.

Second, political appropriations pose the problem of assuming a stable signification uniformly interpretable. According to the critic of the *Washington Post*, Shakespeare is the 'Washington playwright' (Rose 2000). Chris Henley, Artistic Director of the Washington Shakespeare, explained the appeal: 'Washington is a kind of a company town. And the one industry is government and politics. Many of the plays are explicitly about these themes' (cited in Rose 2000). The *Pericles* production certainly was addressed to the politicized D.C. audience, but how specifically and how uniformly did it speak to them? How many members of each age group, in 1998, could be counted on to read the semiotics of Vietnam-era dogtags, porch swings, hippie beads, women's suits with padded shoulders? Furthermore, the production climaxed under the Clinton administration: the last column includes 'Monica Lewinsky scandal breaks' and 'Judge Susan Wright dismisses Paula Jones sexual harassment suit'. Perhaps the audience was intended to infer a parallel between the sexual abuse of a very young girl by a powerful general, or the harassment of a kidnapped princess by the local governor, and shenanigans in the Oval Office. But if the production were revived in 2004, would the advent of President Bush, 'family values', and the events of September 11, 2001, change the resonance of the anti-war attitude and of Thaisa's feminist-inspired speeches? Would the Bush administration, in fact, agree that adulthood in America equals disillusionment?[4]

Certain Bush resonances, in fact, might more easily be suggested by the American Players Theatre's ostensibly non-political production. López-Morillas envisioned the play as a 'life journey … a compelling metaphor for the trials and triumphs of our own lives, [celebrating] the love of family, forgiveness, and the intervention of divine grace to heal the wounds of time and fortune'. Among the stages of adult life was accepting 'the responsibilities of rule and parenthood'. The hero of this production could be identified with a man who admits turning his back on youthful excess, who dramatically renounced alcohol at forty, who eventually found Jesus, who didn't bother to study in college but after various misadventures realized his own inadequacies:

> Yon king's to me like to my father's picture,
> Which tells me in that glory once he was,
> Had princes sit like stars about his throne,
> And he the sun for them to reverence.
> None that beheld him, but like lesser lights

Did vail their crowns to his supremacy;
Where now his son's like a glow-worm in the night,
The which hath fire in darkness, none in light.

(2.3.36–43)

Hero and president both determine to follow in their fathers' footsteps and take responsibility for their countries. The Bush dynasty, and the many holdovers from earlier administrations, might be comfortable with Pericles' final vision of monarchical continuity as he comments on his father-in-law's death: 'Heavens make a star of him! … ourselves/Will in that kingdom spend our following days;/Our son and daughter shall in Tyrus reign' (5.3.80–3).

Neither of these productions was theoretically self-conscious; there were no references to the history of Shakespeare production, interpretation or reception. Banno and McGee certainly did not know that *Pericles* had a history of ideological mounting dating to within two years of its first appearance in 1608. Almost certainly it was for a polemical purpose that *Pericles* was done by the Cholmeley players, a group of recusant actors travelling in Yorkshire in the Christmas season of 1609–10. Their repertory also included *King Lear*, *The Travels of the Three English Brothers* and a 'St. Christopher Play', and they may have silently modified the play to promote a specifically Catholic interpretation.[5] For scholars, perhaps the most provocative issue raised by Washington's 'political' *Pericles* is the relation, or rather the lack of relation, between the connections the directors drew to current events and attempts by New Historicists to read the play within the context of early modern political and religious concerns.

The two productions, in Washington and Spring Green, replicate the divided history of *Pericles*' interpretation. Throughout most of the twentieth century, Shakespeare's romances were viewed generically and archetypally, as representations of the human journey. Northrop Frye summed up such views in his Charles Eliot Norton lectures, *The Secular Scripture: A Study of the Structure of Romance*. *Pericles*, with its imperfections and uncertainties the most 'naive' and transparent of Shakespeare's romances, is the clearest example. For example, of the four usually grouped together, it is the one in which the voyage is not merely a metaphor but the central and repeated action. Similarly, G. Wilson Knight viewed *Pericles* as the first serious treatment of the music–tempest opposition he believed fundamental to the late plays.

By the later 1980s, however, a revisionist view of the romances became common. In the eyes of materialist and feminist critics *The Tempest* is as much about relations between colonists and colonized, superiors and subalterns, patriarchs and female dependents as about myths of immortality or the last stage in an artist's journey. Eventually critics turned the same lens on *Pericles*. For Steven Mullaney the play's occlusion of the source hero's merchandizing and its ambiguous treatment of Marina in the brothel mark its 'evasion of the economic and cultural roots of the popular stage', a radical effort to imagine drama as a 'purely aesthetic phenomenon, free from history and from historical determination' (1988: 145–7). Simon Palfrey insists that the name Pericles, given to a character who in every source going back to the fifth century is known as Apollonius, and often said to be borrowed from the Pyrocles of Sidney's *Arcadia*, instead suggested 'to the educated Renaissance individual … the great Athenian demagogue' (1997: 52). For Palfrey the name signals that Shakespeare's real subject is 'humanist political theory in its republican form: how to define civic virtue and create a sustainable balanced state'

(1997: 48). Constance Jordan considers the common subject of the romances to be 'the restoration of good government' and finds Pericles a failed ruler, one who abandons his subjects to their alien enemies, gives away their property, and is 'complicit with misfortune'. He needs to learn 'the relations comprised by a mixed monarchy' (1997: 36–56).

Although one might conclude that the essentially simultaneous (re)appearance of politicized criticism and politicized productions in the late twentieth century responded to similar cultural forces, the readings of these literary critics and of Banno/McGee are quite different, sometimes even contradictory. New historicist interpretations emphasize Pericles' status as a prince and his behavior as a ruler; Jordan relates Pericles' political problems to James I's difficulties with the House of Commons and suggests that the eventual union of Tyre and Pentapolis shadows the creation of Great Britain. Both American productions discussed here were instead concerned with Pericles as an 'average joe', an 'everyman'. Jordan describes Pericles' kingdom as verging on anarchy due to the absence of an effective leader, yet at the Washington Shakespeare, Helicanus, 'an old childhood friend and perhaps a former girl friend of Pericles', was a 'trusted advisor', running the kingdom well while the king travelled.[6] The feminist imperative to show effective female rule trumped concern with the derelictions of an absent ruler. Similarly, Jordan and Palfrey say little about the brothel scenes, but to Banno these scenes, 'juxtaposing filth and domesticity', push definitions of sexuality and of what constitutes a family, continuing political issues in the USA.

Despite its contemporary *frisson* the Washington interpretation was in some ways less radical than that of the New Historicists. For instance, where Jordan sees Pericles' gift of food to the Tarsians as an abuse of his subjects' property, the production presented it traditionally, as a sign of charitable generosity. Similarly, recent scholarship on travel in the early modern period suggests that the stops on Pericles' voyages around the Mediterranean are meaningful and should be treated with geographical and historical accuracy, rather than merged into illustrative aspects of one country. George Wilkins, Shakespeare's collaborator on *Pericles*, was one of the authors of *The Travels of the Three English Brothers*, about the three adventurous Shirleys who journeyed to and served, among others, the Sultan and the Pope. The 'sympathetic depiction of the Papacy' in that play (Parr 1995: 10) – Anthony Shirley was a notable convert – may explain why it was found with *Pericles* in the Cholmeley players' repertory. The conclusion of *Travels* actually inverts the Washington Shakespeare's innovative separate stages. Stressing the problems of distance and inaccessibility that arose from the action's real locations, Fame, the Chorus, invites the audience to let their 'apprehensions help poor art/ Into three parts dividing this our stage,/ ... Think this England, this Spain, this Persia'. In dumb show the three separated brothers, standing on one stage, then view each other through perspective glasses. Such texts registered changing historical consciousness: as Parr summarizes, 'the travel play is implicated in the material processes of Europe's reconnaissance of the Old World and its "fortunate discovery" of the new. In it traditional ideas become volatile, trendy and debatable' (1995: 4–5).

The Washington *Pericles*' travels, from the redneck kitchen to the brothel, are trendy and material but not always consistent. For example, the final scene, in Ephesus, returns to the emergency room in St. Diana's Hospital, where we find Thaisa as a nurse rather than as one of Diana's 'maiden priests' (5.1.229). The result is aesthetically and interpretively problematic. First, the setting lacks the aura of magic that seems required for the goddess-directed rediscovery of the presumably dead wife. More important, following this production's logic, are we to conclude that an emergency room represents America at the end of the twentieth century? If so, is that because the country is ill, or because the country is a place of resuscitation? Would either view be shared outside of the nation's capital? By the last scene the text's focus on personal relations and re-established family may impede audience concentration on the political significance of the travel metaphor, or the reverse is possible – concentration on America may distract us from the emotional family reunion. In an apparent contradiction to the production's general interpretative stance, McGee's 'Notes from the Dramaturg' conclude with T.S. Eliot's timeless, essentially religious statement that 'We shall not cease from exploration and the end of all our exploring will be to arrive where we started and know the place for the first time'.

Ultimately the most difficult problem facing a director or adapter of *Pericles* seems to be balancing the two halves emotionally. Deeply inventive productions, such as Toby Robertson's 1974 Edinburgh Festival *Pericles*, which framed the play in a Byzantine homosexual brothel, repeatedly demonstrate that the mythic and psychological elements pull against the imposition of a polemical appropriation, or, as in Washington, that ideological readings of the first acts impede audience response to the two most emotional scenes of the play, the reunions of Pericles and Marina in 5.1 and of Pericles and Thaisa in 5.3. Reactions are individual, of course. According to David Skeele, Peter Sellars was drawn to *Pericles* for his inaugural production at the Boston Shakespeare Company in 1983 because the play suited his deconstructive methodology, which emphasized 'the excitement of the individual moment over the cogency of the whole' and an acting style of 'deliberate fragmentation' (1998: 133–4). For one Boston critic this meant that 'the play ... begins to lose its energy about three-quarters of the way through', yet another found 'tremendous emotional force to the great reunion scene' (Kevin Kelly, *Boston Globe*; Jack Kroll, *Newsweek*, quoted in Skeele 1998: 325, 327–8).

Post-modern productions, which tend to avoid a continuous development of emotional engagement, are especially prone to difficulties with *Pericles* if they do not address the uneasy transition between the sections of the play, a transition caused only in part by the difference in authors. Although the first two (Wilkins) acts are linguistically flatter, the shape remains that of Shakespearean romance, with its 'sequence of archetypes' (Frye 1976: 51), its pattern of 'love, loss, and restoration' (Hoeniger 1963: lxxix). To violate or deconstruct this rhythm often evokes distressed responses. This was the case with Brian Kulick's treatment at the Public Theater in New York in 1998, which succeeded for the first half, 'but during the second half... the hazard emerges of stressing design ... to the exclusion of characters and relationships. Suddenly the written text develops poetry ... All at once there is a king, Pericles, who suffers like Lear, and a recognition scene between father and daughter that rivals the intensity of Lear and Cordelia, but emotion and poetry go begging, for the director has prepared neither actors nor audience for their appearance' (Greene 1998). Of the 1991 Public Theater production directed by Michael Greif, Frank Rich wrote, 'the scene that matters most ... the Pericles–Marina recognition scene, is unmoving here. The jokey tone of the sequences preceding this reunion make it impossible for the actors to raise the production's emotional temperature abruptly at this late juncture'. At the Oregon Shakespeare Festival in 1989, Alan Dessen reports, earlier 'high-comic moments' and a 'burlesque treatment' of the brothel scenes did not impede the Pericles–Marina reunion, but 'the trade-offs were most evident in 5.3, where the climactic reunion of Pericles and Thaisa ... elicited significant laughter'.

The crisis in establishing audience affect always comes towards the end. The Washington Shakespeare, provocative in all of its cultural referents, climaxed in the deeply disturbing realistic brothel scene. The reunion, although it had its clever moments, as when to prove she was 'the daughter to King Pericles' (5.1.169) Marina pulled out his dogtag, had neither political referent nor much emotional resonance.[7] Meanwhile the less 'adapted' Spring Green production, pleasant but not notable in its earlier acts, had a gripping scene in the brothel even without textual additions and a deeply moving reunion between Pericles and Marina. The discrepancy could not be blamed on the different authors, because both the brothel and the reunion scene are in the 'Shakespeare' half.

I would suggest a number of reasons why the Washington production faltered toward the end. First, there is the reading itself. Political appropriations run the risk of alienating their audiences through disagreements not over the play but over the external events which such productions interpret and evaluate. Though the details of the American voyage toward disillusionment would be recognizable to an audience of congressional staffers and political aficionados, they might not share this vision of the last thirty years. Or they might feel that the end of Shakespeare's play proposes a happy restoration, one not consonant with the arc of the production but one for which they were still eager. America, after all, is not just their home but in many cases their work.

Next, as already suggested, the constant requirement for the audience to move may have had an alienating effect. Although Shakespeare's audience did not sit still in the dark isolation of a modern day cinema – *Pericles* was a Globe play – the self-consciously disruptive and distancing staging was, perhaps, inherently more suited to satirical/political scenes in Tarsus than to a moving and intimate, semi-mystical father–daughter rediscovery. The evening as event may have come to seem more important than the fable being retold.

The Spring Green production, on the other hand, on the night I saw it received astonishing assistance from its rural setting. At the end of 5.1, having rediscovered Marina, Pericles hears the 'music of the spheres' (217), sleeps, and has a vision of Diana. In the Wisconsin darkness Diana appeared on the second level of the open stage with a full moon directly over her head, and the audience reacted as if there were true magic at the end of Pericles' journey. It was easy to believe, even if briefly, in what the programme called 'the intervention of divine grace to heal the wounds of time and fortune'.

Adaptations that suit their audience and their time do not work on infinitely malleable texts. They can bring plays vividly alive, but they may wrench them so far from their original shape that they appear distorted. Simon Palfrey hesitantly acknowledges that some critical readings of the play may not be fully sustained by the original. *Pericles* 'engages a debate … between a "mixed estate" and absolutist monarchy', but nevertheless, he admits, 'romance's engagement with history is too much taken with things primal and irrational to be contained by either the ends or the eloquence, however admirable, of a "vir civilis"' (1997: 65). While literary critics have learned to tiptoe around any suggestion of authorial intention, reviewers seem quite willing to judge what they see in the theatre against a vision, a 'meaning', that they perceive to pre-exist in a work. For example, Kulick was repeatedly criticized for contradicting *Pericles*' 'fluid essence' by commissioning a 'set built entirely of sliding panels and platforms… better suited to some constructivist epic than this mystical romance' (Sommers 1998). John Simon simply announced that *Pericles* is 'based on the wondrous, the spectacular, the awesome' but

'As the poetical is clearly beyond Kulick's ken, the political becomes primary' (1998). Toby Robertson claimed that his Prospect Theatre 'transvestite production, mirror[ed] the reversal of sexuality that is a feature of the text', but *The Guardian* objected that the 'emphasis on sexual masquerade constantly works against the text' (Skeele 2000: 280–1). Even a sophisticated scholar/critic like Peter Holland, analysing what went wrong in Phyllida Lloyd's 1994 National Theatre *Pericles*, summarizes that 'in the event, the production lost sight of the play' (1997: 214).

To conclude that a production expresses the predilections of a director need not be to condemn it. Conceivably, Shakespeare never considered that Isabella might reject the Duke's hand, but feminist appropriations of *Measure for Measure* have proven powerful theatre. We need not conclude that Shakespeare was a Roman Catholic because the Yorkshire production may have found a way to make his text accommodate the beliefs of one company and audience. It is true that once all of *Pericles* takes place in a bordello, the original brothel scenes tend to lose their shock value. On the other hand, Margaret Healy has provocatively suggested that, on the basis of early modern disease patterns, Lysimachus might have the pox. To stage *Pericles* with such a radically estranged husband for the heroine would fundamentally undermine the romantic/structural reading of Knight and Frye, yet perhaps it could be made to appear consistent with the text's focus on gender and sexual relations. What we think of as the *intentio operis* is limited by the evidence we can find in the text but it is also no doubt limited by our own imagination, context and expectations. The Washington Shakespeare *Pericles* may not have been 'entirely at the service of the story' (Holland 1997: 66). Certainly that at Spring Green seemed more immediately sustained by the text. Yet the political *Pericles* was enormously effective, and its purposes may have been fulfilled by making the play meaningful to its local audience. And while neither production was theoretically or critically self-conscious, they both effectively revealed similarities as well as tensions between recent theatrical and academic responses to *Pericles*. Such tensions in turn highlight the inevitably local nature of both responses.

4 Shylock as crypto-Jew: A new Mexican adaptation of *The Merchant of Venice*

Elizabeth Klein and Michael Shapiro

In 1993, a bilingual troupe in Albuquerque, New Mexico, *La Compañia de Teatro*, produced a radical adaptation of *The Merchant of Venice* entitled *The Merchant of Sante Fe*. The production was set in colonial New Spain in 1670 and the Shylock character, Don Saul, was a moneylender who had outwardly converted to Christianity but who in secret remained a practicing Jew. In other words, he passed as a *converso*, or New Christian, but was in reality a crypto-Jew, a *judaizante*, a *marrano*. In the years preceding and during the run of the production, there had been much talk of individuals in present-day New Mexico who traced their lineage to crypto-Jews of the colonial period. *The Merchant of Santa Fe* was intended to exploit local interest in this topic by adapting Shakespeare's text in accordance with facts and conjectures about the history of *conversos*, as well as to raise issues germane to current American ethnic politics.

Jews have a very long history in Spain.[1] Throughout the medieval period, Jews had had extensive and largely peaceful contacts with their Moslem and Christian neighbors, especially in economic and intellectual spheres of activity, for the most without hostile incident under both Islamic and Christian rulers under the doctrine of *convivencia*, i.e. 'living together with others'. By the thirteenth century, there were about 100,000 Jews in Spain, or roughly 2% of the population (Mackay 1992: 33) In the fourteenth century, however, in response to rising anti-Jewish sentiment, many Jews converted to Christianity, voluntarily or under coercion. In the anti-Jewish riots of 1391, many Jews were killed and several Jewish settlements were ravaged or destroyed. A high proportion of survivors became New Christians, or *conversos*.[2] In order to sever any links between *conversos* and their unconverted Jewish brethren, and perhaps to coerce additional conversions, Ferdinand and Isabella issued an edict on 31 March 1492, giving their Jewish subjects four months either to become Christian or to leave Spain.[3]

Conversos are part of the history of Iberian colonization of the New World, particularly in the establishment of trade. Although Ferdinand and Isabella of Spain banned New Christians from the New World in 1501, in 1509 they permitted them to buy their way into the colonies for a period of two years (Gitlitz 1996: 69 n.57; Roth 1932: 271ff.; Sachar 1985: 229). Charles V reversed this policy in 1522, when he prohibited Christians with even partial Jewish or Islamic ancestry from entering America. The re-issuing of the prohibition in 1539 suggests that it had met with less than total success. As many as half the Spanish inhabitants of Mexico City in the sixteenth century may have been of Jewish origin (Witznitzer 1962: I, 89). Howard Sachar finds compelling evidence that most of these New Christians were secretly professing Jews. Some were even living openly as Jews, and there is a report of a Grand Rabbi in Mexico City in the 1550s (Sachar 1985: 229–31;

Liebman 1970: 2). As in Europe, they may have passed themselves off as 'Portuguese' (Bodian 1997: 175 n.4).[4]

Placing *judaizantes* in colonial New Mexico is more speculative than placing them in Mexico itself. The only recorded accusations of judaizing were levelled in 1663 against Bernard Lopez de Mendizabal, Governor-General of New Mexico. Lopez, whose Jewish grandmother had been burned at the stake in Spain, died in prison in 1664 and was posthumously exonerated in 1671 (Liebman 1970: 22–3; Tobias 1990: 16). The movement of crypto-Jews from Mexico proper to its northern frontier of New Mexico is conjectural. Contemporary historians hypothesize that crypto-Jews wanting to distance themselves from the Inquisition, whose headquarters were in Mexico City, moved to New Mexico in the initial expedition led by Juan Oñate in 1598, in subsequent reinforcements, or in the resettlement following the Pueblo Revolt of 1680 which had forced the Spanish to abandon the region.

In the last few decades, persistent reports have come to light of crypto-Jews or their descendents still residing in New Mexico, as elsewhere in the American southwest. Writing in 1990, Henry Tobias hoped that such anecdotal evidence might be supplemented by archival discoveries:

> However tenuous the evidence reaching the eyes and ears of scholars to date, the future seems to promise more – not less. That, of course, is an expectation and not a conclusion. How much material of a persuasive scholarly nature can be gleaned from records, what may be drawn from existing customs to link the past with the present, remains an open question. Nevertheless, whereas in 1960 the search seemed to lead to a dead end, in the late 1980s a new awareness of both past and present makes scholarly pursuit a worthwhile challenge and a necessary task.
>
> (1990: 21)

While the archival record has still not yielded the kinds of hard evidence Tobias sought, the body of anecdotal material has increased exponentially, largely as a result of the work of Stanley Hordes, State Historian of New Mexico from 1981 to 1985. Hordes recalls how people would come to his office, close the door and whisper about their neighbours' odd doings, such as turning religious images to the wall, lighting candles on Friday nights or refusing to eat pork. It reminded him of denunciations to the Inquisition. Reports like these, and encounters with individuals whose families practiced such rituals without necessarily understanding their source, persuaded Hordes of a Sephardic (i.e. Iberian Jewish) legacy in present day New Mexico. He also found families who claimed to be hidden Jews, families in which informants claim to have been told as children by parents or older relatives, '*Somos judios* – we are Jews', along with instructions to find spouses only from certain families, also believed to be crypto-Jews.

Many of Hordes's informants were unwilling to allow their names to be used. Known to their neighbours and priests as practising Catholics, they feared ostracism and reprisal. They might also have harboured ancient fears that exposure of Jewish identity could compromise their rights to hold land granted to ancestors believed to be Old Christians. To gather more evidence and to assess its value, Hordes and Tomás Atencio, a sociologist, founded a project at the University of New Mexico entitled 'The Sephardic Legacy in New Mexico'. Based on subsequent research, Hordes listed seven commonly found practices as pointing toward crypto-Jewish ancestry, especially found in clusters: 'Friday-night candle lighting, refraining from eating pork, observing a Saturday Sabbath, covering mirrors during mourning, circumcision, playing with a four-sided top, and leaving pebbles on a grave' (Hordes 1993: 137–8).

By the early 1990s, the presence of crypto-Jews in New Mexico had become a highly controversial topic from both Jewish and Chicano perspectives. The Jewish community was torn between scepticism about the authenticity of Chicanos claiming Jewish descent, fear over their possible Christianizing influence and excitement over the return of a 'lost tribe' (Neulander 1994; Halevy 1996). The Chicano community was no less ambivalent. Some feared that claiming crypto-Jewish identity displayed 'a desire to be Gringo' (Flores 1993a: 9). Chicanos who thought they might have Jewish descent were troubled. As one of Hordes's friends remarked, 'It's hard enough being Hispanic; don't let me be Jewish too' (Hordes 1993: 137). Some who discovered crypto-Jewish ancestry felt it had no claim on their present identity. They had been raised as practising Catholics, were comfortable in the Church and did not wish to redefine their identities on the basis of what some of their ancestors are alleged to have done or been. Such was the view of an Albuquerque businesswoman, Millie Santillanes, whose family name, Duran, appears on some lists as one of Jewish origin: 'To reach back over 400 years and embrace a foreign faith is inconceivable. How can anyone disavow 400 years of family history?' (Santillanes 1993: A11). Hordes summarizes the way both communities have consigned these hidden Jews to a kind of no-man's land: 'They are too Catholic for the Jews and too Jewish for the Catholics' (Gruzen 1996: sect. 1, 20).

La Compañia de Teatro was at the time producing a series of plays set in colonial New Mexico which would also dramatize issues relevant to the contemporary Chicano community. Adapting *The Merchant of Venice* would permit them to exploit current local interest in crypto-Jews and their historical background, as well as to probe more general issues of intercultural relations in and for an increasingly multi-ethnic community. Their play would be a radical adaptation of Shakespeare's work, with Shylock conceived as a crypto-Jew. It was to be retitled *The Merchant of Santa Fe* and set in the 1670s in the Spanish colonial settlement of Santa Fe (before the Pueblo Revolt of 1680) and on an estate, or *estancia*, in nearby Manzano. It would play for about two weeks at the KiMo Theatre on Central Avenue, a former movie and vaudeville theatre built in 1927 in a southwestern-accented period style called Pueblo Deco. Additional free performances would be given under *La Compañia's barrio* touring programme in two local churches. This was a local production, both in terms of its agenda and its target audience. However, its significance exceeds the confines of such a specific locality. A closer analysis of this adaptation reveals how local Shakespeares can exploit the controversial but culturally central legacy of a play like *The Merchant of Venice* to address time- and place-specific concerns. Such local appropriations can in turn help the scholarly and theatre-going community establish how our notion of what 'Shakespeare' is or what 'Shakespeare' should sound like is being challenged and adapted to suit an increasingly multi-ethnic and multicultural market. Interesting parallels between this production and the Royal Shakespeare Company's 1993 production of *The Merchant of Venice* analysed by Maria Jones in this volume show that the strategies adopted to make this play relevant in New Mexico are representative of pressures felt far beyond its geographical borders.

La Compañia was founded in 1977 by José Rodriguez, a graduate of RADA in London, under the auspices of the University of Albuquerque, a Catholic college. It is now an independent free–standing community theatre, supported by grants, donations and box office receipts. Ramón Flores, a native of Albuquerque who joined the troupe in 1979, has been its artistic director since 1983, except for a three-year hiatus during which he earned an MFA at Yale. Flores had been thinking of a Chicano version of a Shakespearean text since he started graduate school. In the late 1980s, Flores began reading such historical studies as Americo Castro's books on the ethnic and cultural diversity of Spanish society and Seymour Liebman's work on Jews in Spain's New World colonies, and he was of course aware of Hordes's work and of current discussions of the local crypto-Jewish phenomenon. Flores had presented the idea for the New Mexican version of *The Merchant* at a conference, seconding Louis Valdez's argument that Chicano theatre needed both to confront immediate issues of the community and to celebrate *mestizaje,* or the quality of being *mestizo,* of having hybrid ancestry. As Flores put it, 'The celebration of *el mestizaje* means recognizing and valuing the enormous contributions to the Chicano and Hispanic experience made by not only the native peoples of the Americas and the Spanish Christians, but also the Sephardic Jews, the Arabs, the Berbers, the Sub-Saharan Africans, and the Gypsies, to name the principle groups' (Flores 1990: 1).

Under Flores's leadership, the development of any new script ideally takes about eighteen months. It begins with a *tertulia,* an open meeting to discuss relevant issues, followed by a public reading of the first draft. This cycle is to be repeated twice more, with the director and actors finally beginning rehearsal with the fourth draft. In the case of *The Merchant of Santa Fe,* it was foreshortened to about eight months. The first *tertulia,* 'Crypto Jews in 17th Century New Mexico', held on 13 February 1993 at the Albuquerque Museum, has been preserved on videotape (Flores 1993b). It featured presentations by Hordes and a sociologist at the University of California at San Diego named Ramón Gutierrez, originally from Albuquerque, followed by a general discussion moderated by Ramón Flores.

About a month later, Flores circulated a fourteen-page concept paper among people he felt would be interested in the production. As he imagined it, his version of the play would be set in Spanish New Mexico ten or twelve years before the Pueblo Revolt. 'Our task', Flores explained, 'is to fully expand the story in the context of Spanish Colonial New Mexico while we destroy Shakespeare's anti-Semitic framework'. To achieve the latter goal, he proposed to modify Shakespeare's Shylock, who, according to him, was a slightly humanized version of 'the archetype of the malevolent Jew straight out of medieval anti-semitism' (Flores 1993a: 4) Flores outlined several departures from the Shakespearean original: (a) Shylock's assimilation to Hispanic culture is manifested by his nearly suicidal devotion to the code of *honra* (honor), as he is determined to collect the pound of flesh awarded him by the court and for so doing wins the grudging respect of his enemy Antonio. (b) He is prevented from collecting the pound of flesh by other Jewish characters, who represent a rational and humane Jewish perspective lacking in Shakespeare's version, a perspective amplified by the enlargement of Tubal's role and by the introduction of other Jewish characters, especially a young army officer. (c) Portía reveals her own Jewish ancestry to Bassanio in the final scene in dialogue he had already written:

PORTÍA: You know, *querido,* my grandfather planted this orchard.
BASSANIO: *Ya lo se.* Governor-General Don Juan de Oñate gave him this *encomienda* to
    recognize his years of service. Everyone knows your grandfather was a great

administrator. Don Juan de Oñate could not have established the colony without him.

PORTÍA: My grandfather served the Oñates since the time he arrived from Portugal.

BASSANIO: (*starting to get alarmed*) You mean your grandfather was a *judaizan*-

PORTÍA: Shhh! (*stopping him with her finger to his lips*) *Amor*, welcome to the family.

(1993a: 11–12)

The concept paper also discussed the recent emergence of crypto-Jews in New Mexico, acknowledged Hordes's and Atencio's research, but declared that 'this adaptation will take no position on the continuation of the crypto-Jewish identity into the late 20th century'. For Flores, the more relevant issue was 'how ... the crypto-Jewish experience [is] part of the New Mexican *mestizaje*', thus revealing a pressing concern with ethnic as well as religious issues (Flores 1993a: 11–12).

In collaboration with Lynn Butler, a playwright from Los Cruces, New Mexico, Flores then began work on the first draft of the play. It had a public reading on 17 June and a reading of scenes from the second draft took place on 12 August, followed on 17 August by the second *tertulia*, entitled 'Shakespeare, Anti-Semitism, and New Mexico's Hidden Jews'. The final draft of the script bears the date 22 September, only eight days before opening night, which suggests that during and even late into the rehearsal process, it was still undergoing revision. Flores and Butler's first draft was a complete and radical revision of the Shakespearean original. It contained no blank verse, was written in colloquial prose, ten percent of which was in Spanish, in keeping with *La Compañía's* bilingual tradition. Characters moved easily between English and Spanish, often in the same speech. A few characters with no Shakespearean counterparts, e.g. Clarin, a comical town crier, and Doña Amparo, a brothel-keeper, help to create the atmosphere of colonial New Mexico. In terms of plot, Flores and Butler stuck fairly closely to the Shakespearean original. Don Saul is more or less equal to Shylock in vengefulness, into which he (like Shylock) is goaded, but his villainy is counterbalanced by the humaneness of other male Jews: Erasmo (Tubal), whose staunchly loyal friendship and moderate views echo recent directorial strategies as explained by Maria Jones in this volume, and Lieutenant Manzanares, a *converso* army officer, who is the only newly invented Jewish character in Flores and Butler's adaptation.

In the final draft, Don Saul becomes a far more sympathetic figure. Instead of asking for a pound of flesh as collateral, Don Saul asks Don Antonio to sign his standard bond for loans. Don Saul respects Don Antonio's word but feels obliged to heed the Governor-General's edict that all such agreements be made contractual, so that Spaniards can demonstrate honest and honourable behaviour in dealings with one another and with the neighbouring *Indios*, or Native Americans. Angry that the mere word of a Spanish gentleman will not suffice, Don Antonio offers his life as collateral. Another element which makes Don Saul more sympathetic throughout this draft is the enlarged presence of Salazar, a particularly vicious Jew-hater who is determined to detect the presence of hidden *judaizantes* in Santa Fe and report them to his uncle in the Inquisition. He explains to Rafael how determined they are to conceal their Jewishness:

I've seen Jews burn on the pyres of New Spain, swearing as the flames wrapped their limbs in holy fire that they were followers of Christ. But inwardly, inwardly Rafael, such men keep secret faith with the law of Moses.

(Butler and Flores 1993: 10)

Such nightmares haunt the Jews as well, especially Don Saul's daughter Rebeca (Jessica), as her father tells his friend Erasmo:

> Do you know, when the Inquisition charged Governor-General Lopez de Mendizabal and Francisco Gomez Robledo with being hidden Jews nine years ago, my Rebeca couldn't sleep. And when we heard that the Governor General had died in jail, my poor girl dreamt that I was roasted alive at the stake and that she was dragged through the streets, forced to wear a yellow hood and whipped until the blood streamed from her back.
>
> (Butler and Flores 1993: 31)

In a further departure from the Shakespearean original, since the pound of flesh has been totally eliminated from the final version of the script, Don Saul produces no pair of scales but only a knife with which to take Don Antonio's life. Throughout this final version of the trial scene, Don Saul argues that he needs to avenge an insult to his *honra*, which he sometimes calls his *koved*, using the Hebrew word approximating honour. But as Erasmo had suggested, there is a vast cultural difference between *honra* and *koved*, and Don Saul is following the Spanish aristocratic code of honour far more than any Jewish ethical imperative.

In the final draft, his Jewish friends fail to intervene as they did in the first draft to prevent him from taking Don Antonio's life. Nor will he be deterred by the prospect of his own subsequent death: ' "The *judaizante* won't trade his life for vengeance, eh?" I am *puro Español, y nacimos para morir. A ver*, let's see who dies better' (Butler and Flores 1993: 97). He raises his knife to kill Don Antonio and then lowers it. What stops him is his own inability to kill another man, even one he hates. He tries again and cannot do it, even when he covers Don Antonio's eyes. In the confusion, he and Don Antonio struggle, and the knife passes from one to the other. Don Antonio cannot kill Don Saul either, nor does he want to die at the Jew's hands, and when Don Saul raises the knife for the last time, Don Antonio involuntarily cries out 'No!' (Butler and Flores 1993: 98). The other *castizos* denounce him as a coward for refusing to kill and for his reluctance to die, but he and Don Saul reconcile and shake hands in genuine acknowledgment of one another's humanity and worth. Back at Manzano, Don Antonio even toasts Don Saul as a man of honour, but only Portía and her confidante Nerisa will drink to the Jew. Rebeca sends her father a letter asking for his forgiveness for eloping with a *horko* (Christian) on the grounds that she acted out of love and not out of shame of her Jewishness. Don Saul is touched and under the humane influence of Erasmo, he seems inclined to pardon her. As in the first draft, Portía reveals her 'Portuguese' grandfather.

The new emphasis on ethnic as well as religious concerns emerges once again in Flores and Butler's characterization of Lazaro (Launcelot Gobbo). Lazaro is a *genizaro*, an Indian captured as a child by the Spanish colonists, treated as a servant and raised as a Christian. The word evidently derives from the Turkish *janissary* and the practice was not introduced until the eighteenth century, but Flores and Butler use the anachronism to enable Lazaro to make a political point. Clarin scoffs at any previous religion a *genizaro* might have had, but Lazaro dreams he lived with a family who spoke a strange tongue he came to understand, and he interprets his dream as instructing him to rejoin the surrounding Apaches (Butler and Flores 1993: 104). He proudly identifies himself as Apache, rather than Pueblo, and his sneer at 'those pot makers' (Butler and Flores 1993: 30), which drew a large laugh, pointed to existing tensions over tribal ancestry. He discloses his plan to Nerisa, who is also a *genizara*, and urges her to join him, but she refuses: '*No hables tonterias. Genizara!* I'm married now, *entiendes?* I'm Spanish. *Dejame sola!*' (Butler and Flores 1993: 112). In the actual production, the population of Portía's *estancia* illustrated the rich tapestry of *mestizaje* even more than the text. In addition to the text's under-scoring of Portía's Jewish heritage and Nerisa's Apache parentage, Flores cast Portía's steward Ysidro (Balthazar) with an African-American actor, whose skin colour, shaved head and exotic robe signalled, however anachronistically, the presence of African slaves in New Mexico in the late seventeenth century. The play sees the New Mexican frontier as the last bastion of *convivencia*.

For this reason, in both first and final drafts, the local civilian authority, represented by the Governor-General, and supported by army officers and soldiers, seems relatively indifferent to the presence of crypto-Jews among them. Most of those who know seem not to care. They are far more concerned with the danger from the Apaches, who are restive and hostile and who have recently captured a supposedly impregnable *fortaleza* and massacred all Spaniards within it. Even the Holy Office cannot bother to come from Salinas to Santa Fe to investigate the possibility of a cohort of Jews for several months. Among the Spaniards, only Salazar, a rabid anti-semite, wants to expose hidden Jews to the Inquisition. He is regarded as a pathological case and the Governor-General orders him exiled to dangerous military service as punishment for his trouble-making.

The lack of representatives of Christian anti-semitism further blunts the collision of religious attitudes in the play. In the first draft, Don Antonio finally sees the hostility between himself and Don Saul as one between Christian and Jew. In the final draft, both men defend their *honra*. Barry Gaines, a Shakespeare scholar at the University of New Mexico, described the final draft as more about Spanish honour than about Christian attitudes toward Jews (Gaines 1993). Don Saul in the final draft represents a higher code of Spanish *honra* than the Spanish themselves. He is so much the Spanish gentleman that when Erasmo urges him to flee to Morocco or Turkey, where other Iberian Jews have settled, he refuses:

> No. *Aunque me cueste la vida*, I will not run away. We are Sephardim, Erasmo. And we are *Español*. I cannot separate one from the other. I am what I am. And until we are allowed to go back to Spain, *Aqui me quedo*.
>
> (Butler and Flores 1993: 69)

Struggling to balance the Jewish and Hispanic sides of his identity, Don Saul articulates contemporary American and Jewish-American dilemmas more than the historic experi-ence of *conversos*. Crucially, Flores and Butler's interventions did not only neutralize what they saw as the anti-semitism intrinsic to the Shakespearean original, which is a common strategy among recent and contemporary adapters of *The Merchant of Venice* (see Jones' and Schülting's essays in this volume), but they also altered the relative balance between Jewish–Christian conflict and broader problems of multiculturalism.

Changes in the characterization of Portía's suitors also emphasized codes of honour and *machismo*. In the first draft, the first suitor, Don Renaldo, is a crude caricature of Shakespeare's Aragon. He is followed by Clarin, the town crier, an ineligible suitor because of his class. He is a coarse, low-comic servant, the kind Shakespeare used as a parodic contrast with aristocratic characters. In the final draft, however, Don Renaldo's rival wooer is Floribundo, an outlandishly *macho* buccaneer, and the two become so preoccupied with dueling in the name of honour, a practice forbidden on Portía's *estancia*, that they prefer to go and fight one another rather than take their chances on winning her. As one of them explains, the world contains many women for them to court but only one duel a man can fight to the death. According to Flores, the duel over honour between Portía's comic suitors was added to mock the absurdities of the Hispanic code of honour, and to serve as both parody and foil to the confrontation between Don Antonio and Don Saul in the trial scene. Here, Flores and Butler hoped to touch a live nerve in the Chicano community. This code, or 'what you are willing to die for', as Flores explained in a newspaper interview, 'has been responsible for deaths in his own family, in the family of friends, and in the ranks of Albuquerque's Hispanic gangs' (Reed 1993: 8).

Revisions were aimed at the concerns of both Jewish and Chicano communities. In the final version, Butler and Flores had gone far beyond Flores' original plan to counter any anti-semitic attitudes Shylock might evoke simply by surrounding him with other Jews espousing and embodying more humane perspectives. The final draft presented a Jew who was a fine upstanding Spanish gentleman, a light unto the Iberian nations, striving to balance both the Iberian and Jewish aspects of his identity. Susan Seligman, local director of the Anti-Defamation League, had worried that the production might exhibit anti-semitic biases, a fear raised by Richard Edwards and other members of Albuquerque's Catholic–Jewish Dialogue. In the end, Seligman was pleased with the final version, calling it 'a positive vehicle for promoting Jewish and Hispanic relations in New Mexico' (Steinberg 1993: 12).

Although some local reviewers were lukewarm toward the production (Reyes 1993: E4; Zimmerman 1993: 12), in retrospect, *La Compañia* should be congratulated for reworking Shakespeare's *The Merchant of Venice* further and more radically than productions which simply update its setting. Like other recent productions and adaptations, it presented its Jewish protagonist in terms of modern as well as early modern Jewish history. Butler's programme note articulates this bi-fold approach:

> How could Shakespeare's stereotypical Jew still stand in the face of the 20th Century Holocaust, the establishment of the state of Israel and the recent accord between the PLO and Israel? But we also wanted to make our Shylock, Don Saul, true to his time, when to be openly Jewish was to invite the Inquisition to ruin one's reputation, property, and life.

But Butler's note also presents the Jewish protagonist in terms of current debates over multiculturalism in America: 'Don Saul embodies the tension between staying true to one's separate culture or faith and the desire to belong to the mainstream culture' (Butler 1993: 5).

In short, in addition to confronting 'the Jewish question', the troupe also displayed a willingness to grapple with other contemporary concerns, such as Don Saul's Hispanic identity, the relations with Native Americans, the presence of African slaves, the treatment of women and the fatuity of *machismo*. Moreover, in addressing these issues, *La Compañia* remained in dialogue with various sectors of its community throughout the production process. One can argue that the production's weaknesses resulted from too many compromises, too great a willingness to negotiate the demands of different factions within the mix of ethnic politics of present-day America, nowhere more visible than in Albuquerque. But surely many of the 2000 or so spectators who saw *The Merchant of Santa Fe* at the KiMo theatre or during its *barrio* tour were encouraged by this appropriation of a Shakespearean text to reflect more deeply on their own ethnic identities, on the historical bases for those identities, and on how those identities exist in relation to those of others with whom they live in close proximity.

5 Negotiating intercultural spaces: *Much Ado About Nothing* and *Romeo and Juliet* on the Chinese stage

Ruru Li

Locality is a useful concept which can help us understand what constitutes genuinely intercultural theatre. Successful intercultural performance stretches the boundaries of the cultural field (as defined in the introduction to this volume), by creating new theatrical and cultural spaces through a complex negotiation of possible positions within the field (Bourdieu 1993). While the notion of locality is becoming increasingly relevant in performance studies, critical investigations of intercultural appropriations often ignore the essentially dynamic nature of these negotiations. Those who accuse intercultural theatre of stealing, manipulating or appropriating other cultures fail to acknowledge the degree to which both cultures actively interact with each other.

This chapter establishes how two Shakespearean productions directed by David Jiang (Chinese name Jiang Weiguo) in mainland China in 1986 and post-colonial Hong Kong in 2004 negotiated the distance between Shakespeare and theatrical conventions which are native to traditional and modern Chinese drama.[1] Jiang's experience indicates that an intercultural project constrains the director's artistic freedom because it requires painstakingly minute negotiations between often opposed preconditions and conventions which characterize the target and the source cultures. Yet, when such negotiations are successful, the result can be outstanding.

The two productions discussed in this chapter, *Much Ado About Nothing* (1986) and *Romeo and Juliet* (2004), represent two distinct styles of Shakespearean performance in China. *Much Ado* was adapted to suit the conventions of a regional type of traditional Chinese operatic theatre. By contrast, the recent production of *Romeo and Juliet* is more in line with modern Chinese spoken drama, which started at the beginning of the twentieth century under the influence of the Western dramatic traditions.

Looking for Trouble[2] sinified *Much Ado* into *huangmeixi*, a local musical form from Anhui province. The director carefully adapted Shakespeare's text to portray convincing Chinese characters in a Chinese setting. This production premiered at China's first Shakespeare Festival in 1986, by which time people felt they had finally emerged from the dark shadow of the Cultural Revolution and were full of hope for the future. Such an optimistic cultural climate probably led the practitioners to choose a romantic comedy and to overlook its potentially darker and satirical undertones. And yet 1986 and China's First Shakespeare Festival also marked a period of intense transition and adjustment. In 1986, after China had been cut off from the rest of world for decades, artists had little sense of what had been happening abroad. 'Shakespeare in jeans' had been denounced as a form of capitalist decadence and Chinese attitudes towards Shakespearean performance were still profoundly affected by the memory of the productions staged in the 1950s by Soviet practitioners, who had been invited to teach in the main Chinese drama academies. Socialist-realism had aimed at (re)constructing the ideal world of the European Renaissance. Consequently, actors had to pretend to be Westerners. Furthermore, China is a country where the acknowledgement of authenticity and acceptance of authority are strongly reinforced by traditional Confucian principles. Such principles were cynically absorbed and endorsed by the communist regime. As a result, the idea of producing a sinified Shakespeare was opposed by many scholars, because they felt that the greatest literary master of the Renaissance, extolled by Marx and Engels, would be tarnished by traditional Chinese theatre which was a relic of the feudal system. Clearly, the cultural context of the 1986 Shakespeare Festival represented a complex 'field of struggles' through which the director and scriptwriter of the *huangmeixi Much Ado* had to navigate warily.

Back in 1986, *Looking for Trouble* represented a ground-breaking experiment, carried out at a time when intercultural appropriations of Shakespeare were still regarded as a highly questionable and potentially flawed practice. Jiang remembers how he consciously departed from what his contemporaries thought was possible or even desirable to do while transferring Shakespeare to the Chinese stage: 'Even then I knew I would be unable to present either an authentic Shakespeare play or a pure *huangmeixi* performance. But I did not dare admit this because everyone else claimed they were doing real Shakespeare'.[3] Jiang was inspired and encouraged by the fact that *huangmeixi* is a relatively recent dramatic form, which originated from the tea-picking ballads in the Anhui/Hubei area. Compared to much older forms, such as *jingju* (best known in the West as 'Peking Opera') or *huiju* (regional opera in the Anhui area), *huangmeixi* would prove much more flexible and therefore more suitable for the experiment Jiang had in mind.

And yet *Much Ado* was not a natural choice as it does not immediately appear to be compatible with the rules and conventions of traditional Chinese opera. First, *Much Ado* includes multiple plots whereas the golden rule for traditional Chinese playwriting is 'one person [main character] and one thing [story-line] throughout the play'.[4] *Huangmeixi* showcases the actors' singing, which is sometimes accompanied by dance. The simple rule of 'one person [main character] and one thing [story-line] throughout the play' is meant to help the audience focus their attention on the performers' skills in these arts. Second, the storyline of *Much Ado* revolves around specific European ceremonies, such as the masked ball, for which there is no Chinese equivalent. The third and greatest challenge, however, was Beatrice.

Bicui, in the adaptation, is a proper Chinese name which conveniently provides the transliteration of the name Beatrice. The main problem for Jiang was how to *culturally* translate a young aristocratic woman, full of social confidence and verve, who demands to be treated like the other young aristocratic men in the play, into a character compatible with the traditional Chinese stage. It is also worth stressing that Beatrice's determination and will are clearly expressed not while she is in disguise, as many other Shakespearean heroines do. Traditional Chinese theatre has a strong repertoire of female characters who adopt a male disguise in order to surmount challenges that are deemed to be beyond a woman's physical and intellectual powers, but it had never accommodated the direct challenge presented by a figure like Beatrice.

Presenting a convincing Bicui proved to be Jiang's most challenging task. And yet his decision to attempt an intercultural encounter between Shakespeare and *huangmeixi* offered him the opportunity and the inspiration to introduce a brand new type of female character in traditional Chinese opera. Shakespeare's text was also transformed by its encounter with *huangmeixi*. The new possibilities offered by aria singing, music and dance as they are used in Chinese opera provided a Shakespearean female character with more means to express her inner world than merely speech. Besides, the *huangmeixi* repertoire is centred on the *dan*, or female role, and following this theatrical convention, *Looking for Trouble* gave Bicui a more prominent and active role than Beatrice in *Much Ado*. Thus, in the adaptation, it is Bicui – instead of Friar Francis – who has the wit and wisdom to arrange the faked death of Hailuo (Hero) and the recognition scene at the monument. As a result, Judith Cook's comments on Beatrice as a 'Lady of spirit' (1990: 26) seem to apply even more readily to Bicui than to Beatrice. The transformation of Beatrice into Bicui seems interestingly in line with recent mainstream theatrical appropriations which have similarly foregrounded Beatrice's exceptional voice within the strictly patriarchal context of Shakespeare's Messina.[5]

The adaptation sets the story in a remote area on the Chinese border, a *liminal* space where many ways of life unacceptable in mainstream China become conceivable. Bicui is brought up by her uncle because her parents died when she was little, and this explains why she is allowed more freedom to say and to do whatever she wants. She is a 'young mountain eagle' in her uncle's eyes.[6] In this geographically and culturally liminal area, women enjoy more freedom and are allowed to develop relationships with other young people more openly. Thus the 'merry war' between the Chinese Beatrice and Benedick becomes more credible. Yet, Bicui is still subject to rigorous gender-specific pressures and strict codes of behaviour and, from time to time, her uncle threatens to send her to the court in the capital to be formally educated if she fails to observe the rules.

The adaptation opens with a bustling scene of preparation for a masked ball. In the absence of a Chinese equivalent for a ball, the adapters drew on a local shamanic tradition to make this event intelligible to a Chinese audience. As the curtain rises, Bicui spells out her views on love, marriage, truth and deception by singing the following aria:

> Masks often hide a person's real heart,
> And a real heart usually cannot be seen through a false facade.
> No wonder a lot of marriages cause real grudges between two people,
> People cannot tell a false facade from a real heart.

The same motif reappears in the singing during the dance when Bicui and Bai Lidi (Benedick) meet again. Bicui takes off her mask and sings. 'Bicui never cheats people,' Her mask is her true face.' The Chinese word for a 'mask' literally means 'false face' and the word-play in the lyric effectively suggest that the pursuit of truth is Bicui's ultimate objective.

The special cultural and theatrical space created by this adaptation made it possible for Bicui to be a radical nonconformist. In her manifesto, inspired by the following lines in the Shakespearean original – 'a star danced' (2.1.316), 'Adam's sons are my brethren' (2.1.59) and 'Would it not grieve a woman to be overmastered with a piece of valiant dust …' (2.1.56–7)[7] – she describes herself as 'coming to this world fearless and undaunted', as 'a wild flower that is no good in an artificial garden' and as a monkey 'unwilling to be tied down'.

However, neither Shakespeare's original play nor contemporary China (merely ten years after the end of the Cultural Revolution) supported the ideal of a masculine heroine.

Chinese people had seen too many man-like female Red Guards or revolutionaries on and off stage during the Cultural Revolution. Most heroines in the revolutionary operas were women with no feelings, no families, assuming traditional man-warrior gestures and body movements on the stage. Moving away from this model of femininity was another challenge facing the director and his company. Bicui needed to be both radical and conventionally feminine in order to appeal to audiences who flocked to the traditional theatre because they were fed up with masculine revolutionary heroines. The arbour scene, when Beatrice is tricked into believing that love has finally arrived, gave the adapters an opportunity to bring out a more conventionally feminine aspect of her character. Bicui was given a twenty-four-line aria:

> … I was born free from anxiety,
> And where has this slight inkling of sadness come from?
> My face was always cold but now is burning – rosy clouds are rising,
> My mind was calm but now is confused as if waves were rolling over it;
> The silk of love is woven.

While singing Bicui dances gracefully as if she were floating on air. At this moment, the music becomes louder and faster, the trees start swaying, and numerous small bells tied to their branches start ringing to add one more dimension to the music. Bicui runs among the swaying trees, branches and bells. The whole stage is full of energy and movement. She is intoxicated by her first experience of love, and so is the whole world. At the end of this scene, she stops and kneels facing upstage. She then gracefully executes a full backward bend. Her head touches the stage floor with arms and shawl outspread. Bicui's rapture reaches a musical and a visual climax amidst the fairy-tale setting.

Out of the five Chinese operatic adaptations of Shakespeare performed at China's first Shakespeare Festival in 1986 the *Huangmeixi Much Ado* was notable for its success in negotiating an intercultural space between a Shakespeare play and a Chinese indigenous theatrical form. Jiang did not opt for a Westernized presentation like the *yueju Twelfth Night* and the *jingju Othello*, in which actors donned wigs, prosthetic noses and false eyelashes, and imitated Western ways of bowing, kissing hands, duelling and dancing. Nor did Jiang aim to present *Looking for Trouble* as an authentic traditional *huangmeixi*, as the *kunju Macbeth* and the *yuejue Winter's Tale* did. Before the rehearsals started, Jiang explained that Shakespeare and *huangmeixi* should be combined in equal measures, 'half and half', and he amusingly described himself as mediator between two cultures (1994: 379). Critical reviewers commended this production for the excellent way in which it had dealt with the intricacies of Shakespeare's original plot-lines, for its convincing presentation of an unprecedented type of heroine on the Chinese stage, and for maintaining the strength of the traditional Chinese theatre. Indeed, *huangmeixi* developed to accommodate alien elements in a Western canonical text. Ma Lan, who played Bicui, won the 1986 Plum Blossom Prize, the highest theatrical award in China. Yet, audiences' reactions were rather mixed. The production proved extremely popular when it was staged in Hefei, the capital city of Anhui province, where *huangmeixi* was the main local theatre. Young peasants who came to the city from the countryside to see this unusual production responded positively to its innovative quality. By contrast, a tour to the North for workers in the Yellow Sea Oilfields elicited less encouraging feedback, possibly because *huangmeixi* is an unfamiliar theatrical tradition in that area and audiences prefer very famous traditional repertoire to any innovative production.

Jiang presented his latest Shakespearean production with the Hong Kong Academy for Performing Arts at the Lyric Theatre in March 2004.[8] Unlike his operatic adaptation *Looking for Trouble*, his production of *Romeo and Juliet* followed the conventions of spoken drama. Spoken drama (or *huaju*), since its original development under the influence of Western theatrical conventions at the turn of the nineteenth and twentieth centuries, has always been the principal vehicle for staging Shakespeare in China. The distance between the Shakespearean text, on the one hand, and the local dramatic tradition and its target audience, on the other, was therefore far less than in *Looking for Trouble*. Besides, *Romeo and Juliet* has been one of the most frequently performed Shakespearean tragedies in Chinese spoken drama, except during the Cultural Revolution, when even Shakespeare's works, praised by Marx and Engels, along with all Chinese and Western masterpieces, were banned. Following the Communist Party's seizure of power over the mainland, the 'balcony scene' staged by the Shanghai People's Art Theatre in 1953 became the first Shakespearean sequence to be presented in the new People's Republic of China. Influenced by Soviet Shakespearean scholarship, Chinese scholars and theatre practitioners regarded Shakespeare as a spokesman of Renaissance humanism, which triumphed over the old Medieval feudalism. Thus, Chinese Romeos and Juliets were portrayed as 'Renaissance giants',[9] that is as progressive individuals whose young lives were destroyed by a feudal society. In 1980, director Huang Zuolin[10] rejected the Western interpretation of *Romeo and Juliet* as a tragedy about star-crossed lovers and defined the play as 'an optimistic tragedy', because he believed that Romeo and Juliet embodied 'the idealistic quality of Renaissance humanism. ... Although they died, their ideal won' (1983: 273–4). As late as 2000, Fang Ping, the editor of a translation of *The Complete Works of Shakespeare*, commented in his 'Introduction' to the play:

> The love between Romeo and Juliet reflects the significance of anti-feudalism. Marriage based on love was a new phenomenon at that time. Through a series of scenes of fighting caused by the feud between the two families, and the sharp conflicts between the old and new generations within the family over marriage, we can see that it was a time when feudal power was still rather strong. The play is therefore *not only an individual tragedy or a tragedy of two lovers*. It is a tragedy of progressive human beings ahead of their time, who were determined to pursue their ideals at the cost of sacrificing their own lives. The epic significance of the play implies *the necessity of the development of history.*
>
> (Fang 2000: 5, original emphasis in Chinese.)

The official interpretation authorized by the regime often led to the omission of Rosaline, whose silent presence would seem to tarnish Romeo's character. Erotic allusions and sexual metaphors in the original also tended to be suppressed, Mercutio's Queen Mab speech was cut altogether, while the old bawdy Nurse was often replaced by a more conventionally kind and sympathetic female character.

Xu Qiping's 1981 Tibetan version,[11] was the first to emphasize the role of sexual passion over the purity of the lovers. Xu's production predictably caused much controversy. For decades, and until very recently, Chinese approaches to *Romeo and Juliet*, in particular, and to Shakespeare, in general, were deeply affected by the literary theories of Marx and Engels and by communist ideology. As a result, the style of the presentation of the play always aimed at (re)constructing the atmosphere of fifteenth-century Verona, although some directors did occasionally use specific stage devices borrowed from traditional Chinese theatre. Thus, inspired by the theatrical convention that in ancient China a young girl could with her parents' permission throw an embroidered ball to the man she chose to marry, Zhang Qihong in her 1957 production arranged for Juliet to drop a long white scarf during the balcony scene, the colour of the scarf suggesting the purity of her feelings (Meng 1994: 168). In Xu's 1981 production, the dramatic convention in Chinese stagecraft of 'changing face' using paint or thin masks in order to visualize the character's emotional state was emulated at the end of the ball scene by having different coloured lights aimed at Juliet.

Jiang's production departed from this traditional approach to *Romeo and Juliet* and was profoundly affected by the peculiar history and cultural connotations associated with Hong Kong. Hong Kong, a former British colony and now under the rule of the Chinese Communist Party, is increasingly open to the ever-growing influences of twenty-first century globalized economies and cultural markets. The performers of the 2004 production were young people in their twenties, born and brought up under the influence of Hong Kong pop-culture. Most had seen *West Side Story*, and all were familiar with Baz Luhrmann's *Romeo + Juliet*. Jiang, once again, created a production which was neither traditionally Chinese nor too close to Western cultural influences. His production was both a reaction against mainstream cinematic appropriations in the West and against conventional Chinese interpretations. In opposition to the Chinese ideal of pure and non-sexual romantic love, all crude allusions to sex in the original were kept in the production. Although the Production Office in the Academy insisted that a sign reading 'The performance contains some uncivilized language' was displayed at the entrance to the auditorium, Jiang's production was allowed to go ahead. Unlike recent cinematic adaptations, which, according to Jiang, glorify violence, the ubiquity of death, destruction and decay, his production attempted to transform *Romeo and Juliet* into a redemptive love story. In the programme notes, Jiang stated: 'The concept of our production is based on the belief that love is forever.' The theme of 'love for ever' was visualized through the way the production's setting shifted through time: '... we lead the audience to follow the characters, scene by scene, stepping from a 15th century street and church into today's square and hall, and even into the sky of the future' (Jiang 2004: 5). The opening fight, the ball, the duel between Mercutio and Tybalt, and the tomb scene were selected as moments when the style of costumes changed, thus suggesting substantial temporal leaps. Towards the end of the play, performers wore the casual outfit worn by the younger generations in contemporary Hong Kong. Jiang's strategy was inspired by the role played by time in the Shakespearean original. The text constantly refers to haste and its consequent dangers. 'Romeo and Juliet are two teenagers ... but they grow up within four crucial days in their lives and they finally understand what responsibility means.' In Jiang's production, the death of the young lovers is no longer seen as a cruel sacrifice demanded by a feudal society, or as the result of social conflict, but as a voluntary decision, as an expression of the lovers' own development.

Particular attention was paid to the staging of the balcony scene. Jiang's setting for the balcony scene was inspired by the sense of distance and height evoked by the following lines: 'It is the east, and Juliet is the sun', 'O that I were a glove upon that hand,/That I might touch the cheek' and 'The orchard walls are high and hard to climb'. The set included five structures – the tallest incorporating a curved 4.5 metres high staircase – which could be readily moved and rearranged to suggest different locations. Romeo climbed the tall staircase which spanned across a sheer wall. The sharp contrast between the giant wall and Romeo, and the gap separating him from the tiered structures forming Juliet's balcony, suggested the great barrier between the lovers and their determination to overcome it. The two lovers were thus physically isolated from each other, although within their individual locations they had the space to stand, sit, walk, or to run around. The set design created a visual spectacle complementing the poetry since the protagonists could climb to the highest points of their stage structures in order to be much closer to each other, but the chasm between them appeared all the deeper.

Jiang's work in the operatic *Much Ado* and the spoken drama *Romeo and Juliet* demonstrates that a careful negotiation of ideological, aesthetic and political distance can create effective, ground-breaking and theatrically spell-binding intercultural theatre.

6 'It is the bloody business which informs thus ... ': Local politics and performative praxis, *Macbeth* in India

Poonam Trivedi

In the Indian literary tradition, translation, adaptation, rewriting and transformation are sanctioned practices of literary creation. Unlike the Western tradition in which even translation is a 'fall' from the origin and a condition of 'exile', the Indian literary tradition recognizes these practices as legitimate modes of alterity. The Indian theory of literary growth and evolution through translation and adaptation is best seen in terms of a banyan tree, as a 'natural process of organic, ramifying, vegetative growth and renewal, comparable perhaps with the process by which an ancient banyan tree sends down branches which in turn take root all around it and comprise an intertwining family of trees: *quot rami tot abores*' (Trivedi and Bassnett 1999: 10). Adaptation and revision of a literary text are thus neither parasitic nor transgressive but rather a familiar norm. The words used for literary creation, representation and translation in Sanskrit literary theory, which represents the main source of most Indian literatures, *anukriti*, *anukaran* and *anuvada*, all share the same root *anu* (to come after), underlining not just a fundamental equivalence of the three processes, but also the view that the very act of literary creation is a rescription, an imitation. Newness in this tradition enters via appropriation and retelling. In the medieval period, with the emergence of the regional languages, Sanskrit epics were freely adapted, rewritten and even subverted to suit local concerns. This practice of creative freedom to reinvent within a hallowed tradition was seminal to literary and cultural growth.

It follows then, that the initial indigenous response to Shakespeare in India was to adapt and Indianize. Shakespeare was introduced to India in 1775 as part of the entertainment apparatus of the trading enterprise, but stayed on centrally enshrined in the colonial English language education policy. The performance of Shakespeare was less governed by official dictat than by classroom study and there exists a continuous tradition from 1852 onwards of the performance of Shakespeare's plays in Indian languages, predictably transformed and relocated. The earliest Shakespeares were freewheeling adaptations, which changed names, places, scenes, plots and even characters and often added song and dance to facilitate local reception. Some, however, were critical appropriations which challenged colonial hegemony.[1] Although from 1900 to 1920, with the spread of English language education, Shakespeare was staged more faithfully, adaptation into an indigenous theatrical idiom remained the mainstream mode of Shakespeare translation and performance. In the post-colonial period, after independence in 1947, this adaptive tradition has evolved into a deconstructive 'play' with the text and themes of Shakespeare.[2]

Macbeth has been the most popular tragedy after *Othello* in India and has been performed in a variety of modes. Most of the notable early versions were free adaptations, like *Rudrapal* (Bengali, 1874) and *Manajirao* (Marathi, 1897), where translation and structural rearrangement bore the main burden of localization. Later versions like *Barnam Vana* (Hindi, 1979) and *Gombe Macbeth* (Kannada, 1988) appropriated the play into indigenous theatrical forms – in these two cases into the south Indian theatre form of *yakshagana* – and assimilated the ideas of the play into Indian philosophic traditions.[3] The two productions under consideration in this essay – *Maranayakana Drishtanta* by H.S. Shiva Prakash in Kannada and Lokendra Arambam's *Stage of Blood* in Manipuri – went a step further and extended this adaptive tradition from the theatrical and philosophic sphere, into the political. They used the enactment of violence in *Macbeth* to draw parallels with the bloodshed, in the first case, in the participants' own lives, and in the second, in the larger political and social life of a northeastern state of India. Their intent was to mobilize a cathartic self-reflexivity and a critique of ideologies of violence which lead to individual crime and internecine and secessionist warfare. The success of these productions marks the distance the 'colonial book' of Shakespeare has traversed in India: from being an instrument of imperial coercion to becoming a voice against post-colonial oppressions. Canonical Shakespeare was, for the first time, openly deployed, in an activist manner, to speak for the subaltern. It also underlined the resilience and strength of the indigenous adaptive tradition which assimilates an alien entity and inflects it to very specific local needs.

Maranayaka was first staged in July 1998 by actor–director Hulugappa Kattimani as the centrepiece of a rehabilitation programme for the inmates of Mysore prison, most of whom were serving life sentences for murder. This experiment achieved such singular success that permission was secured for the inmate-actors to travel under armed escort to the state capital, Bangalore, for a public show at its prime cultural centre. *Maranayaka* was then staged on 26 February 2001 for a theatre festival at Kasargode, Kerala, by most of the same group of actors, some of whom had since been released but had chosen to continue their work with community theatres.

The Stage of Blood evolved over a period of three years from a pilot performance on the floating islands of Loktak Lake, Manipur, in 1995, to a fully fledged show on a floating stage at the Ningthem Pukhri Reservoir, Imphal, on 25 June 1997, and a later revival on the Thames at the Waterman's Arts Centre, Brentford, from 20 to 24 August 1997. *The Stage of Blood* was a protest play, a rallying cry to northeasterners to look to the ritual blood letting caused by the insurgency movement in Manipur. By drawing attention to the 'performance' of violence at individual and at state level, both productions aimed to deconstruct and reconstruct mindsets and ideologies given to bloodshed.

Maranayakana Drishtanta, or *The Parable of Maranayaka* (1989), was particularly successful thanks to a careful cultural mediation between Shakespeare's text and the prisoners's own worldview. Writer–teacher Shiva Prakash chose adaptation over translation because he had found that on stage, in live performance, 'faithful Shakespeare' sounded archaic. Earlier in 1987, he had done a free translation of *King Lear* for the well-known director, B.V. Karanth. Now, inspired by Shakespeare's poetry he attempted to write his own verse.[4] Influenced by native Kannada narrative traditions, he turned the play into a parable against violence. *Maranayaka* follows *Macbeth* until about the middle of the play, cutting out the sub-plot, after which it takes a different course. Maranayaka, a commander and a kinsman, quells a rebellion against his king, Bhadrappanayaka, by the king's younger son, but is not suitably rewarded. Instead, the elder son is nominated to the throne. The king goes to celebrate the victory at Mara's house. On the way Mara meets three *kateries* (witches, blood-drinking demons) who predict the kingship for him. Mara's wife, Mangale, too has a vision of the kateries and hears the prediction. Mangale is pregnant and the kateries warn her that an obstacle may prevent the birth. As she goes into labour during the feasting, the king's drunken laughter floats up; this is the bad omen, she thinks, as she is being assisted by the kateries, who now double as midwives. She then demands that her husband kill the king, whom she identifies as the obstacle mentioned by the kateries. In a dramatic sequence, the birth of the son takes place while Mara is doing the deed; he returns to hold his son with hands stained with the king's blood. This interpolation exploits the interplay of 'fair and foul' in Shakespeare's play to further underline the interchangeability of good and evil and how birth and death spring from the same source, a concept central to Indian philosophy. Mara is crowned king, but at the celebratory banquet the ghost of the dead king appears to reveal all and then leads Mara to the bedchamber where he discovers his new born babe slaughtered by the deposed prince. The Queen seeks revenge and rushes after the killer into the forest. Mara follows and meets the kateries who mock him. At this point a new character, a Jain monk[5] who meditates in the forest, and who turns out to be the deposed brother of the dead king, is interpolated to channel Mara's anger and anguish. Coming into the forest he finds that his wife has hanged herself after murdering her child's killer. The monk advises Mara to look for the famed *sanjeevani* (life-giving) root in the forest. While the monk's gnomic utterances implicitly recommend repentance and atonement, Mara is persuaded by the kateries to dig for the root. He literally digs and digs but gets entangled. In desperation, he starts cutting the trees, but they seem to multiply. In the end he is enmeshed and smothered by the trees which fall on him.

Shiva Prakash's adaptation exploits and extends Shakespeare's central motif of the interplay between good and evil: Mara kills to protect his unborn son as much as to get the crown. His motives are muddled and his ambition becomes more complex and less self-willed, a part of a primitive force which both generates and destroys. These philosophic shifts, familiar to the prisoners, helped considerably in instigating the self-introspection sought by the rehabilitation programme. The workshop, said director Kattimani, was premised on the belief that like Macbeth/Maranayaka, the prisoners, too, were *swamibhaktas* (loyalists), who through accidental turns of fate had been pushed into bloodshed. Although most of the prisoners had been incarcerated for murder, they were not professional killers; they were rather guilty of crimes committed in a rash moment of passion or petty political skirmishes.

The forest and its equivocal nature also acquired local resonance. From being a symbol of both deception and restoration in Shakespeare's play, the forest was re-imagined as a site of primeval desire and darkness. Crucially, the word for forest in Kannada, *kaadu*, is synonymous with haunt, bother, trouble. While the forest seemed to hold the promise of regeneration (the sanjeevani), it ultimately leads Mara astray. The kateries, who first meet him in the forest and then follow him back there, represent its malevolent dimension. This power of the forest drew on another recognizable local set of beliefs: many of the prisoners were from the northern thickly forested area of Karnataka, where animistic worship of the forest as a deity by the local tribes is not uncommon. Accordingly, the forest, as opposed to a vanquishing army disguised as a forest, brings about the main character's demise. The trees themselves smother Mara who digs up their roots and cuts them down, destroying their organic environment.[6] The performed text reworked the adaptation's prologue, which was spoken by Macbeth's spirit/ghost, who continues to haunt the forest and narrates its life story as a warning, and the epilogue, which was spoken by village folk, in order to locate the play more firmly within the context of the prisoners' lives. The performance itself was framed by a dramatic opening sequence set in a jail, with prisoners bullying and threatening each other, until one of them tries to restore order by offering to tell them a story. At this point the play proper began. The ending, which returned to the prison sequence, showed the prisoners awed and chastened by Maranayaka's tortured end.

As mentioned above, *Maranayaka* was first staged in 1998 at Mysore Central Jail and was subsequently revived eight times outside the prison. It was also staged as the *piece de resistance* at a theatre festival and seminar called 'Shakespeare on the Indian Stage' at Kasargode, Kerala (24 February – 2 March 2001), which I had the privilege to attend. The original production emerged out of director Kattimani's urge to use his theatrical experience for an activist purpose. He is an actor with the Karnataka State Repertory Company, Rangayana, at Mysore. When Kattimani proposed this theatre workshop as part of a rehabilitation programme,[7] he had to break down resistance at both the official and the individual level. The state police needed a lot of convincing, this being the very first time anyone had approached them to literally 'play' with the prisoners. The inmates themselves were initially sceptical and unenthusiastic. They had already had enough drama in their personal lives to get excited about dramatic fiction. Kattimani too later confessed to some anxiety at the start about working with people known for their violent tendencies. However, Kattimani won their trust by deciding to eat and live with the inmates for the full period of the forty-five day workshop. Kattimani's experiment turned out to be hugely successful among the inmates. 'The last forty-five days (of the theatre workshop) have been the most fruitful days I have spent in the jail. It gave me something positive to think about and I wish such activities continued throughout the year', said Walter Da Cunha, who played Duncan and who had already served twelve years in prison for murdering a bar owner for failing to serve him chilled beer (Anon 1998). The actor playing Macbeth/Maranyaka, Shivalinga Gowda, a young man who had been serving a ten-year sentence for a murder committed during a political riot, acknowledged that many of the scenes, particularly the ghost scenes, would recall to his mind the spirits of the dead making him reflect on his past actions. 'These few months changed me more than the last ten years. Now I feel I can fit back into society once again. Earlier, I had felt my life after prison would be as meaningless as before, but now I am filled with a new sense of enthusiasm', he said after the first public performance at Bangalore, 'I am transformed, both my mind and body feel rejuvenated' (Lankesh 1998). By the time of the Kasargode performance, he had been released on parole and had started a business selling milk. The 'milk of human kindness' was restored to him in more ways than one and it would not be an exaggeration to see this as a social and spiritual rebirth through Shakespeare. However, the original performance and its several revivals were overshadowed by the fanfare of state officialdom and consequent media attention. The state police now held Kattimani's experiment up as a feather in their caps. As the then District Inspector General of Police said in a press conference after the show, 'There is a risk we take in letting these men perform outside the prison; but I now know that they are not thinking about escaping, but about what will happen to their parts if they leave!'[8]

Lokendra Arambam's *The Stage of Blood* was produced under the auspices of an international collaboration between the Forum for Laboratory Theatres of Manipur and International Arts, London, for the celebrations of the fiftieth anniversary of Indian independence in August 1997. Though this foreign collaboration may make it seem to fit the exportable 'ethnic' Indian model, this production was in fact conceived as a radical assertion of dissidence. Manipur is one of the smaller states in the northeast of India. Its geographical seclusion has allowed it to develop its own distinct identity, particularly in the arts. It was the last northeastern state to succumb to British expansionism in 1891 and after independence in 1947 it saw the rise of a militant Left Front which initially resisted assimilation into the Union of India. The late 1960s saw the rise of an insurgency movement countered by increased state surveillance and repression. By the 1980s, revolutionary and counter-revolutionary movements were threatening the stability of the whole region, which remains precarious to this day. The theatre in Manipur, particularly since the 1970s, has responded to the turmoil and civil unrest by producing radical theatrical experiments. The director, Lokendra Arambam,[9] one of those at the forefront of this alternative theatre, was brought up on the adaptive tradition of Shakespeare performance. In 1930, when Manipur was a princely state under the British Raj, his father adapted *Macbeth* (one of the first in the Manipuri language) as *Bhagyachandra* – named after the then ruling king – in which not the king but only the usurper Macbeth is killed and the whole play becomes a eulogy to good rule. In the post-insurgency atmosphere of the 1990s, Arambam chose not only to appropriate Shakespeare's text but to rewrite in it 'another text' ... 'to use its signs and symbols to transform it and place it in my culture and transform that too.' 'Love and hostility is my attitude towards Shakespeare', Arambam explained in his lecture at Kasargode. Privately, Arambam also indicated that his appropriation was triggered by his rage at the brazen abuse of power seen when the son of a government minister, known to be a rapist, was publicly felicitated by party sycophants. In a further elaboration of his position, Arambam added that, '*Stage of Blood* is a continuation of my urge to do politically sensitive plays in which I reflect on our situation; ... It is *Macbeth* wrenched, twisted and subverted into a metaphor of the anarchy in Manipur.'

According to a programme note, Macbeth in *Stage of Blood* is a representative of a repressive state, who has lost his soul. Lady Macbeth is his alter ego/conscience and is played by the same actor. Malcolm and Macduff are not individual representatives of the righteous, but part of the unnamed unknown forces of the oppressed. Macbeth is killed by a collective of reed-mat covered men and warriors. The didactic/propagandist thrust was kept to the fore: Macbeth's story was narrated, literally, back to front, using an indigenous convention, the cyclical 'syllogism of the magic mind'. The play began with a dead Macbeth reawakening to re-enact his life of ruthless ambition, intrigue, self-definition and self-annihilation. At the end, when Macbeth is killed, the boat procession, which brought his body on stage at the beginning of the play, comes back to take him to his burial. It thus offered a paradigm of the alienation of people of peripheral societies who are doomed to self-realization through cyclical and self-destructive acts of violence.

The polemics of this rewriting of Shakespeare were rooted in local and even topical politics. Its performative praxis was entirely governed by local beliefs, rituals and practices. The environmentalist staging – in the open air, on a raft, in a lake – which subsumed the whole play was symbolic of the philosophy of the Meiteis, the indigenous tribe of Manipur. According to the Meiteis, organic natural forces, Earth, Water, Wind, Fire and Sky, are deeply in communion with human life. Tragedy ensues when this equilibrium is disturbed. As explained by Arambam, the stage was seen as Mother Earth, isolated, naked, and a site of the relentless struggle for domination. The surrounding Water was not just the seed of life but also the tomb where the spirits of the dead were subsumed. The seven weird sisters, representing the seven main tribes in Manipur, were the Winds whose exhortations and buffetings lead Macbeth to meet his tragic end. The Fire, which Macbeth lit before the murder of Duncan, was the spark of human confrontations. The Sky, the good of the world, was ignored by the ambitious characters. The spirit of Banquo as the Sky was a mute witness to Macbeth's world of intrigue. The events and the motifs in Shakespeare's play were effectively woven into the political and collective unconscious of the Meiteis.

Though the conceptualization may have seemed somewhat esoteric to the untutored non-Manipuri viewer, the performative language of movement and gesture based on a fusion of *thang-ta* (martial art), Manipuri dance and shamanistic rituals was so physical and graphic that the narrative became suggestively intelligible. Performed by professional actors trained in ensemble work, the choreographed violence was alternately vigorous and lyrical. Coupled with tribal costumes, atmospheric lighting and haunting music, its visual and dramatic impact was stunning. The text, a pared down prose version of seventeen scenes organized around Shakespeare's main scenes and soliloquies, prepared by Somorendra Arambam, did more than translate Shakespeare. It heightened and clarified it. The only interpolation occurred after the murder of Duncan and before the climax of the dance of the revolution, when Macbeth lets loose a reign of violence by quoting Ross's lines at 4.3.164: 'Alas poor country ...' in a mocking, ironic vein, and ending with 'Birnam wood shall not come to Dunsinane/I shall continue suppressing rebellions/And the people shall I oppress ...'. As Macbeth utters these lines, boats appear in the distance, the dead rise up, roll the reed-mats around themselves, and transform themselves into a collective force which advances towards Macbeth and destroys him.

The subversive potential of this appropriation emerged from its local resonance. Macbeth was not just the butcher who met a deserved fall. Surrounded by the living, life-giving water, man's petty, transient existence, riddled by violence, was implicitly compared to and belittled by the power of the natural elements and cosmic forces. Reflections on the water were powerfully expressive of the fragile duality of Macbeth as an individual and as a representative of the state: while pondering whether to murder Duncan – 'if it were done ...' – the actor stood at the edge of the floating stage and addressed his own reflection in the water before dousing it with a torch. In the Meitei worldview life begins and ends in water, change and continuity are cyclical, and life and death are but stations on the soul's journey. The re-enactment of Shakespeare's violent plot was ultimately shown to be gratuitous, pointless. Significantly, Macbeth and Lady Macbeth were played by the same actor, who deftly slipped in and out of the roles by repeatedly donning and discarding a red shawl. This doubling of roles suggested that responsibility for violence cannot ultimately be attributed or confined to a gendered psyche. The use of an undifferentiated chorus of actors to play the other roles introduced a 'collective opposition' against Macbeth. Macduff, Malcolm, the other nobles, the soldiers and the servants were all part of this chorus which alternatively brandished spears, shot arrows, jumped, thumped, rolled about, went into a trance or covered themselves with reed-mats, all in ensemble unison. This collective 'revolutionary force' according to Arambam was meant to present, not virile images of men in arms, but 'resilient, soft and subtle forces of resistance, capable of withstanding pressure, able to bend, represented by the pliant and flexible reed-mats and bodies under them' (Lecture, Kasargode). Arambam's chorus can be seen as a potent image of the collective strength of the common man, vested in humble reed-mats, confronting violence and destruction. Arambam has always asserted that his theatre's agenda is to give the common man a platform: 'my *Macbeth* brings the people in, it shows the revolutionary forces of the future' (Lecture, Kasargode). A two-thousand strong audience applauded the first performance in Imphal as an authentic community experience. In London, Arambam's strongly local redaction received mixed responses, ranging from a quizzical hauteur – 'the cheek of it' exclaimed *The Times* (Kingston 1997) – to a quiet appreciation – 'it might not be the *Macbeth* we know and love, but as a resonant, hallucinated experience, there has been nothing like it' said *The Guardian* (Cartwright 1997).

The impact of *Stage of Blood*, unlike *Maranayaka Dristhanta*, was not on the immediately verifiable level but on the aesthetic, theatrical and ideological plane. It was the first consciously progressive use of Shakespeare, a colonial text, to protest a felt neo-colonialism. However, both these productions of *Macbeth*, in terms of their frame-breaking innovativeness, their artistic and programmatic success and their extension of the canvas of theatre are the most unusual to come out of India in recent times. They both show how Shakespeare can serve political and social activism.

Adaptation, or appropriation, is not a prerogative of the East. The English have subjected their own national poet to a series of revisions, burlesques and parodies since the seventeenth century. Yet these rewritings have never been able to shed the taint of deriving their value from the cultural capital of the 'original' text; they have always been seen as illegitimate and parasitic. In the Indian literary tradition, adaptation is an accepted practice which allows rewritings to co-exist without challenging the status of the 'original' ur-text. And what is more, in the multilingual context of the subcontinent, it functions as a localizing, indigenizing and, ultimately, democratizing factor: just as the Sanskrit epics had been reworked in the regional languages, so was Shakespeare adapted into local cultures. Contemporary translation theory, too, argues for adaptation to be seen as a 'creative process' which, particularly in relation to drama, seeks to 'naturalize' into a new milieu, the purpose, as well as the meaning, of this kind of intercultural communication (Bastin 1998: 6, 8). Though the indigenous Indian theatre had begun by accepting Shakespeare on its own terms, e.g. *As You Like It* was appropriated into *yakshagana* as early as the 1860s, adaptations were largely governed by literary and aesthetic imperatives. The Parsi theatre (1870–1910), on the other hand, rewrote Shakespeare for popular and commercial success. Today, however, a more focused and purposeful spirit annexes and adapts the plays for identifiable social and political issues. The process of adaptation has entered another stage in which Shakespeare may be seen speaking for those very subaltern people and theatre forms that earlier in the colonial period he, as an icon, was responsible for suppressing. The promotion of English medium education, as promulgated by Macaulay in 1834, was a strategy to undermine the development of Indian languages and literatures and the consequent emulation of Western theatre led to a decline of indigenous theatre forms. Now, adapted Shakespeare may be seen 'giving back' that agency that he symbolically took away during the colonial period.

Shakespeare constitutes a unique case of an author who continues to be read and performed across time and space. These world-wide proliferating Shakespeares have challenged critical practice.[10] Shakespeare studies need to acknowledge the simultaneous existence of 'Other Shakespeares', which like the branches of the banyan tree may have become free standing, but nevertheless remain tethered to the mother trunk. They also need to investigate their value beyond the local. As Stuart Hall has pointed out, the 'post-colonial' marks not only the anti-colonial struggles of a binary form of representation, but more crucially for the present, the 'move from one conception of difference to another …, from difference to différance' (1996: 247). World-wide Shakespeares challenge us not just with their difference but also by intimating 'brave' new worlds of deferred possibilities.

Part Two

Local Shakespeares for national audiences

7 Relocating and dislocating Shakespeare in Robert Sturua's *Twelfth Night* and Alexander Morfov's *The Tempest*

Boika Sokolova

The eruption of volatile ludic energies, released by the political change of 1989, was paralleled by the revival of Shakespearean comedies on the Bulgarian stage. Considering this development during the early 1990s, Evgenia Pancheva found that, at that time, comedy had come 'too suspiciously close to tragedy' and discovered a Shakespeare 'hushed down, borrowing from himself and others, trimmed to alleviate – or exacerbate? – the wounds of a guilty, slanderous, politicizing, revengeful, sexually aroused banished and re-acknowledged, thinking Bulgaria' (Pancheva 1994: 260). Ten years on, Shakespeare is still trimmed, full of borrowings, radically rewritten, with the same taste for sad endings.

Yet, the cultural climate has undergone a sea change since the early 1990s: the iconoclasm and enthusiasms of the first post-communist years has given way to a more sober picture of impasse, disappointment and lack of acknowledgement. Economic pressures, too, have left their mark as the old state-funded theatre system collapsed, making survival in the profession dependent on market success. In this context, two Shakespeare productions at the Ivan Vazov National Theatre in Sofia, during the 2001/2 season – *Twelfth Night*, directed by Georgian theatre veteran Robert Sturua, and Alexander Morfov's *The Tempest* – provide interesting food for thought about how directors work in a changing world.

Robert Sturua, who has had a long and distinguished career in the theatre, makes it no secret that he regards revamping the Shakespearean original as an integral part of his job as a director. Following perhaps an old instinct, fostered in a world where every change had to be historically and politically accounted for, Sturua, even now, justifies his approach by alluding to Shakespeare's use of his sources as an example of a fundamental authorial/directorial prerogative, and by pointing out that Shakespeare's theatre itself appropriated the past by means of bold anachronisms. He also claims to have been affected by the Elizabethan practice of developing, cutting and reshuffling plays in the course of rehearsal (Kozova 2001). Overall, he sees himself as a mediator whose task is to tease out readings and interpretations which are merely latent in the Shakespearean source. Alexander Morfov, who belongs to the post-1989 generation of Bulgarian directors, does not need Shakespeare to justify his choices. According to him, directing, to use a term lately proffered by Terence Hawkes, is an individualistic act of 'presentism' (Hawkes 2002) through which audiences are lured 'into the field of his own fantasy.'[1] The director, in other words, is not a mediator between the audience and the Shakespearean original, but an active co-creator of meanings. Like other directors of his generation, Morfov cuts, rearranges and adds to Shakespeare freely and unapologetically.

Sturua's *Twelfth Night* was originally performed to great acclaim in his native Tbilisi. Versions of Morfov's *Tempest* were staged in St. Petersburg and Skopje and received major prizes both in Russia and Macedonia. There is a new dynamic of cultural exchange within the East European theatre, fostered by closeness of cultural traditions, personal connections, general social circumstances, similar artistic and material concerns and new money-making possibilities. From this point of view, the encounter between two director–managers, like Sturua and Morfov, is not accidental. Sturua has been at the helm of the Rustaveli theatre in Tbilisi for over twenty years while Morfov was artistic director of the National Theatre in Sofia for four years and during the season under consideration.

What You Will: or Robert Sturua

I borrow this title from a review in the Sofia press (Nikolova 2001) because it successfully identifies tensions at work in Sturua's *Twelfth Night*. These are already visible in Stefan Despodov's poster for the production. It foregrounds the lower end of a crucifix with the body visible from the waist down. Rooted in what looks like a barren stretch of land, the cross towers imposingly over the viewer. The golden yellow background strengthens the suggestive religious iconography. In the background, sketched in darker ochre, dancers and figures on stilts look like shadows, compared to the robust flesh of the figure on the cross. The poster gestures to a *vanitas* composition, which opposes the substantial nature of Christ's sacrifice to the superficiality of the world for which he died. The title *Twelfth Night* appears at the top in bright blue letters. As the eye travels to the right, large letters in dark blue announce: 'A Robert Sturua production'. Suggestively, the name 'William Shakespeare' is confined to small print on the very edge of the poster.

The theatre programme offers further insight into what the poster has already identified as clearly expressed directorial intentions:

> The theatre I have lately been trying to make is connected with the events in Georgia. In some ways, they resemble those occurring in Bulgaria. Lately, I've had the feeling that we as humans are at the mercy of higher powers, as if Fate has been playing with us. [...] That is why, my thoughts turned to the man whose 2000th birthday we recently celebrated [...]. I decided to dedicate a play to his birthday. The idea was to create a mystery type play, based on texts about Passion Week without any other dramaturgical basis. [...] We had already been negotiating a Shakespeare title with the director of the National Theatre Alexander Morfov [...] and I suggested *Twelfth Night*. The moment I pronounced the words I realised that this play was written for the end of the Christmas season, for Twelfth Night when the Wise Men come to visit the baby Christ, [...] when the Nativity celebrations traditionally come to a close. [...] I took the Gospels by Luke and Matthew and started creating the gospel scenes and introducing them into the main plot. Thus, this stage version of *What You Will, Or Twelfth Night* came into being.

(Sturua 2001–2)

Sturua's approach is a mixture of the familiar and currently fashionable. On the one hand, he seems to have retained a penchant for socio–political topicality as suggested by his references to 'recent events in Georgia'. Familiar, too, is the choice of Shakespeare to perform cultural work in support of a contemporary cause. Also, despite the radical quality of his appropriation, Sturua claims that the intersection between the events at Orsino's and Olivia's courts and the added biblical scenes, outlining the progress of Christ from birth to crucifixion, reveals a moral sub-text *already present* in Shakespeare's play. What seems fashionably new is the transcultural nature of the adaptation and the Christian overtones, enhanced by directly relating *Twelfth Night* to the millennium. Shakespeare's Illyria thus becomes even more delocalized in order to accommodate two loosely connected plots and two time sequences. The set, created by Sturua's collaborator of many years, Georgi Alexi-Meskhishvili,[2] reinforces the metaphysical quality of his vision. The stage is enveloped in glistening white satin, to become an all-place where a few stylized lambs on the edges provide a visual seasonal metaphor. Against such pristine background, indigo skies, bright costumes and red helium-filled balloons make for an aesthetically exquisite contrast. In keeping with Sturua's and Meskhishvili's ideas, Ghia Kancheli's[3] incidental music creates the feeling of 'a transcendental unimaginable-magical future', of 'theatrical eternity itself' (Decheva 2001).

Not surprisingly, critical response has been rather mixed. For some, the whiteness of the biblical scenes is as emotionally 'empty as a Siberian night' (Nikolova 2001), while the red balloons call forth discrepant associations 'of celebrations in the style of the 4th July' (Vasileva 2001). Other commentators find that this abstract fluidity of space enhances the opposition between the darker and the lighter elements in Shakespeare's play and between the human and the divine levels of experience, which Sturua's additions bring to the fore to create a dramatic parable (Hristova-Radoeva 2001). As the contrasting critical views suggest, to appreciate fully the visual and musical sophistication on display one needs to share Sturua's conviction to have successfully identified the *true meaning* of Shakespeare's play.

The set, props and music defy logic unless seen from a specific interpretative angle, which reconfigures the play, through the narrative about the life of Jesus, into a parable of human materialistic shallowness and forgetfulness of his sacrifice. In an interview, Sturua quite unambiguously defines 'the message' of *Twelfth Night* by construing Viola's disguise as the master metaphor of the whole play: 'Her aim is to come close to Duke Orsino, described by her father as an ideal man, but her small deceit produces a deluge of events which threatens a catastrophe. Shakespeare seems to suggest that whatever we do, however small our sins might be, small or great, they produce cataclysms' (Pramatarova 2001). It is worth stressing the extent of the alterations needed to make the play 'render' what Sturua takes to be the play's *true* meaning.

One of the consequences of revision is that Shakespeare's characters are turned into stylized 'marionettes in the hands of Fate'. The idea of the theatricality of human existence is also underlined by the raised stage reminiscent of 'a circus arena … where characters move like dolls' (Decheva 2001). Maria, for example, is a sexless, slightly sinister clown, sporting heavy make-up, spiky red hair and a bright red satin costume.[4] Her movements are deliberately exaggerated, her enunciation squeaky and jarring. Noisy and alienated by her mask, Maria is the physical and behavioural antithesis of Biblical Mary, who glides across the stage in quiet self-absorption. More generally, Sturua's strategy of interweaving narrative and temporal sequences aims at what Mikhail Bakhtin calls *menippea* – an ambivalent generic mixture of spatial, temporal and psychological levels producing a universality, encompassing both the serious and comic

(Bakhtin 1979: 102). This aspect of the structure of the production has been compared to Mikhail Bulgakov's novel *The Master and Margarita* (1929–40) with its heady mixture of sacred and profane, philosophical and satirical, real and magical (Kostova 2001). However, what makes Bulgakov's novel a masterpiece is his radical *critique* of the spiritual dearth of Soviet life, achieved through breath-taking shifts of linguistic and emotional register corresponding to effective and rhetorically persuasive twists in the story line. Sturua's three-and-a-half hour stage-traffic shuttling between the Shakespearean and biblical plots undermines both narrative meaningfulness and contemporary relevance. As blond-wigged angels are hoisted down on swings to cross paths with Illyrians who themselves acquire angelic wings as they fall in love, '[y]ou are never quite certain whether what is on the stage is what is' (Kasimova 2001). Sturua's menippean polyphony does not transcend the bizarre and the spectacular, and the cross which towers in clouds of smoke at the back of the stage in the final moments of the play appears as merely another *coup de thèâtre*. Christ, the corrective 'stranger', remains an unaccommodated 'other' within a production which places him at its supposed emotional and moral centre.

Dislocations are also latent in the way the performance text was produced. For the production in Tbilisi, Sturua himself translated Shakespeare's play into Georgian. In Sofia, instead of using the current Bulgarian translation, which is linguistically agile and performatively sound, Sturua chose to have his Georgian version translated into Bulgarian with borrowings from the available translation. His overhaul of the text therefore results in an act of complete self-authorization. Even the much publicized allusions to the Georgian/Bulgarian context ultimately translate into a generically Christian condemnation of the vanity of material pursuits, a highly unspecific and easily exportable message. Sturua's production, in other words, bears the marks of being conceived as a marketable aesthetic product, an easy-to-carry commodity which exploits Shakespeare's iconic status and the loosely escatological interests raised by the beginning of a new millennium. The marketability of the product cannot be under-estimated; after all, Sturua's team, who spent a fortnight working at the National Theatre in Sofia preparing the production, have been reported by several newspapers to have netted $60,000, a sum few east – and west – European directors can dream of (Tsolov 2001; Vasileva 2001).[5] In Sturua's hands, the subversive sub-text characteristic of the communist stage has morphed into a seemingly universal one, as William Shakespeare, Jesus Christ, the disillusionment of East Europeans with the moral state of their world, are recycled into an all-fitting supranational directorial brand (Kennedy 1995), bearing the logo: 'Made by Robert Sturua and Co'.

Alexander Morfov: *The Tempest,* or the director as a young man

Alexander Morfov's arrival on the Bulgarian stage coincided with the political overturn of 1989, when the unsettled nature of post-communist times disconcertingly mixed artistic excitement with the politics of commercialization. A veritable tempest of impos-sibilities became the stuff of daily experience. Morfov is predictably obsessed with Shakespeare's late play. In about eight years, he created six versions of *The Tempest* (four of them on the stage of the Ivan Vazov National Theatre). These *Tempests* are a land-mark in the stage history of the play in Bulgaria. In the hundred and twenty odd years of local Shakespearean productions, *The Tempest* had been put on only once, in the 1950s, before Morfov granted it unprecedented cultural currency. Thus, the turbulence of the 1990s and the advent of a new generation of theatre directors have given the Bulgarian stage a new Shakespeare.

Like Sturua, Morfov thinks of his work in the context of his country's life, as an alternative to the confusion in its everyday existence. 'Times are so painful', he writes, 'they constantly remind us of the impossibility to live normally. This impossibility … must be spiritually counterbalanced … . Perhaps, this is the reason why I keep making theatre' (Morfov 1996–7). Even more drastically than Sturua, he cuts, rearranges and amends Shakespeare's text, inserts additions of his own and collages from other Shakespearean texts, which foreground comic situations, sexual encounters or lyrical moments. Unlike his elder colleague, he offers no transcendental cures, or moral advice. In fact, Morfov's intervention is often tongue-in-cheek and invites the audience to join in as equals. On the poster, a tear-like little boat is shown floating in the left eye of an old man wearing a crown. To a Bulgarian this is a clear allusion to the phrase, 'Do you see a ship floating in my eye?', meaning, 'Do you really believe that I am so gullible?'. The audience are therefore warned that they are going to see a story about a ruler and a ship, but one that shouldn't be taken at face value.

For the performance, the picture-frame stage of the National Theatre is left open and, as the audience drift in, they can see the stage hands in black T-shirts and jeans move around Svetoslav Kokalov's set – a rough looking raised platform with a mast and a few ropes, suggesting a battered ship tilted on one side. The island is reduced to a wrecked ship, though the revolving stage will reveal different nooks and crannies. An actress, Miranda, is reading a script as if rehearsing her part. She is conversing with an imaginary partner about love. An older actor, Prospero, adjusts the straps of his dirty dungarees, which are a size too large, and wraps himself in a scruffy cape made of patches. The stark light which stage and auditorium share underlines the uncomfortable poverty of their tattered clothes. As Miranda offers her imaginary partner to play him some music, Prospero asks her to do so for him. Shaken out of her happy trance she tries to run away; Prospero stops her by beginning to tell their story (1.2.35 ff.),[6] but the audience are not yet certain whether the play has actually begun, since there is neither dimming of lights in the auditorium, nor a clear shift from the world of the National Theatre into the fictive world of Morfov's *Tempest*. But the play *has* started and it slowly gains momentum as Prospero unravels his past life and moves up to the high point on the deck. As he describes how his brother tried 'To have no screen between this part he played/And him he played it for' (1.2.107–8) by a subtle change of light his shabby cloak becomes a royal robe and the rough hull of the ship turns into a mysteriously strange place. The outside world vanishes, and the audience are lured into the play world, dominated by Prospero's resonant blank verse.

Soon, Morfov shifts gear, by changing the linguistic register and alerting the audience to the theatrical nature of their experience – this time, by altering the acting style. While with Prospero the play moves in a psychological/naturalistic direction, the love scenes between Ferdinand and Miranda are composed as puppet show. The director, who was formally trained in puppetry, uses his expertise to create a comic counterpoint to Prospero's grand narrative. The actors playing the lovers are handled like dolls by the spirits/stage hands who move them, speak their parts, jest with them by placing their limbs in suggestive positions underlining the sexual desire aroused by their encounter. Similarly, the comic scenes with Stephano, Trinculo and Caliban are played in the style of circus clowning, while 'the mast and tackle of the ship turn into the props and suspensions of a circus dome' (Dobrev 2000). The actors are given leave to indulge in improvised sketches until the tone changes again and we move back into Prospero's blank verse narrative.

Throughout Morfov initiates the audience into the ways theatre works by baring the ropes of illusion and then letting loose its power. In this production, the tempest, which follows Prospero's revelations of 1.2, is similarly created through openly theatrical means. The orchestra pit at the National, full of musical instruments and machinery for wind and storm effects, becomes the place where the spirits generate a percussionist tempest in full view of the audience. Everyday objects turn before their eyes into the stuff of theatre magic. The tempest begins with the spirits finding some scattered music sheets. Rhythmically, they crumple the paper – we hear the first crackling of leaves as the wind rises. With wide circular movements, they start swiping the floor with the paper balls – the sough of the wind becomes frightening, the rhythm changes. The cords of the instruments in the pit are plucked, the wind machine is set in motion, the tempo gets faster and faster, the clattering and the swishing sounds culminate in an explosion of throbbing music – Carl Orf's *Fortuna* from *Carmina Burana*. A sheet of water pours down the sides of the stage, the hull of the ship rocks. Then, the furore of sound and move-ment comes to an abrupt stop – the music, the spirits, the water suddenly vanish.

The idea of oppression is central to Morfov's reading.[7] Prospero oppresses Miranda, Ariel and Caliban; Miranda oppresses Caliban; Stephano and Trinculo boss over Caliban. Caliban as the only native, is forced to adapt to all, even to the comic fools. Morfov has added a fine touch by turning Stephano into a 1930s black-face music-hall clown. Himself oppressed in his own world, the 'black' man is only happy to proclaim himself King Stephano I and reign over Caliban. Morfov has also expanded the comedy in the scenes involving the lost aristocrats by creating additional 'encounters with natives' – the silent spirits disguised in African tribal costumes. The aristocrats (who don't know who they have encountered) lavish racist abuse on the natives while outwardly putting on a show of seeming politeness. The intruders are exposed as arrogant and disrespectful, in spite of their miserable plight.

Caliban is a vibrant comic centrepiece.[8] He is not a monster and some have seen in him the 'little man of the twentieth century, whose body and soul have incorporated the horrors of being; not a tragic character either – for he is resigned to his fate, even his rebellion is somehow fictitious' (Dobrev 2000). The 'shapelessness' of his survival strat-egy is underlined by his baggy costume, long-sleeved overalls reminiscent of a straight jacket and, significantly, of Prospero's own garb. In the eyes of the local audience, 'African' is a metaphor for 'Bulgarian' and the enhanced arrogance of the aristocrats who come from the 'white', 'civilised' world to teach the locals 'manners' (i.e. economic strategies) alludes to the endless string of dignitaries from the World Bank and other international institutions who briefly visit to tell the natives how to run their lives and then go away. Among these, there are often 'comic fools', like Stefano and Trinculo, who also have a go at bossing over and using the local Calibans. Yet, Caliban's 'earthy materiality' relentlessly undermines any attempt to rule over him. In the rebellion scenes he exposes the inadequacies of the comic characters and 'brushes [Prospero] aside, as a boring spokesman of ideological recitatives' (Dobrev 2000). Although Morfov's Caliban echoes recent post-colonial and new historicist critical approaches, his character actually draws on the long local tradition of folk and literary comic underdog characters. Caliban openly plays for the laughs of the audience who are invited to see the play from his point of view. By textually and visually augmenting the comic scenes Morfov gives them a prominence they do not have in Shakespeare, following, once again, a tradition in the Bulgarian treatment of the comedies whose stage history shows a marked preference for the comical/satirical, rather than the lyrical/romantic register, which, in the pre-1989 context, had the sly subversive effect of dif/fusing – de/fusing master narratives (Shurbanov and Sokolova 2001). In the world where Morforv works and where competing narratives have proliferated, the need to question their validity is even stronger.

Suggestively, Morfov's *Tempest* does not end with the stable realization of Prospero's grand plan, underscored by his farewell to the audience. Instead he speaks some of his lines from 4.1:

> These our actors,
> As I foretold you, were all spirits, and
> Are melted into air, into thin air:
> And, like the baseless fabric of this vision,
> The cloud-capped towers, the gorgeous palaces,
> The solemn temples, the great globe itself,
> Yea, all which it inherit, shall dissolve,
> And, like this insubstantial pageant faded,
> Leave not a rack behind. We are such stuff
> As dreams are made on.
>
> (4.1.148–58)

As Prospero speaks, the lights are turned on and, once again, stage and auditorium become a shared space, the turn-table starts to revolve, and the actors take their original positions. As if trapped on the island/stage, the characters/actors prepare for a replay of the story of love, treason, oppression and foiled rebellion. The backdrop of painted clouds gently folds aside to lay bare the recesses of the theatre with their magic-making ropes and pulleys, the audience is returned to a city called Sofia, on its own island of failed hopes. The production projects a sense of location by inviting the audience to share the same space with the tired actors. Morfov's *Tempest* admits the provisional nature of the 'happy hour' solution it offers and goes circularly back to its beginning, in a gesture of thoughtfulness which is not for all seasons, but for his audiences' unsettled and uncertain present.

It is worth stressing that artistically accomplished, imaginative and radical as Morfov's approach may be, it is not immune from market pressures. Comedy, especially broad comedy, attracts wider and younger audiences who throng the theatres to see their favourite actors in enlarged comic roles, *even* in a Shakespeare play. Morfov used this stratagem in *A Midsummer Night's Dream*, which he revised so as to foreground the mechanicals. Filling a theatre has become a crucial imperative for the artistic director of a European national institution, where Shakespeare is a *sine qua non* on the playbill. Some newspapers have drawn attention to another, somewhat disguised, commercial element in the director's approach: the lines written by him have been treated as 'authorial' and have earned him royalties. Shakespeare clearly offers two practical advantages over the work of living authors or work protected by copyright: the opportunity for fashionable revamping and adaptation and financial gain on the strength of the dead author's reputation.

In twenty-first century Bulgaria, Shakespeare's plays seem to have been subjected to a cultural processing resembling the moment of their original production. Their revival reminds one of interactions, characteristic of early modern collaborations between author/s, adapters, companies and entrepreneurial impresarios, a process recently described as Shakespeare's 'co-authorial reconstitution' (Bate 2003). Only now, the playwright's co-authors are moderns. Elizabethan cultural and market forces modelled Shakespeare's drama into what it is; cultural and market forces at other historical junctures continue to affect its afterlife. In their transformations on the Bulgarian post-communist stage, the two Shakespeare plays under discussion show clear signs of yielding to the drastic pressures of a prolonged socio-political and economic transition, to the new freedom of director managers and to the marketability of theatrical products across national borders in a globalized world. Sturua's *Twelfth Night* articulates through harshly bright images a puzzlingly bizarre sense of fatality and eventually finds uncertain refuge in the certainties of Christianity. Through an enhanced sense of theatrical metaphor and a feverish quest for new forms of expression Morfov's *Tempest* thrives instead on a playfulness which is profoundly destabilising. Shakespeare's plays are still there, still celebrated as culturally significant events; yet posters, though in small print, signal the now rather tentative place of the sixteenth-century partner in this modern alliance and often tend to introduce Bulgarian audiences to theatrical entertainment 'After William Shakespeare'. In the gap between 'by' and 'after William Shakespeare' lies a vast gamut of possibilities – from intercultural theatrical experiences substantially based on the texts produced by him and his company, to their relegation to sources, like the ones he used in order to serve the needs of his theatre.

8 'I am not bound to please thee with my answers': *The Merchant of Venice* on the post-war German stage

Sabine Schülting

In 1998, the Gorki Theatre in Berlin announced a production of Rainer Werner Fassbinder's controversial play *Der Müll, die Stadt und der Tod (Garbage, the [C]ity and [D]eath)*. This news caused an outcry which was not confined to the German capital alone. Among others, Andreas Nachama, then chairman of the Jewish community in Berlin, maintained that the play had 'Goebbelsque' qualities (Lau 1998). The dispute reproduced – albeit on a smaller scale – former controversies over Fassbinder's play. *Der Müll, die Stadt und der Tod* shows the miseries and the hopelessness of life in modern Western societies where the individual suffers from alienation and human relationships are modelled on the logic of capitalist exchange. The debates revolved around the character of A., 'The Rich Jew', a real estate investor, who figures as the cynical and ruthless representative of the inhumane system – when *Der Müll, die Stadt und der Tod* was first published by Suhrkamp in 1976, it was immediately criticized as anti-Semitic. In the same year, *Schatten der Engel (Shadow of Angels)*, the film adaptation of Fassbinder's play directed by Daniel Schmid, was the official German contribution at the Cannes film festival. When the festival refused to comply with the demand of the Israeli delegation to withdraw the film, the Israelis left under protest. In 1985 the Schauspielhaus Frankfurt planned a production of *Der Müll, die Stadt und der Tod* and, again, a heated controversy arose. Whereas the Jewish community as well as other organizations (including both the conservative and liberal democratic parties of Germany) protested against the production, the play was defended by leftists, who insisted on the freedom of art. On the night of the premiere, the theatre was occupied. A fervent discussion followed until the audience was finally sent home. After an official letter of protest from the Knesset to the German government, a number of (unsuccessful) lawsuits against the theatre, and a petition of renowned theatre directors and managers from all over Germany in support of the play, the theatre eventually announced that the production would be postponed until further notice.[1] By the end of the 1980s, the debate had slowly died down, but it was kindled anew in 1998. More than a decade had passed and the setting of the dispute was now Berlin; yet, the arguments, both in favour and against, had remained the same. The Gorki Theatre finally yielded to the protests and cancelled the production. Interestingly enough, the play seems to have been rather unproblematic outside Germany. It has so far been staged in the USA, in several European countries and even in Israel (see Jessen 1999).

William Shakespeare's *The Merchant of Venice*, on the one hand, and Fassbinder's *Der Müll, die Stadt und der Tod*, on the other, have little in common. It is only the character of the rich Jew which loosely links the two plays and which can account for the fact that

German productions of both *Der Müll, die Stadt und der Tod* and *The Merchant of Venice* almost inevitably become political events in which Germany's past and present relationship towards its Jewish population is at stake. Today, Antonio's contempt for Shylock together with Shylock's psychic, physical and economic destruction can only be read as a disturbing recollection of the Shoah. Some critics have thus doubted whether the play should be shown to a German audience at all: in 1960, the manager of the theatre at Mannheim decided to take *The Merchant of Venice* off the programme because he did not want to pour oil into the flames of a re-emerging anti-Semitism. In 1985, the critic Rolf Hochhuth demanded, 'Don't play it any more', and the director Heinz Hilpert said that he would only put the play on stage when '40 Jews sit in the stalls and laugh about it' (cited in Weiß 1995: 276; my translation). The question remains as to whether it will be possible to find *The Merchant of Venice* funny ever again. Can its characters pronounce their lines without evoking anti-Semitic violence? Isn't the comic resolution in the play inextricably bound up with anti-Semitism? In recent years, these reservations against the play seem to have decreased so that there are at least two or three German productions of *The Merchant* each year. However, even in 2003, Wilhelm Hortmann introduced his review of German *Merchants* since 2000 with a reference to Max Reinhardt's *Kaufmann von Venedig* and a melancholic reminiscence of the 'happy days' when a Jewish director could produce *The Merchant* as a colourful fairy tale (Hortmann 2003: 217).

Germany's 'problems' with *Der Müll, die Stadt und der Tod* and *The Merchant of Venice* have been informed by more general controversies about Germany's past. The so-called *Historikerstreit* was the most far-reaching of these debates, which was provoked by the demand of some historians to 'normalize' and 'historicize' the German attitude towards the Third Reich. In particular, they claimed that the Shoah had not been unique but could be compared to other genocides of the twentieth century, in particular to the Gulag under Stalin.[2] This debate was revived in 1998, when the writer Martin Walser was awarded the Peace Price of the German Booksellers' Association. In his speech during the ceremony at the Paulskirche in Frankfurt, Walser criticized the 'instrumentalization' of the German past and the ritualization of remembrance by both the media and left intellectuals. Walser argued that for them these repeated references to the Shoah had become a form of self-congratulatory exculpation (cf. Walser 1998). After his speech, Ignaz Bubis, the late chairman of the German–Jewish Committee, accused Walser of 'spiritual arson'. The controversy between Bubis and Walser was carried out in the media and focused on sensitive issues such as the German–Jewish relationship and the problem of German national pride. Since then, the debate has evolved, reaching a new peak in 2002 with the publication of Walser's novel *Tod eines Kritikers*, which was also accused of anti-Semitism, and the verbal attacks on Michel Friedman, then vice-president of the German Jewish Committee, by the liberal politician Jürgen Möllemann and Jarmal Karsli, a former member of the Green Party. Interestingly enough, by blurring the boundaries between victims and perpetrators, or, rather, by focusing on 'the victims of the victim', Fassbinder seems to have anticipated some of the arguments advanced during these recent controversies. In *Der Müll, die Stadt und der Tod*, the Shoah is indeed instrumentalized by the Jew for his economic success. A. admits: 'The city protects me, it has to. In addition, I am a Jew' (Fassbinder 1998: 58–9; my translation).

Through the figure of the rich and bloodthirsty Jew, both Fassbinder and Shakespeare's plays cite from the anti-Semitic tradition in Western Europe, in which

Jews were accused of poisoning wells, committing ritual murders and desecrating the host. In the 1930s and 1940s, Shakespeare's play could thus easily be adapted for the purposes of fascist propaganda, as the 1943 production at the Burgtheater in Vienna shows. A contemporary critic wrote:

> The masque alone – the pale pink face, framed by his bright-red hair and beard, the restlessness of his small sharp eyes, the greasy caftan with the yellow ritual cloth – [...] the clawish gesture of his hands, the bawling and murmuring voice – all this converges in the pathological picture of the racial type of the Eastern Jew, together with the whole outer and inner uncleanliness of the man, while the danger lurking in the humorous is underscored.
>
> (Cited in von Ledebur 1982: 283; my translation)

It is obvious how Shakespeare's play was successfully appropriated in order to justify the ideological basis of the genocide. One could thus argue that theatre managers, directors and critics are absolutely justified when they try to ban the play from the German stage.

An alternative approach to the problem of this play's fraught legacy in post-war Germany is offered by the feminist philosopher and critic Judith Butler. In her book *Excitable Speech* (1997), Butler focuses on the potential of hate speech. With reference to J. L. Austin's speech act theory, she argues that it is not a figure of speech when we say that words wound. '[S]peech does not merely *reflect* a relation of social domination; speech *enacts* domination, becoming the vehicle through which that social structure is reinstated' (Butler 1997: 18). Racist or anti-Semitic speech is injurious since it 'quotes' cultural stereotypes, thus endlessly reproducing and consolidating discrimination. The victim is forced to remember a history of violence – both institutional and physical – and she/he is threatened with a repetition of this violence in the future. Butler posits a close link between hate speech and trauma. In psychoanalysis, trauma describes the state of shock after a stressful event, which the subject cannot overcome. In repetitive dreams, for example, the traumatized subject relives the same event again and again. According to Butler, hate speech functions in a similar way. The individual is also subjected to recurrent injuries, in which violence is both substituted and re-enacted by linguistic signs. This implies that the violence of hate speech does not result from an autonomous or sovereign power, which exists prior to the speech act, but, rather, from the repetitive and citational character of the speech act itself. Only because the speaker refers to – or 'quotes' – traditions and conventions, she/he can assume authority and 'hurt' the addressee. With regard to Shakespeare's play this would imply that the text itself is not intrinsically violent. However, the play has exercised violence since it cites from anti-Semitic traditions which more often than not have been closely intertwined with political and social discriminations against the Jewish population as well as the material violence of pogroms. Butler maintains that although the repetition of injurious speech re-enacts the injury, it can nevertheless reveal how hate speech works. A repetition can show that the word itself is not violent, but that it only gains this power through a history of endless citation. The emphasis on the performative nature of any speech act implies that it is ultimately open to appropriation and radical resignification. This also applies to post-war productions of Shakespeare's *Merchant of Venice* which have tried to foreground the violence associated with and exercised by the play.

My essay explores the extent to which adaptation in recent German productions of *The Merchant* can function as a strategy of repetition and resignification. My analysis focuses on Otto Schenk's 1968 TV version, starring the Jewish actor Fritz Kortner as Shylock, George Tabori's 1978 adaptation of the play at the Munich Kammerspiele, Peter Zadek's *Kaufmann von Venedig* at the Burgtheater in Vienna in 1988 and Hanan Snir's *Kaufmann von Venedig* at the Deutsches Nationaltheater in Weimar in 1995. Although these examples cover four decades and also different media, I shall not try to posit a historical development. I shall rather discuss them as different ways of repositioning Shakespeare's *Merchant* in post-war Germany.

In the first decade after the Second World War, 'a predominance of noble Shylocks' could be seen on the German stage, 'half-brothers of Gotthold Ephraim Lessing's *Nathan der Weise*, near-innocent victims, more sinned against than sinning'. These 'expiation Shylocks', as Wilhelm Hortmann argues, 'satisfied a deep need for making moral amends' (1998: 54–55). Only since the end of the 1960s has this tradition been deliberately broken. In the 1968 TV version of *Der Kaufmann von Venedig*, the presence of the Jewish actor Fritz Kortner in the role of Shylock contributed to rendering Shakespeare's *Venice* as a clear allegory of fascist Germany. Before the war, Kortner[3] had already played Shylock in Vienna in 1916, in Max Reinhardt's production of 1924 and in Jürgen Fehling's *Kaufmann von Venedig*, which premiered on 27 November 1927 at the Staatliches Schauspielhaus, Berlin. Fehling had meant to show a gentle and humane Shylock as an argument against the growing anti-Semitism in the Weimar Republic. However, Kortner rejected Fehling's approach. In his autobiography, he reports that, contrary to Fehling, he wanted to play a Shylock whose increasing inhumanity would be shown to be a reaction to the inhumane attacks from which he had suffered. Kortner succeeded and this *Merchant*, he writes, turned out to be 'terribly contemporary. Its reference to the racist fascism which was now striving for power electrified both friend and enemy' (Kortner 1979: 297; my translation).

Kortner left Germany in 1938 and emigrated to the United States, but returned to Europe after the war, in 1949. When he played Shylock in Otto Schenk's TV version in 1968, he was seventy-six years old and had already retired from the stage. His interpretation of the role showed clear parallels to the Berlin production before the war: once more, Shylock appeared as a 'traditional' Jew with *tallith* and *kippa*. Kortner's Shylock is a deeply religious man whose original benevolence eventually gives way to hatred because he has to suffer endless anti-Semitic attacks. In the overall production, which tells the story of Bassanio and Portia as a rather shallow comedy, frequently verging on the folklorist, he is an obvious outsider, and Kortner's acting – serious, intense and 'operatic' (Schütze 1994: 70) – underscores this contrast. For this reason, the film has been criticized for 'frittering away' (Schütze 1994: 70) Kortner's dramatic potential, yet I wonder whether this apparent lack of aesthetic coherence cannot also be read as a general comment on Shylock-figures on the post-war German stage and screen: the film shows Shylock as a killjoy, disturbing the sentimental *Heimatfilm* atmosphere and confronting the audience with a past it would rather forget. When in the last scene Shylock not only loses his fortune, but is also forced to consent to his conversion, he raises his eyes towards heaven in mute despair, then draws his *tallith* over his face and asks permission to leave. The camera follows his exit through a vacant hallway, its bareness suggesting the 'disappearance' of the Jews and the absence of the victims of the Shoah in post-war Germany. To the extent of even visually remembering his Berlin Shylock of 1927 – Kortner's Shylock had the same thin beard and dishevelled hair – the film became an act of cultural memory, which established a direct link between the increasing anti-Semitism in Germany in the 1920s, the emigration of the Jews in the 1930s, Nazi pogroms and the genocide as well as the conflictual relationship between Germany and its Jewish population after the war.

Although Peter Zadek addressed similar questions in his 1988 *Kaufmann von Venedig* at the Vienna Burgtheater, his production worked in a completely different way. The setting was transferred to Wall Street. Portia's question – 'Which is the merchant here, and which the Jew?' (4.1.169) – drew the audience's attention to the fact that Gert Voss as Shylock was indeed a broker like the others: he wore the same dark suit, read the same newspaper, and had the same briefcase and mobile phone. His defeat at the end of the play was the failure of a businessman, who accepted his bankruptcy without batting an eyelid. When at the end of the trial scene, Shylock dropped to his knees, this was not an act of submission. Rather than asking for mercy, he just bowed down in order to sign the cheque for Antonio. One critic wrote:

> Shylock goes – but this time he does not bear his people's tragedy on his shoulders. He does not go (like other Shylocks) to gloomily meet his destruction, he also does not go towards Auschwitz. The Christians know (and this is why they are so embarrassed) that they will not easily get rid of this Jew. [...] Shylock goes – but he will always come back.
>
> (Heinrichs 1988; my translation)

In Zadek's interpretation, Christian society cannot ward off the 'foreigners', since the boundary between the self and its others has become blurred. Shylock remains; he is a member of a society which has to come to terms with its prejudices.

In both George Tabori's and Hanan Snir's adaptations of *The Merchant*, the concern with German history was stressed through their setting and *mise en scène*. Snir's Weimar production of 1995 was a play within a play: Jewish prisoners in a concentration camp – by implication, Buchenwald, near Weimar – had to stage Shakespeare's play in order to amuse the SS officers. Originally, George Tabori had devised a similar scenario for his 1978 adaptation of *The Merchant of Venice*. His initial plan had been to play the trial scene at the site of the Bavarian concentration camp at Dachau (near Munich). However, when permission was denied by the municipality, the play was transferred to an improvised stage in a rehearsal room at the Munich Kammerspiele. Through these relocations both directors gave the play a new local and historical habitation. However, Snir was widely criticized for his rather schematic and all too obvious adaptation. After having performed Shakespeare's play for the Nazis, Jessica, Shylock and the other Jewish characters were killed on the open stage. Despite these gratuitous and rather crude modifications Snir produced a rather conventional *Merchant*.

George Tabori's production, on the contrary, represented a thorough investigation into Shakespeare's play, which blurred binary oppositions and resisted all attempts at economic, psychological or sociological explanations of anti-Semitism (cf. Michael Krüger in Tabori 1979: 30). Whereas Snir's production ended with the confrontation between a contemporary Antonio and Shylock's ghost, who nodded at his former torturer, Tabori's play stressed the impossibility of giving merely one reading of Shakespeare's *Merchant* and coming to a unilateral conclusion. The title of Tabori's adaptation was a quotation from Shylock's speech in 3.1: *Ich wollte, meine Tochter läge tot zu meinen Füßen und hätte die Juwelen in den Ohren: Improvisationen über Shakespeares Shylock.*[4] In the eighteen scenes, some based on Shakespeare's play,[5] others such as 'KZ-Ezählung' ('Concentration Camp Narrative') or 'Kristallnacht'[6] explicitly referring to Nazi Germany, Shylock was played by the whole cast, thirteen actors in all, who offered as many interpretations, or, rather, improvisations, including a monstrous caricature of a Jew, a Jewish prisoner in a concentration camp, and a survivor. Jessica, in turn, metamorphosed into a (male homosexual) inmate of a concentration camp, so that the couple Lorenzo and Jessica were transformed into quite a different pair: a Nazi torturing a Jewish prisoner. The Portia sub-plot was cut altogether, since it was believed that its happy romanticism could not be adapted to the violence of German fascism.

Tabori's production underscored the performative and processual character of the adaptation. For example, Shylock's outrage at Jessica's elopement, which in the Shakespearean original is only reported by Solanio (2.8.12–22), was played twelve times, always in a different way. One actor expressed his grief in a low and subdued voice. Another actor ran over the stage screaming and howling. A third actor spoke in dialect; a fourth imitated Fritz Kortner playing Shylock; a fifth transformed the scene into a musical. In addition, there were also slapstick and pantomime versions (see Hensel 1978). In his seminal study *Shakespeare on the German Stage*, Wilhelm Hortmann has read these improvisations as a means of providing 'comic relief as well as a reinforcement of the emotional impact of the scene by reflecting it through different personae and media' (1998: 61). Although the audience may have experienced relief, I would rather argue that these variations are much more significant than Hortmann's reading seems to suggest. By foregrounding the processes of remembering as well as the problems of performing the play, Tabori showed both the critical potential and the disturbing effects of an adaptation based on strategies of repetition and resignification.

Ich wollte, meine Tochter... began with the 'Ballad of Shylock', a song based on a seventeenth-century text by Samuel Pepys, during which the actors, all playing Shylock, prowled through the audience. With their long hooked noses, their greedy looks and their gestures, they represented the typical caricatures of Jews as reproduced by Nazi newspapers like the *Stürmer*. The first scene thus already showed how the citation of the anti-Semitic tradition was visually inscribed on the body of the other. But Tabori's Shylocks were not politically correct, and their despair, aggression and offensive behaviour questioned the post-war (German) stereotype of the Jew as an object of pity (Rothschild 1997: 7). This denial of victimization did not merely represent Tabori's attempt to give dignity to the Jewish character, but it was also a deliberate attack on the expectations of the audience, who were not allowed to indulge in a sentimentalized *Merchant*. In the conservative daily *Die Welt*, one reviewer of the production concluded that only the fact that Tabori was a Jew himself and that his relatives had been killed at Auschwitz protected him from the accusation of anti-Semitism (Anon. 1978). The critic was not willing to accept the disturbing quality of the performance, which was meant to confront the audience with an uncomfortable and, indeed, *violent* recollection of the German past that could not be held at bay and began to physically affect the spectators. So, for example, puppets were undressed and their clothes thrown on a pile before their 'naked bodies' were destroyed and the fragments distributed among the audience. Towards the end of the play, Shylock – having been sentenced to convert to Christianity – was undressed, baptized and then turned into a kind of monster, a Bavarian goy, with his white christening shirt, rouge and powder, bleached hair and Bavarian stock-ings. Tabori himself has commented on this detail of his production:

> The naked Shylock is embarrassing for the author, for the audience as well as for the other actors. You don't want to see this, but you have to, and you say: 'Not again, please!' or 'What's the point?' or 'Spare me that!' [...] An English critic once called the theatre the medium of embarrassment: it confronts the spectator with what he would rather ignore. After all, who would like to spend his weekend with Shylock?
>
> (1979: 11; my translation)

In the trial scene, Shylock was not alone, but he appeared in a group of people, who dragged themselves onto the stage. Shylock carried another Jew over his shoulder and pulled two victims of a concentration camp after him (see Schödel 1978). He thus assumed the role of both witness and victim.

These two figures – the survivor and the victim – stand at the centre of Giorgio Agamben's *Remnants of Auschwitz: The Witness and the Archive* where they are discussed as the two opposing figurations of the dilemma of giving testimony. Agamben rejects the thesis that Auschwitz is unspeakable, arguing that this position would support the orig-inal attempt of the Nazis to eliminate all witnesses (1999: 157).[7] With reference to Primo Levi, Agamben sees the survivor as a subject who has the ability to speak for those who cannot speak but whose testimony needs the authenticating presence of the silenced victim, the 'Muselmann':[8] '*The authority of the witness consists in his capacity to speak solely in the name of an incapacity to speak – that is, in his or her being a subject*' (1999: 158; italics in the original). Testimony, he stresses, is not concerned with factual truth but, rather, with the possibility or necessity of language 'where there has been desubjectification' (Agamben 1999: 58). According to Agamben, the modern form of biopower with the camp as its model can be summarized in the formula '*to make survive*' (Agamben 1999: 155), i.e. the separation of 'animal life from organic life, the human from the inhuman, the witness from the Muselmann, conscious life from vegetative life maintained functional through resuscitation techniques' and 'of the living being and the speaking being' (155–6). Testimony explicitly refutes this separation and stresses the indivisible bond between bare life and the human, the witness and the Muselmann, the speaking subject and the trau-matized and silenced victim of racism: 'to bear witness is to place oneself in one's own language in the position of those who have lost it' (Agamben 1999: 161). Tabori's improvisations, one could conclude, do not merely show how Shylock is silenced in the course of Shakespeare's play. In addition, they emphasize that post-war German productions of *The Merchant of Venice* can bear witness to the Shoah by resorting to a continuous and painful search for new words. *Ich wollte meine Tochter* ... as well as other recent relocations of Shakespeare's play[9] on the German stage suggest how central its role still is not only in prompting heated discussions, but also in enabling processes of re-membering Germany's past.

9 Katherina 'humanized': Abusing the Shrew on the Prague stage

Marcela Kostihová

The Taming of the Shrew is the third most frequently performed Shakespeare play on the Czech stage: with seventy-eight productions since 1945, it is surpassed only by *A Midsummer Night's Dream* and *Twelfth Night*. In the 2000–1 theatre season, there were no fewer than six *Tamings*[1] country-wide, three competing in Prague alone. These numbers raise an inevitable question: what fuels the cultural interest in one of the most problematic of Shakespeare plays? Diana Henderson has usefully established that the interest in *The Taming of the Shrew* in Western Europe and North America intensifies at times of growing backlash against feminism.[2] The increasing Czech fixation on Katherina and Petruchio's abusive relationship similarly suggests a deeply rooted reluctance to accept social changes inspired by feminist movements in the West.

Czech culture is recovering from gender equality policies enforced by the communist regime. These policies pushed women into the workplace even as they barred traditional career opportunities for men. Instead of restoring conventionally patriarchal gender roles, the end of communism has prompted further social disruption by creating new professional opportunities for both men and women. Further, in order to join the European Union, the Czech Republic has had to introduce new legislation to ensure gender equality in the workplace and the domestic sphere. Besides affecting the roles of women in Czech post-communist society, the recent political upheavals have added to a general anxiety about masculinity and, inevitably, Czech national identity.

Recent productions of *The Taming of the Shrew* reveal how Shakespeare is being used to explore conventional gender roles at a time of intense political, cultural and economic change. In a society where traditional dominant masculinity was undermined by four decades of communism and is now threatened by cultural influences from the West, *The Taming of the Shrew* is often used to fuel a nostalgic fantasy. The play is often read as being simultaneously about an uppity female forced into a subservient position and about a disempowered male subject, who reclaims his rightful dominant position within the patriarchal family. Shakespeare, often used in the past to articulate a subversive stance against a totalitarian regime, is now invoked to stem the influence of current Western values. Far from emulating Western Shakespeares, Czech Shakespeares often serve as a corrective and a reminder of the 'true' core of Western cultural identity, as it was understood and imagined from behind the Iron Curtain.

Off stage, resistance to feminism surfaces in debates about *pozitivní diskriminace*. Literally translated as positive discrimination, this term is the equivalent of affirmative action. In May 2001, the secretary for labor and social affairs, Vladimír Špidla, established a new committee for 'equal opportunities for men and women',[3] a clear step towards the requirements set by the European Union. The press voiced strongly negative responses. Pavel Zídek, for instance, wrote: 'it is women who have special rights while men often experience discrimination'. 'Considering that women choose marriage freely,' he continued, 'the traditional family unit within which they do most of the housework and childcare would seem to be a satisfactory arrangement' (Zídek 2001: 3). The assumption underlying these comments is that gender inequality is natural and desirable, whereas gender equality equals discrimination against men, as it denies them access to traditional networks of power and resources

Public opinion is clearly divided between official willingness to implement new legislation and a popular commitment to the 'ways we always were'. This division is further underscored by recent research on domestic violence, which demonstrates that it is both widespread and widely condoned as a problem to be resolved privately by the individual family unit.[4] Czech lawmakers officially admit that their interest in domestic violence stems from a desire to join the European Union. Society at large similarly sees this 'trendy', 'Western' concern merely as political correctness that further undermines traditional family values. Wary of the socialist experience of artificially imposed gender equality, which brought state-run day-care and required women to join the work force but failed to translate into equal division of domestic labour or equal pay for equal work, Czech society is now struggling to accept further intervention into domestic relations.

The three 2001 Prague productions of *Taming* discussed in this chapter reflect local attitudes towards domestic violence, gender relations and the role of the Czech Republic in the newly reorganized Europe. Each production struggles to perform the play as a comedy while retaining the troubling sequences of Katherina's 'taming'. Whether framing the play as Sly's masculinist dream, suggesting that Katherina's love for Petruchio overcomes all obstacles, or showing Katherina as the ultimate winner of the war of the sexes, these productions betray a cultural anxiety about the perceived societal disorder resulting from a gender imbalance in private relationships. My analysis, which draws on personal observations, reviews and original interviews, aims to establish how Shakespeare is used to address local issues and concerns at this crucial juncture in the recent history of the Czech Republic.[5]

The *Taming* directed by Michal Dočekal was performed in a small but well known alternative theatre called Komedie, which is dedicated to non-traditional, often postmodernist interpretations of a predominantly traditional repertory. This is the first Czech production to include the Induction and the Epilogue from the anonymous *The Taming of A Shrew*. As a result, Katherina's taming can be interpreted as the dream of the drunkard Sly, played by the same actor who plays Petruchio, who becomes the projected fantasy of Sly's ideal model of a dominant, self-confident and eloquent masculinity. The dream-like qualities of the play are emphasized throughout by the reappearance of the Lord and his crew. This production also makes clear that, in order to perform Petruchio, Sly needs to learn how to assert his masculinity in relation to his new status: instead of abusing women physically, the upper-class Petruchio abuses them psychologically.[6] In other words, the 'classy' model of masculinity embodied by Petruchio does not need to make an argument for male dominance; it rather takes if for granted.

The 'success' of Petruchio's taming is visible both in Katherina's appearance and behaviour. The energetic, assertive woman donning short spiky hair and glasses, boots and overalls at the beginning of the play becomes a model of conventional femininity, as suggested by her glittering low-cut gown, high heels, long hair and a made-up face that resembles a blank mask. This taming process raises an interpretive dilemma for the audience: is Katherina's 'authentic self' expressed by her initial spirited personality or by her subsequent ultra-feminine composure? If Dočekal's audience decide that the 'real' Katherina has short hair and wears boots, then this production has the potential to function as a critique of conventional gender roles and of the taming process as flawed and inherently abusive. In fact, the violence of the wooing/taming scenes is reminiscent of Emily Detmer's comparison between *Taming* and the Stockholm syndrome.[7] Detmer shows that Katherina, like the victim of a kidnapping, 'begins to subordinate her wishes, ideas, and actions in order to stave off the next outburst' of violence and abuse on her captor's part (1997: 276n). In this respect, Dočekal's production can be read as an attempt to investigate the chilling realities of domestic abuse resulting in the loss of the victim's personal identity.

However, most reviewers preferred to think of the earlier, alert and outspoken Katherina as the one wearing a harsh disguise, hiding her 'natural' feminine self, which then surfaces in response to Petruchio's 'wooing'. Illona Francková sees the taming as a process of self-discovery whereby the initially unwomanly Katherina awakens to her own femininity and accepts the appropriate position of the 'submissive but triumphant' wife who 'will be subservient to her husband in speech and action, but not thought' (Francková 2000: 11). Similarly, Martina Musilová, who believes Katherina's initial lack of femininity to be 'unusual in Czech culture', argues that Petruchio 'educates her and with a fatherly superiority forces her to accept a desirable and life-saving order' (Musilová 2000: 53). Few reviewers question the viability of Katherina's taming or the assumption that women's subordination is a cultural given, integral to women's welfare within a balanced and harmonious social order. They rather see Katherina's taming as a slightly caricatured and exaggerated representation of the usual interaction between the sexes.

Crucially, the theatre practitioners involved in this production had different views on how Shakespeare's play should be read and staged. During an interview, Dočekal pointed out that he sees *Taming* as a completely 'sexist, anti-feminist play ... a comedy in which nothing is funny'. The newly translated epilogue confirmed his view that *Taming* is 'a play dreamt up by the sleazebag Sly, who is imagining that he is someone he is not' (Dočekal 2001). For Dočekal, the play becomes viable only when the taming is represented as a form of social critique, exposing rather than glorifying aggressive masculinity. Despite Dočekal's feminist agenda, his cast had very different views on the play. David Matásek, as Sly-turned-Petruchio, regards the taming as a viable method to ensure Katherina's discovery of her natural self and of her appropriate position in society, which many women are regretfully abandoning. Pointing to the falling birthrate in the Czech Republic, Matásek argues in favour of the 'natural' procreative and familial role for women which he sees as essential for the survival of society. Remembering with aversion women's roles supported by the socialist regime, such as the 'monstrous' large-machinery operators and construction workers, Matásek argues that women were forced into these roles as a result 'of the lack of men ... or some ideological coercion which claimed that a woman is equal to man in terms of productivity ... . They forgot that there is one immensely important thing, called a family'. Despite the potential for freeing women from this bind, capitalism did not bring much improvement, as women 'put on their little suits and managerial positions in large companies, and again forgot all about the family'. According to Matásek, Shakespeare's play warns against the imminent breakdown of conventionally patriarchal gender roles, which he sees as a direct consequence of the introduction of capitalism and westernization (Matásek 2001–2).

Alena Štréblová, who played Katherina, reported that she struggled immensely with her part. Perceiving Katherina as 'an outcast, ... as a woman who does not want to be a woman because she is afraid of her own femininity', she then endorses the taming process, through which Petruchio validates and rewards her feminine side. Štréblová went on to describe 'ideal relationships' where 'the more the women stoop, the more they gain in individuality ... and that is how they earn their right to be respected by their partners' (Štréblová 2002). Within the context of Dočekal's production, Štréblová's views should have found validation in Katherina's final speech, which, according to Štréblová's reasoning, would secure Katherina Petruchio's respect. Yet, both in rehearsal and in production Matásek refused to act respectfully during the last scene. Admitting that the production does not show much of the self-sacrificing mutuality she detects between Katherina and Petruchio, she blamed Shakespeare. Despite Dočekal's feminist agenda, this production revealed unresolved tensions among the actors, between the actors and the director, and, more crucially, divided views on the viability of the sexual politics which all parties involved thought Shakespeare's play purports to promote.

The second production, directed by Michal Lang in another small and mostly independent theatre called CD 94, attempted to perform the play 'traditionally'. Lang's Katherina, clearly bothered by the prospect of spinsterhood, quickly accepts Petruchio's courtship. The taming process is merciless: Petruchio's definition of Katherina as a commodity – 'She is my goods, my chattels; she is my house,/My household-stuff, my field, my barn,/My horse, my ox, my ass, my anything' (3.2.219–22)[8] – is chilling, sadistic and firm. The production emphasizes her complete isolation. Even Petruchio's occasional kindness merely increases Katherina's dependency on him. In the last scene, Katherina appears in a dress and cap given to her as reward for her obedience. Looking lovingly at her husband, she delivers this controversial speech as a genuine appeal to both women on stage, Bianca and the Widow, and to women in the audience.

The critical response to this production was overwhelmingly positive. Reviewers celebrated the virtues of the normalized nuclear family that results from Petruchio's taming. Taking his cue from the play, Pavel Čírtek compared Katherina to a bird of prey, to 'a wild, unbound creature which needs to be tamed'. He calls her 'a woman who at first only senses, but eventually learns how to regain her seemingly lost pride' (Čírtek 1997: 12). Jana Soprová reassures those feminist critics who have dismissed *Taming of the Shrew* as irremediably misogynistic that the audience is ultimately prepared to believe that Katherina and Petruchio 'really like each other. [...] Although Katherina submits, she gives the surprised Petruchio such a lesson that he is unlikely to ever torment the lovely creature again' (Soprová 1997: 13). Zdeněk Tichý goes as far as regarding this *Taming* as one of the 'merriest performances' around (Tichý 1997: 19). Even those who deem the taming passages brutal still perceive Katherina and Petruchio's relationship as ultimately positive, at least once Katherina budges. Vítězslava Šrámková is disturbed by Katherina and Petruchio's violent fighting, but she commends Katherina for her wisdom as she is the first to recognize the futility of unending fights and gives in, pursuing the 'better and more rational alternative of the relationship – love' (Šrámková 1997: 15).

The director, Michal Lang, believes that *Taming* provides a universally recognizable rite of passage into adulthood. For both Katherina and Petruchio, the taming interlude functions as a 'gate of sorts':

> When a man tames a woman, they both grow up. Even when the man's development
> is not readily seen, it *is* there, it is. That is why I chose to do the play. When Katherina
> presents the monologue, when she takes it seriously, and Petruchio kneels, he is meek.
> That is maturity. That is the point at which the little boy becomes a man.
>
> (Lang 2001)

Lang sees the conflict as pertinent to both sexes. Commenting on the social relevance
of the play, Lang notes that Czech culture is infantile, because it no longer has proper
rites of passage. Men and women are allowed to remain children, which is the 'goal of
Western consumerism'. Once again, a 'straight' reading of Shakespeare is interpreted
as an active act of resistance against the influence of Western economic models and
cultural values.

Petra Špalková readily admits that the play is anti-feminist. Seeing her Katherina as a
proto-feminist character 'who clearly surpasses the rank of the submissive woman', she
perceives the taming as a bitter recipe for 'how to deal with feminism in the Czech
Republic'. From further conversation, however, it becomes clear that, for Špalková,
'feminist' is not necessarily a positive attribute. Though she agrees that Katherina's initial
spirit is broken, she also argues, echoing Štréblová at Komedie, that Katherina 'wins' by
submitting to Petruchio, bringing an emotional connection, peace, and 'the happiest
marriage of the three on the stage'. She sees the process of taming as one of 'cultivation',
during which 'one man and one woman learn to live next to each other' (Špalková
2001–2). At Lang's bidding, Špalková usually delivers Katherina's final speech to 'the
men in the audience with their briefcases, cell phones, and manicured hands', first
reminding them of a man's duties to women: a man is, in Shakespeare's words, 'one that
cares for thee/And for thy maintenance commits his body/To painful labor both by sea
and land,/To watch the night in storms, the day in cold' (5.2.147–50).[9] Špalková's
Katherina suggests that women's unwomanly behaviour arises from the softening of
Czech masculinity, which no longer requires sacrifice of bodily comforts. Once the men
reclaim their dominant positions, as Sly does by doubling as Petruchio, women will
relinquish the tasks and behaviours that do not belong to them, thus restoring conventional gender roles. In this context, domestic violence is a justified means to a worthwhile
end, that is, the establishment of a stable society built on traditional nuclear families at
a time when the Czech Republic is faced by the prospect of a cultural redefinition of
national as well as personal identity.

Vladimír Strnisko's *Taming* at the open-air Prague Summer Shakespeare Festival casts
Slovak actors as the Minolas and Czech actors as the rest of the characters. Strnisko
therefore adds a political dimension to his production by addressing cultural developments after the peaceful but far from amiable division of Czechoslovakia in 1991. Even
more interesting within the context of this essay is the fact that Strnisko's version
provides an alternative reading of the play by omitting Sly and by shifting power
relations between the two central characters. Katherina is in her forties, self-possessed,
confident and experienced. In red leather pants under a flowing white dress, she is the
most vibrant character on stage. Petruchio, in contrast, dressed in blanched blues, is
young, ambitious and not sure how to handle Katherina. Except for occasional
moments during the taming scenes, Katherina is in control throughout the play.

While Petruchio sweats, stumbles and grasps for pertinent comebacks, Katherina pursues, threatens and laughs. Unlike her counterparts in the other productions discussed in this chapter, this Katherina knows how to fit into the world around her, and has simply been refusing to do so. Katherina remains her assertive self to the end of the play, even as she is openly affectionate with Petruchio. Petruchio is far from sure whether she will come at his bidding and is genuinely stunned by her monologue. Katherina's speech is over-earnest and brief, breaking off in mid-sentence to initiate the unbelieving Bianca and Widow into the secrets of social subversion. The play closes with an outburst of laughter coming from this newly formed group in response to Petruchio's claim of absolute power over Katherina. The stage darkens as uncertainty returns to Petruchio's face and quickly spreads to the other male characters, whose confidence in their ability to control their women seem suddenly shaken. The final laugh, in other words, crosses the boundary of what Lynda Boose has called the 'characteristically' revisionist approach which allows for a modest degree of subversion in Katherina's actions so far as it remains invisible to the men on the stage. Such revisions, Boose argues, 'desired ... not so much a way of undoing Kate's ventriloquization of male superiority as a way of making it more palatable. Kate's subjugation must be endowed with signs of resistance, but a resistance that Petruchio *will not recognize*' (Boose 1994: 193; my emphasis).

Strnisko's directorial intervention radically changes the interpretation of the final scene. The first two productions had gradually isolated Katherina so that at the end she stands alone, utterly dependent on her husband. Strnisko's production, however, targets this isolation as a pitfall. By establishing a subversive connection with the other women, Katherina resists her husbands' attempt to polarize the women against each other ('Petruchio: To her Kate!/ Hortensio: To her, widow!') (5.2.33–4).[10] On the contrary, she learns how to manipulate her husband and shares her newly acquired skills with the other women. As a result, the taming process itself becomes a constructive experience for Katherina, as she emerges stronger and more self-possessed than she was at the beginning of this production. In Strnisko's *Taming*, male abuse breeds female confidence, and not conventionally patriarchal ideals of domesticity as in the other two productions.

Of the three performances, this one fared the least well with the critics who refused to recognize it as a viable rendition of Shakespeare's play. Despite the fact that all three productions used the same translation of the play by Martin Hilský, reviewers argued that the language of Strinisko's version was too vulgar and too sexual, suggesting that this production failed to represent Shakespeare faithfully. The majority of reviewers commented that the production degraded 'one of the most beautiful of Shakespeare's plays' to a 'seedy farce' (Vlastník 2000; Machalická 2000: 21; Jeníková 2000: 2). Their response suggested that, in denying Petruchio ultimate mastery over Katherina, this production does not only depart from traditional Czech appropriations of *The Taming* but also from the Shakespearean original itself. In an interview, Strnisko claimed that he would not have opted for such a rowdy production, in the style of *commedia dell' arte*, if he had directed *Taming* in a more conventional venue. Nevertheless, he also stressed that the vulgarity the reviewers condemned is, for the most part, not added but already in Shakespeare.

Yet, as with Dočekal's production, the director's views were not always shared by members of his company. Michal Dlouhý, for example, who performed Petruchio both at CD 94 and at the Shakespeare Festival, insisted that in both productions proper masculine dominance was achieved as 'Petruchio won. He won for himself. He got what he wanted. And he won in front of the others'. However, when asked to compare the two productions, he admitted that he preferred Lang's traditional interpretation. There, Petruchio

> is not mean, he is not brutal. What you see is self-confidence. All the taming, all the things he does to Katherina he does only for her, to change her view of the world, to make her approachable, to make her human. He is not there to break her; he breaks her only in so far as she changes into a normal, pleasant person who can finally adjust to her environment.
>
> (Dlouhý 2000–1)

Strnisko's production is more challenging for Dlouhý. However, even this Petruchio, Dlouhý insisted, is not afraid of Katherina. His discomfort is merely feigned to manipulate Katherina into showing 'her true colours so that he knows exactly how to tame her'. Asked to explain what he thought about the relevance of *Taming* in contemporary Czech society, Dlouhý argued that *Taming* rightfully

> suppresses a bit women's emancipation, since it is not natural. *Taming* shows that women do not have to do all that men do … although this has been a trend in the last few years when women have begun meddling in gentlemen's matters. This play could be a healthy mirror showing that a woman is a woman, a man is a man, and that blending such distinctions is not appropriate.
>
> (Dlouhý 2000–1)

Like Matásek and much of the Czech press, Dlouhý voices the prevalent cultural understanding of male–female relationships and the unshakeable assumption that Katherina and Petruchio are connected through bonds of true love, forged by their survival of the rocky taming. In this context the two characters' transformation and even Katherina's brutal abuse are necessary to make them able to function harmoniously around others. Katherina's initial outspokenness as well as Sly's decadent masculinity are interpreted as insurmountable obstacles, which prevent them from functioning as well-rounded human beings.

As both the actors and the reviewers suggest, the majority of Czech women seem to share a very similar cultural space with contemporary theatrical appropriations of Shakespeare's Katherina. Discouraged from expressing independence or engaging in patterns of behaviour which are not allowed by currently popular gender codes, they find (sometimes subversive) agency in their subservience to nominally dominant masculinity. Published data on domestic violence further underscore the unfortunate reality that Petruchio's methods – physical as well as psychological – are used and condoned as acceptable measures for 'taming' ostensibly unruly women. The current need to enforce normative gender roles stems from a profound cultural anxiety about the possibility of chaos resulting from the radical changes which are occurring at several different levels of contemporary Czech society.

For better or worse, this anxiety and its consequences are fuelled by a need for stability. Czech culture, despite (or because of?) colonizations by various empires from the Hapsburgs to the USSR, has traditionally identified itself as Western European.

On one level, its current journey towards the European Union is not a step into a great unknown; rather, it is widely perceived as a return to a long-lost cultural home. On another level, though, Czech culture is torn by a shattering paradox, as assumedly Western values at the core of Czech national identity, represented, among other things, by a commitment to traditionally patriarchal gender politics, are at odds with the explicit ethical code enforced by a new twenty-first-century European Union on its new member states.

Recent Czech appropriations of *Taming* are fundamentally unstable, showing directors and actors often working at cross-purposes. The three productions analysed in this essay show that even when directors and actors opt for a traditional, 'straight' interpretation of *Taming*, there is no unequivocal, stable textual point of origin for them to reclaim. Points of origin gradually tend to lose their authenticating function. '(Western) Europe', as an ideal geographical and cultural entity, which Czech nationals aspired to rejoin while under a communist regime, no longer exists, if such entity ever existed at all. Even as the Czechs are becoming aware that there is no 'Europe', no elective homogeneous homeland to rejoin, they are also coming to terms with the fact that 'Shakespeare' itself is no safe haven but a field of 'genuine struggles'.

10 *Shooting the Hero*: The cinematic career of *Henry V* from Laurence Olivier to Philip Purser

Ton Hoenselaars

Critical investigations of Shakespeare's *Henry V* have increasingly come to recognize the importance of theatrical and cinematic appropriations, native as well as foreign, but they still tend to ignore off-shoots generated by these appropriations in other genres and in the broader field of popular culture. It nearly goes without saying that such spin-offs are neglected at the critic's own peril; often they may generate valuable new insights into the more familiar Shakespearean material, and give rise to fresh investigation and debate. One such unfortunate oversight is Philip Purser's 1990 novel entitled *Friedrich Harris: Shooting the Hero,* a first-person fictional tale about the making of Laurence Olivier's 1944 film epic. This novel places the film and its crew in the context of wartime propaganda, and, by establishing a direct connection between the German film industry run by Joseph Goebbels and the charismatic acting skills of Laurence Olivier, it ultimately invites a reconsideration of the political significance of the most problematic of Shakespeare's history plays and one of its most popular cinematic reincarnations. Purser's largely unexperimental novel represents a useful case study because it problematizes the phenomenon of hero worship which has deeply affected the reception of Shakespeare's play throughout the twentieth century, and which even iconoclastic approaches like John Sutherland and Cedric Watts' *Henry V, War Criminal?* have been unable to challenge.

Shooting the Hero is a Second World War spy novel like Geoffrey Household's *Rogue Male* (1939), presenting a clash between British and German interests during the Nazi years. This conflict of interests is effectively suggested by the novel's main character, Friedrich Harris, who is half German and half Irish. Clearly, the German part of his name is meant to recall his distinguished royal German forebear whom Thomas Carlyle celebrated as Frederick the Great ('my illustrious namesake', as the narrator in the novel puts it [241]), just as the British part of his name is a reminder of 'Bomber Harris', who coordinated the allied bombing campaign against Germany ('Official propaganda against the air-raids reducing our cities to ruins had lately begun to name the English air marshal Harris as the arch-villain' [236]).

Shooting the Hero recounts Harris's memories of the shooting of *Henry V* ('the Olivier movie above all Olivier movies' [2]), at which he was present as Joseph Goebbels's film-adjutant preparing *Kolberg,* the most expensive German propaganda film of the Second World War, a venture comparable, perhaps, only to Olivier's *Henry V* (Welch 1983: 213–35). The novel's plot begins in 1943, in Goebbels' film viewing room in Berlin. The occasion is the Reichsminister's announcement that they are planning the greatest film ever made, a film that will even eclipse *Gone with the Wind.* He shows the spectators present, including Veit Harlan, the film *Lady Hamilton* (dir. Alexander Korda, 1941) starring

Laurence Olivier. Goebbels wants to find out why Germany has 'no actors of such heroic magnetism' (23), and announces the plan to give Olivier a central part in *Kolberg*, to be directed by Veit Harlan. Goebbels believes that Olivier 'would certainly be the most valuable player in any film designed to popularize new world-political situations that might arise, for example England and America supporting [Germany's] crusade against the Bolsheviks' (28). For this purpose Olivier must be made to come to Germany from neutral Ireland where he is shooting the battle scenes for *Henry V*. Friedrich Harris is entrusted with the task, and sent to Ireland after a period of training in medieval warfare:

> Your foremost objective is to persuade Mr Olivier to come to us voluntarily. Failing that, you will bring him against his will. Failing this, you will endeavour to prevent his film of *Henry V* from being completed. In the last resort you will at least deny his further services to Churchill and the warmongers.
>
> (50)

One of the novel's main strategies is to exploit the detailed accounts of the making of *Henry V* by Olivier and his biographers. In the process, it manipulates precisely those instances where Olivier and his biographers express their apprehensions about the past they are trying to recreate, or where they confess their inability fully to understand and explain strange incidents – 'the usual number of cock-ups', as Olivier calls them (1986: 190). Moreover, the novel is quick to exploit those moments in the memoirs and biographies where Olivier would seem to quote speakers or introduce agents into the narrative who ultimately remain unidentified or anonymous.

One case in point is the instance in Olivier's *Confessions* where he speaks of his strategy vis-à-vis a daunting film crew of seven hundred. In order to impress and ultimately to control these men from the outset, Olivier climbed onto a beer-crate, and made an impressive and brave announcement to the effect that he would never ask them to do anything hazardous that he would not do himself. Cottrell calls it '[s]tirring stuff' (1975: 193), and notices a special case of identification between Olivier and Shakespeare's king. As Anthony Holden has it, this was 'a rousing inaugural address worthy of Henry himself' (1988: 175). Olivier, however, not without self-irony, comments on his own grandiloquence as follows: 'The warmth and strength of the applause that greeted this mighty line should have been a warning to me. I was taken literally' (1982: 101). He then proceeds to tell the related incident where he asked one of the actors to jump from a tree onto a passing horse and rider:

> My gallant rider looked at me pleasantly but steadily, and as usual it came: 'We'd like to see you do it first, Mr Oliver?' – all the peasants pronounced the name thus.
>
> (1982: 101)

In the event, Olivier jumped from the tree, sprained his right ankle, and told the bystanders: 'There, you see? Easy, really' (1982: 102). In an attempt to explain the event, John Cottrell is tempted to commit a generalizing act of national prejudice:

> there were obvious hazards in committing oneself publicly to promises like that, especially before so many men with the mischievous, sometimes perverse, Irish sense of humor.
>
> (1975: 193)

In the Philip Purser novel, however, the incident involving an unnamed and presumably Irish film crew member is deftly presented as Friedrich Harris's Germano-Irish attempt to sabotage the shooting of *Henry V*: 'From the back of the group of us, in my best Irish brogue, I called out: "Would you mind showing us exactly how you mean, Mr Oliver?" '(96). Although the wording is slightly different, the effect is the same, as becomes clear also from the response of the fictional Olivier, in severe pain: ' "There you are", he cried rather desperately. "Nothing to it." '(96).

Another instance in the novel where Purser capitalizes on the anonymity and confusion of the biographical material is Olivier's account of the accident that occurred when, during the shooting of the scene with a French horseman setting light to the English camp, one rider had to charge in the direction of the camera:

> I told the young rider to come as close to the camera as he could; again through the finder I could tell it wasn't very exciting. This time I said, 'Look, boy, aim to hit the camera this time, will you? Your horse will manage to miss it at the last moment.' I watched again through the finder; the horse was looming beautifully large and frighteningly close – and smack! – right into the camera.
>
> (Olivier 1986: 102)

The impact of the camera left a large scar on Olivier's upper lip (often covered by a moustache). In Purser's novel, the description of what Holden has called 'one of the worst incidents' of Olivier's career (1988: 174), is presented as the result of a clash between the German protagonist Friedrich Harris, whose mission it is subtly to persuade Olivier to transfer his talents from the British to the German propaganda war, and Dominic, Harris's Irish contact on the set, who labours under the conviction that it is 'about time somebody did something towards this stupid operation' (135). In Purser's fiction, it is Dominic who rides the horse, and tries to hurt Olivier on purpose.

Shooting the Hero closely follows Olivier's autobiographical and biographical writings. However, the novel also challenges the various accounts by Olivier and his biographers in at least two significant ways, thus bringing into focus some of the political complexities that Olivier ignores or unconsciously represses, matters involving Anglo-Irish and Anglo-German relations.

As the son of an Irish patriot who fought England during the First World War by enlisting in the Army of the Rhine in Solingen, the son also of a father who ended his life in an English prison, Friedrich Harris is consumed by a deep hatred for England. This explains his long residence in Berlin, where, thanks to his uncle's connections, he has worked in the film industry, getting involved in the making of anti-English and pro-Irish films like *The Fox of Glenarvon* (*Der Fuchs von Glenarvon*, dir. Max W. Kimmich, 1940) and *My Life for Ireland* (*Mein Leben für Irland*, dir. Max W. Kimmich, 1941). Harris's dual nationality introduces a sensitive political issue which is activated further on his arrival in Ireland. As Harris tries to persuade Laurence Olivier politely to come to Berlin, his Irish contact named Dominic (a moderate Republican whose father fought in the Spanish Civil War), finds his strategy too slow to be convincing, and independently tries to attack the actor on horseback. Nor is this the only reference to the Irish question. The IRA, too, are on Olivier's tail, and stage a hijack that is surprisingly unsuccessful. It would be wrong to argue that *Shooting the Hero* provides subtle political analysis of any intrinsic value or relevance; however, it does highlight the political irony implicit in Olivier's making of *Henry V* on Irish soil. Shakespeare's play, of course, makes explicit reference to the Irish rebellion across the narrow seas which the Earl of Essex, on behalf of an expansionist Elizabethan government, was meant to crush, and as Andrew Hadfield has therefore put it, the Shakespearean play 'appears to be at least as much concerned with Ireland as with France' (1997: 50). It is against this background that Olivier's utterances must be classified as complacent, certainly when, speaking about shooting Shakespeare's political play in Ireland, he alleges that those working on it 'were inspired by the warmth, humanity, wisdom and Britishness just beneath the surface of Shakespeare's brilliant jingoism' (Olivier 1986: 190).

Admittedly, Olivier carefully represents the scene from *Henry V* where the three British nationals – the Welshman Fluellen, the Scot Jamie and the Irishman Macmorris – engage in a debate about nationhood. Olivier's reading, however, stresses the way in which, via their discord, these three came to represent a united nation behind the warrior king.[1] This is confirmed by Olivier's comments at the time he made the film. Asked how, in wartime, it was possible to make a propaganda film in which the English king invaded and conquered the land of his Second World War ally, France, Olivier said that the film was in the interest of 'Anglo-British relations' (Geduld 1973: 17; Durgnat 1970: 109).

If Olivier's interest was mainly to suggest the way in which Henry V managed to busy giddy minds with foreign quarrels, Philip Purser deftly uses the discussion among the three Britons as a guide to the narrative's conflict. In particular, Purser playfully translates Macmorris's famous words – 'What ish my nation?' – into the dual nationality of the main character of Friedrich Harris. This accounts for Harris's involvement in the Germano-Irish plot against Olivier, but it also explains his sexual involvement with the Irish wife of an English army commander preparing the Normandy invasion, appropriately named Mrs Macmorris. Even if the novel fails to explore the inherent political issues in any serious detail, it does invite the reader to look again at Olivier's wartime rhetoric on matters Anglo-Irish.

In addition to matters Anglo-Irish, the novel also alerts us to the overlap of matters Anglo-German. In 1937, Charles Laughton had commented on Olivier's stage performance of Henry V with the words: 'Do you know why you're so good in the part? Because you are England' (Holden 1988: 123). Purser's novel subverts this Anglocentric statement (which Olivier liked to quote) by suggesting that the same charismatic actor might have also graced the propaganda of Britain's enemy.[2] At first, the situation suggested in the novel seems utterly fictitious, but a closer look at the available information indicates a number of intriguing points of contact that may have inspired Purser.

In film history, and even more so in Shakespearean reception history, there are striking instances of overlap between the English and German traditions. As Anthony Holden, for example, remarks in his biography of Olivier:

> It is an intriguing footnote to the history of the Second World War that while *Lady Hamilton* became one of Churchill's favourite diversions, Hitler would apparently order screening after screening of *Fire over England*.
>
> (1988: 169)[3]

This hint at a German interest in the products of the English film industry – imitated and mirrored at the beginning of the novel where it is Goebbels who uses *Lady Hamilton* to explain his views about the future of the German film industry – does not stand by itself. When we take another look at the mythmaking accounts of Laurence Olivier's career, and concentrate on the embellishment of the narrative where it concerns the actor's skills at playing Henry V, a richer discourse opens up.

In his biography, for example, Anthony Holden discusses in some detail Olivier's habit of making patriotic speeches on behalf of the English government. These 'rabble-rousing duties' would culminate in the Harfleur speech from *Henry V*: 'A stirringly sub-Shakespearean address would invariably be followed, in grandiloquent Churchillian vein, by "Once more unto the breach" ' (1988: 172). Olivier himself also mentions these one-man stints in his book *On Acting*. He describes how, following the reading of some now lesser known verse, he would slip into the Feast of Crispian speech. The actor's craft of illusion – or was it the rhetorician's art? – was consciously aimed at a clearly identified audience:

> I knew how to pace it all perfectly and was able slowly to whip up my wartime audience, urging them forward with me:
>
> > And hold their manhoods cheap, while any speaks,
> > That fought with us upon Saint Crispin's day.
>
> During the applause I would hold my gesture and remain still. Then, when I felt the applause reach its peak and begin to wane, I would launch into 'Once more unto the breach …'. By the time I got to 'God for Harry …' I think they would have followed me anywhere. Looking back, I don't think we could have won the war without 'Once more unto the breach …' somewhere in our soldiers' hearts.
>
> (1986: 65–6)

On the basis of utterances such as these, where the histrionic impersonator is transfigured into the politician leading his troops into an ongoing war, Holden reminds us of the following:

> A clip which survives of one such performance at a Royal Albert Hall rally organized by Basil Dean in 1943 – to mark the twenty-fifth anniversary of the Red Army, then holding off the Germans – shows the uniformed Olivier in frenzied histrionic form, looking for all the world as if he were intent on out-ranting the enemy leader.
>
> (1988: 172)

Olivier and his patriotic circus based, among other things, on Shakespeare's *Henry V*, in an apparent act of imitation and emulation, begins to assume not just the monarchic or 'imperial' traits that all of his biographers recognize, but those of the nation's common enemy (Spoto 1991: 145–7). The words that Shakespeare penned for Henry V ('This day is call'd the feast of Crispian', 4.3.40)[4], together with the voice of England's Prime Minister (producing the 'grandiloquent Churchillian vein') and combined with the striking gestures of Olivier (who was 'in frenzied histrionic form'), evoke, excel and outclass Adolf Hitler himself.

This instance of narrative identification of the actor, his part, and two contemporary political figures who were also one another's enemies, should not be read as a veiled indictment of Olivier's political loyalties. Rather, it ought, perhaps, to be interpreted as a complex image that captures *Henry V*'s profoundly problematic status in the Shakespearean canon, which remains underexposed in Sutherland and Watts' exploration of Henry V as a potential 'war criminal', as they consider the ethical and political implications of 'the most contentious element in the play for British audiences, namely Henry's apparently criminal massacre of his helpless French prisoners in what seems suspiciously like an attack of pique, or at best cold-blooded strategic calculation' (2000: 109).

The problematic status of *Henry V* was first established by William Hazlitt who, two years after the Battle of Waterloo, called Henry not only 'very amiable' but also a 'monster', and it was more fully recognized after the First World War, when memories of the play were evoked on either side of no-man's land – in the English trenches, where Edwardian schoolboys-turned-soldiers would repeat King Henry's invocation of St. George, but also in Germany, from where the Chancellor 'quoted *Henry V* when his troops stood before Calais' (Engler 2000: 107). However, the Second World War activated traditional uses of the play's political and militaristic interests anew. There were, of course, G. Wilson Knight and Laurence Olivier who exploited its rhetoric in their public addresses, but also Winston Churchill who manipulated Henry's victory against all odds into a model for wartime Britain when he alleged that 'Never in the field of human conflict was so much owed by so many to so few' (Knight 1967: 91). Olivier in turn exploited Churchill's propagandist use of the play in the making of his film, thus turning his most popular of Shakespearean adaptations into his own belligerent contribution to the conflict. Paradoxically, Sutherland and Watts do not seem to regard this highly idiosyncratic and localized use of *Henry V* as one of 'the most contentious elements in the play for British audiences' (2000: 109).

More alert in its response to *Henry V* in the context of the Second World War was Peter Zadek's analysis of heroes and of hero worship in his 1964 production of *Henry V,* entitled *Held Henry* ('Henry, the Hero'). Zadek – who had grown up in England after his parents fled the Nazis in 1933, returned to Germany in 1958 to make a name for himself as a controversial avant-garde director (Loehlin 1996: 48) – presented *Henry V* as 'a pacifist collage, an ahistorical multimedia show against heroism and militarism' (Hortmann 1998: 222) complete with portraits of fifty rulers, including Elizabeth I, as well as images of ancient and modern heroes. These images included Elvis Presley, Billy Graham, soccer star Uwe Seeler, Wernher von Braun, Frederick the Great, Atilla the Hun and Churchill. Moreover, the production featured 'a screen at the back showing Hitler's troops marching into Paris, and "Harry" taking the salute' (Hortmann 1998: 222). This production conflated Shakespeare's medieval monarch and the dreaded leader of Nazi Germany by means of overlapping images drawn from both the German motion picture propaganda machine and from traditional Shakespearean (hence canonized) battle rhetoric, thus making it difficult if not impossible to establish which leader served to level criticism at the other. It is true that Zadek, as Loehlin puts it, 'made *Henry V* into a part of Germany's confrontation with its own past and present' (1996: 151), but it seems inappropriate to overlook the provocative comparison between the German and British war efforts which Zadek clearly brings to his audience's attention.[5] As much as *Shooting the Hero* and Olivier's biographical and autobiographical materials suggest, this German instance of 'foreign Shakespeare' invited contemporary, politico-cultural questions of a more serious nature than those that elevate Henry's historical massacre to 'the most contentious element in the play for British audiences'. Instead of challenging the play and its impact on contemporary English culture, Sutherland and Watts's question represents a neatly sanitized, but still largely acritical, desire for hero worship in keeping with a nineteenth-century tradition which elected as its target objects the charismatic medieval English king and the nation's canonized play-wright. Purser's novel helps us realize how Olivier's wartime performances, on and off screen, revitalized this tradition. However, and most interestingly, it is on this very point that Philip Purser's novel betrays its origins, and more or less explicitly subscribes to the tenacious English devotion to its cultural heroes.

In *Shooting the Hero*, Friedrich Harris never kills Laurence Olivier. Given a final oppor-tunity to do so – during the decisive blows exchanged between Olivier-as-Henry and Friedrich Harris-as-Constable of France at the end of the Battle of Agincourt sequence – Harris unexpectedly refrains from killing the actor: 'I could see each fine black corn of hair in the shaven skin of his neck, the tiny crater left by a spot. And my arm would not move' (206). The motivation for his apathy is precisely the hero worship syndrome that Zadek's production of *Henry V* exposed as affecting all levels of society, from the world of politics to the soccer field:

> It was the certainty that we must all have heroes, for without heroes there is no hope. So who would choose to slay the King; who would dare to shoot the hero, on whosoever side he be?
>
> (244)

Despite its useful emphasis on ideological fault lines, telling omissions and overt propa-gandistic gestures in Olivier's film, Purser's novel shows that the ubiquitous need for heroes more or less subliminally links state and military hierarchies with the cinematic star system.

However, the novel is not a generic tribute to one of the greatest English actors of the twentieth century; it is a tribute to this same actor playing the part of Henry V. While it praises Olivier's wartime role, it is also extremely critical of the actor's postwar achievements. The opening of the novel anticipates the debunking representation of the actor in the classroom scene of *Last Action Hero* (dir. John McTiernan, 1992):

> When I watched him in one or other of those stupid roles of his old age; when for example he played the Jewish poppa in a vile remake of *The Jazz Singer*, or on television a Roman elder in some laughable epic continuing over two or three evenings; when he was inveigled on to one of those ceremonies at which today's film makers 'salute' each other, and he would address them in the quavering voice he affected on such occasions; when I saw these things and remembered how once he could strike fire, summon music and bring down thunder with one cry, then I would groan aloud that I had not killed Laurence Olivier when I had the chance.
>
> (1)

Friedrich Harris: Shooting the Hero ultimately represents an attempt to fictionally preserve the image of Laurence Olivier at his 'finest hour', as Winston Churchill would have said. However, it also represents an attempt to criticize the post-war years, including peacetime Hollywood stardom. Perhaps nothing better illustrates Harris's attempt to do so than his attitude to Kenneth Branagh's remake of *Henry V* of 1989. Harris refuses to name the Belfast-born actor–director when he states that 'some young English [sic] smart-arse was remaking the English title. Jesus, is nothing sacred? I shall take care not to see it' (2). As Donald Hedrick has noticed, Branagh's film reveals 'tactical indecision', which is possibly due to Branagh's failure to confront the very issues and concerns which Purser's novel effectively foregrounds.

It may well be that the need for heroes accounts for the tenacious position of Shakespeare in the literary canon, in general, and of his controversial war play, in particular. As Thomas Healy remarks in his discussion of the fortunes of *Henry V*:

> While Shakespeare allows us to re-examine our differing pasts in important ways, a sense can also develop of the inescapability of these pasts and the ideological structures the plays articulate, no matter how adapted for new productions. Is Shakespeare the ally we seem to want to make him? Perhaps the time has come, not to dispense with Shakespeare, but to disestablish him, whether as the voice of order or of dissidence?
>
> (1994: 193)

Rather than disestablishing Shakespeare, recent appropriations from Olivier's to Purser's show that important cultural and political positions are still being advanced through plays like *Henry V*. It is indeed a measure of the continued vitality and centrality of Shakespeare that not only offshoots (like the cinematic adaptation of *Henry V* by Laurence Olivier), but also offshoots of these offshoots (like Philip Purser's *Shooting the Hero*) can be effectively used to gauge the extent to which a stable sense of national identity is threatened at times of intense crisis or change.

In recent years, Shakespearean drama has been increasingly used to explore the fascist element in European politics. In 1992, Terence Hawkes discreetly but effectively read *Coriolanus* within the context of the ominous developments in the 1920s. Julie Taymor's *Titus* (1999) explores the history of fascism from the Roman period, via Mussolini, to the present day. And, from a slightly different perspective, Loncraine's interpretation of *Richard III* suggested what might have become of Britain if Oswald Mosley had been as successful as Shakespeare's hunch-backed king. In a similar way, *Shooting the Hero*, along with the biographical and autobiographical materials upon which it draws, may alert one to a discourse that also links *Henry V* to a range of Second World War notions of charismatic authority, hero worship and movie stardom, and not always unproblematically so. Perhaps it is due to the play's special place in the definition of British nationhood, supported by a brand of bardolatry akin to the hero worship at work in various guises in the afterlife of *Henry V*, that such insights have not been able as yet to emerge in current critical discourse.

11 Lamentable tragedy or black comedy?: Friedrich Dürrenmatt's adaptation of *Titus Andronicus*

Lukas Erne

In 1970, the Swiss dramatist Friedrich Dürrenmatt (1921–90) undertook a dramatic adaptation of Shakespeare's *Titus Andronicus* which has hitherto suffered from critical neglect and still awaits its first translation into English.[1] The same applies to his earlier adaptation of Shakespeare's *King John*.[2] Despite the world-wide fame Dürrenmatt acquired in the course of his career, Dürrenmatt's dramatic practice, both in general and, more specifically, in his response to Shakespeare, is emphatically 'local' as defined in the introduction to the present volume (pp. 3–11). Yet just what local position his adaptation of *Titus Andronicus* occupies is perhaps less easy to determine.

Dürrenmatt was born and always lived in Switzerland, a country with four national languages and linguistic communities – German, French, Italian and Romansh – making problematic the notion of a 'national audience'. Even if we focus on the roughly two-thirds of Switzerland's inhabitants who are German speaking, linguistic and national identity remains an issue. Dürrenmatt memorably called German his 'father tongue' – the language Swiss Germans use, hear or read in the public realm, at school, on television or in the newspapers – to distinguish it from his 'mother tongue', Swiss German, the language of the private sphere in which Swiss Germans feel most intimately at home. Dürrenmatt once pointed out that he would have liked to write his plays in the Swiss dialect.[3] Yet this, as he well knew, would have prevented the spread of his fame beyond the boundaries of Switzerland where only just some four million speakers of German reside, as opposed to roughly eighty million in Germany. As Dürrenmatt succinctly put it, 'Ich lebe in der Schweiz, aber nicht von der Schweiz' (Dürrenmatt 1996: 2.273), I live in Switzerland, but not off Switzerland. Dürrenmatt elsewhere suggests that his *Titus Andronicus* does not exclusively address a Swiss audience. His play, he wrote, 'represents an attempt to render Shakespeare's chaotic early work fit for the German stage without having the Shakespearean atrocities and grotesqueries passed over in silence'.[4] 'German' serves here to delimit the German-speaking linguistic community (Germany, Austria and a large part of Switzerland) rather than a nation. Nevertheless, it deserves pointing out that Dürrenmatt's *Titus* premiered not in his native Switzerland but in Germany.[5]

Before investigating what specifically it is about Dürrenmatt's adaptation that allows us to characterize it as a 'local' response to Shakespeare, it will be necessary to come to an understanding of the nature of Dürrenmatt's adaptation. Ruby Cohn (1976: 34) has written that Dürrenmatt is 'fairly faithful to Shakespeare's events', and Jonathan Bate (1995: 60) goes even further, maintaining that Dürrenmatt's *Titus* 'is very close to the original'.[6] These statements require scrutiny and refinement.

According to most modern editions, Shakespeare divides his play into fourteen scenes which Dürrenmatt reduces to nine.[7] Six of Shakespeare's scenes, 1.1, 4.2 to 4.4, 5.1 and 5.2, have corresponding scenes in Dürrenmatt (Scenes 1 and 5 to 9). Two disappear entirely, 3.2 (the so-called 'Fly-scene' which was first printed in the Folio of 1623) and 5.1, dramatizing Aaron's defiance after his arrest. Dürrenmatt condenses the six remaining scenes into two: 2.1 to 2.4 becomes a continuous sequence in Dürrenmatt (Scene 2) in the course of which Chiron and Demetrius murder Bassianus and rape and mutilate Lavinia. And 3.1 and 4.1 are reduced to one scene (Scene 3) in which Titus, hoping in vain to save his sons Quintus and Martius, is tricked into cutting off his own hand, and ends with Lavinia revealing the identity of her ravishers. This leaves one of Dürrenmatt's nine scenes unaccounted for, Scene 4, which has no equivalent in Shakespeare. In it, Lucius, who has left Rome to raise an army from among the Goths, is shown in dialogue with Alarich, their leader. To sum up, Dürrenmatt's play begins with three long scenes, roughly corresponding to the action up to 4.1, and ends with six shorter scenes, covering the rest of Shakespeare's play.

Dürrenmatt thus transforms the overall shape of Shakespeare's play without radically departing from it. But how specifically does Dürrenmatt, who read Shakespeare's play in the early nineteenth-century translation of Wolf Graf von Baudissin, adapt the text of *Titus Andronicus*? The relationship of Dürrenmatt's play to the original radically changes in the course of the play. A brief look at the first scene will serve as a representative example. Some passages are very close to the original, indeed identical. The first seventy-two lines, for instance, correspond word for word to Baudissin's text. After this opening sequence, Dürrenmatt's departures from the original are at first minor: Tamora's initial speech loses two lines and shows local substitutions and rearrangements of words. Titus's opening speech is abridged and partly rewritten. Of Lucius's three-line speech at 1.1.130–2, only the first three words remain. A little later, Dürrenmatt for the first time allocates a speech to a different character, substituting a six-line speech by Aaron for a speech of the same length by Lucius. Less than half-way through the scene, Dürrenmatt entirely reconceives a short dramatic movement (1.1.191–256; Dürrenmatt 1980a: 124–5).[8] A little later still, Dürrenmatt first expands a short Shakespearean passage into a much longer one of his own (1.1.291–6; Dürrenmatt 1980a: 127–9). By the time Dürrenmatt reaches the end of the scene, next to nothing is left of the original language or action. Whereas the original scene ends on a precariously – and provisionally – restored order as Saturninus and Tamora seem to forgive Titus and plan to hunt together the next day, Dürrenmatt shows Titus in total isolation, all characters leaving him one by one until he is left alone to bury the son he has previously killed. Some later scenes revert to a much closer correspondence between adaptation and original. Much of Scene 8, for instance, follows Shakespeare almost speech by speech, even though most speeches are abridged and many are rewritten. Nevertheless, Dürrenmatt's departures from the original are such that his adaptation can hardly be described as 'very close to the original'.

Every adaptation is an interpretation. How then does Dürrenmatt *reinterpret* Shakespeare's play? The question of genre is central to Dürrenmatt's adaptation. In an oft-quoted essay, Dürrenmatt argued that comedy is the only genre that suits our modern world: 'Tragedy presupposes guilt, measure, overview, responsibility. In the muddle of our century, in this clean sweep of the white race, no one is responsible any more. No one can help it, and no one wanted it. Everyone can be done without. ... Only comedy does us justice'.[9] Accordingly, Dürrenmatt turns Shakespeare's tragedy into a grotesque black comedy. Whereas the original title page of *Titus Andronicus* referred to the play as a 'Lamentable Roman Tragedy', the subtitle of Dürrenmatt's adaptation reads 'Eine Komödie nach Shakespeare', a comedy after Shakespeare.

The fate of Aaron, the villain, illustrates this generic shift: in Shakespeare, his two appearances in the last act are of central importance for the restoration of order as required by tragedy. Taken prisoner by a Goth who leads him to Lucius, the villain is made to reveal all his misdeeds. In the final scene, punishment is meted out to the unrepentant Aaron. Through the dramatization of Aaron, Shakespeare produces the meaning that is proper to tragedy, with both the intrigue and the moral drama thus finding their resolution at the play's close. In Dürrenmatt, by contrast, Aaron has his final appearance as early as Scene 5 in which he is presented with the Queen's bastard son whom he has fathered.[10] As in Shakespeare, Aaron kills the nurse who brought the babe. Yet unlike Shakespeare, Dürrenmatt, a few lines later, has Aaron declare his intention of leaving Rome and of returning to Africa where he and his son will be 'Nicht Sklaven Roms, doch freie Kannibalen' (169), not 'Rome's slaves but free cannibals'. Dürrenmatt's Aaron thus not only fails to disclose his villainies and escapes unpunished, but even the killing of the nurse – duly motivated in Shakespeare by his desire to rid himself of potential witnesses against him – appears grotesque and gratuitous in light of his and his son's imminent departure to Africa.

Dürrenmatt sometimes achieves a comic effect through language, as when Titus, at the beginning of the final scene, offers to serve Saturninus 'another little kidney, liver, brain or rib'.[11] Much of the time, however, the laughter Dürrenmatt strives to provoke arises from his dramatization of scenes of violence. The adaptation, in other words, treads a fine line between laughter and horror. This is particularly true at the end of the play. It may be tempting to argue that the speed at which the various characters are killed creates a comic effect: Titus kills Lavinia and Tamora before being stabbed by Saturninus who, in turn, is killed by Lucius, all in little over twenty lines of dialogue. But, in fact, the killings in Shakespeare's play are no less but even more condensed. What *is* different in Dürrenmatt, however, is that he adds one more killing: Lucius has returned to Rome with an army of Goths led by Alarich who, as we have seen, Dürrenmatt introduced in Scene 4. Once all the other main characters have been killed, Alarich stabs Lucius and commands his soldiers to kill all Romans. In Alarich's chorus-like concluding speech, he comments that 'im stupiden Lauf der Zeit' (197), 'in the stupid course of time', revenge will lead to further revenge, that after he and his fellow Goths will have destroyed the Romans, others, the Huns and the Turks, will come and destroy the Goths, leading to more and more pointless violence in a pointless world. The killings in the last scene are thus grotesque not because they happen in quick, mechanic succession, but because they turn out, contrary to those in Shakespeare's play, to serve no purpose, to lead to more killings which lead to more killings. In the original *Titus*, by contrast, Marcus announces the restoration of order immediately after Tamora, Saturninus, and Titus have been killed: 'O let me teach you how to knit again/This scattered corn into one mutual sheaf,/These broken limbs again into one body' (5.3.69–71). Before the end of the scene, since 'The common voice do cry it shall be so', Lucius is crowned 'Rome's royal emperor' (5.3.139–40). It may thus be argued that popular consensus and the visible centre of Rome's unity are carefully restored before the play concludes.

Yet Dürrenmatt's comedic adaptation is more than an idiosyncratic response by the Swiss playwright. Dürrenmatt's *Titus Andronicus* is in fact related to a distinctive stance in the reception history of Shakespeare's play. Peter Brook's immensely successful 1955 production, starring Laurence Olivier, was both indicative and constitutive of a revival of interest in Shakespeare's earliest tragedy, but a traditional view of the play as extremely crude if not downright grotesque lingered on. At the same time as Antonin Artaud's Theatre of Cruelty, Beckett and Ionescu's Theatre of the Absurd and Jan Kott's *Shakespeare Our Contemporary* provided a context within which *Titus* fitted better than ever since the sixteenth century, this context also favoured a certain kind of reading of Shakespeare's play, exemplified by Dürrenmatt's adaptation and prominent in contemporary criticism of Shakespeare's play. For instance, when J. Dover Wilson edited the play for the New Cambridge Shakespeare series in 1948, he argued that the excessive violence had been dramatized with a burlesque intention.[12] Even though disagreeing to some extent, J. C. Maxwell (1953: xli), editing the play for the Arden Shakespeare, second series, in the following decade, similarly held that 'it would be rash to say that a uniform attitude of deadly seriousness is presupposed'.

That this attitude was still alive when Dürrenmatt came to write his adaptation is best illustrated by an article Daniel Scuro wrote in 1970 – the year of Dürrenmatt's *Titus*. A retrospective appreciation of the achievement of Peter Brook's 1955 production, Scuro's article has recently been reprinted in the Garland collection of critical essays on *Titus Andronicus*. According to Scuro, Brook's production turned dross into gold by 'cutting the text and ordering the stage so that bathos was never allowed to enter' (Scuro 1995: 402). Scuro's view of Shakespeare's play transpires even more clearly when he writes that the 'grotesqueries of the original text (Act III, Scene ii; Act IV, Scene i) were tastefully edited' (403). The possibility that Brook's *Titus* might have been a success because of, rather than despite, the original text nowhere enters Scuro's discussion. His argument is affected throughout by the presupposition that Shakespeare's play in and of itself is grotesque. Peter Brook (1987: 72), for one, begged to disagree, commenting that 'When the notices of *Titus Andronicus* came out, giving us all full marks for saving [Shakespeare's] dreadful play, I could not help feeling a twinge of guilt. For to tell the truth, it had not occurred to any of us in rehearsal that the play was so bad'. A whole strand of criticism on *Titus Andronicus* from Dover Wilson to Scuro thus suggests that when Dürrenmatt wrote his adaptation in 1970, many students of Shakespeare's play must have felt that the Swiss dramatist was only following Shakespeare in choosing to write a black comedy rather than a tragedy. As we have seen above, Dürrenmatt subtitled his *Titus* 'eine Komödie nach Shakespeare', which can be understood as meaning either that the play (a comedy) is adapted from Shakespeare or, more specifically, that the object of the adaptation is a comedy by Shakespeare. In view of certain critical tendencies in the course of the twentieth century, the latter reading should not be discounted.

The similarities between readings offered by various critics and the reading implicit in Dürrenmatt's adaptation calls for a consideration of the relationship between adaptation and original on the one hand and between the subject and object of literary criticism on the other. An adaptation that omits, changes, adds, transforms, deflates and highlights parts of the original may be a way of assessing the specific inflection of a local critical appropriation. Dürrenmatt, trying to show how grotesque the world of *Titus Andronicus* is, alters the original in significant ways. What reading adaptation and Shakespearean original side by side can therefore provide is insights into the exact nature of a critical reception that adopts a view of Shakespeare's play that is similar to that inherent in the adaptation.

This analytic method can best be illustrated by a brief examination of the character of Lavinia. What this examination shows is that if Dürrenmatt's reinterpretation of *Titus* crystallizes in the generic shift from 'lamentable tragedy' to dark, or grotesque, comedy, then his main device for achieving this shift is the foreclosure of the play's potential emotional impact by discouraging any empathetic engagement with the main characters. Significantly, Lavinia, who is the emotional centre of Shakespeare's play in most recent productions, is reduced to a relatively minor character, appearing only in the first three and the last two scenes. In 3.1 of Shakespeare's play, an extensive sequence, from the entrance of Marcus with the mutilated Lavinia to the entrance of Aaron almost a hundred lines later, dramatizes the empathetic response of Titus, Lucius and Marcus to Lavinia. The grief is physically enacted in a variety of ways, with Lucius 'falling to his knees' and Marcus and Titus in tears, all dramatically expressing what Titus calls 'a sympathy of woe' (3.1.149) in what is potentially Shakespeare's most moving and intimate family scene before *Hamlet*. Dürrenmatt omits nearly the entirety of this sequence and, in what remains, radically alters Titus's emotional response to his daughter. To Lucius's interjection 'Ihr Anblick tötet mich!', 'The sight of her kills me!', he responds 'Ihr Anblick tröstet mich' (152), 'The sight of her comforts me', and goes on to explain to Lucius that his mutilated daughter is a reassuringly appropriate expression of the world's overall corruption. Dürrenmatt seems to introduce Lavinia only as a pretext to move on immediately to the symbolic significance of her role. Dürrenmatt uses Lavinia to make a point, to explain; Shakespeare makes her an icon of suffering and spends considerable time and ingenuity in dramatizing the on-stage audience's response to her, thereby facilitating and directing the empathetic response of the off-stage audience.

A further device used to bring about this response is direct address. In three speeches and a total of some forty lines, Shakespeare's Titus interacts with and speaks to his daughter. Dürrenmatt's Titus, by contrast, never addresses but only speaks about her. The contrast is all the more striking as Dürrenmatt here introduces another character – absent from Shakespeare – to whom Titus talks instead: Publius, who fought as one of Titus's soldiers against the Goths and, when he lost a leg in battle, was excluded from the army 'ohne Pension' (153), with no pension. Publius, down-to-earth and disruptiveof Saturninus's intentions, serves as a foil to Titus. As a powerless victim of the war, he has none of the illusions to which Titus is still subject. Instead of dramatizing Titus's emotional response to his daughter, which humanizes both Lavinia and her father, Dürrenmatt engages Titus in a conversation in which intellectual responses to the casualties of war are contrasted.[13]

These and many other changes seem ultimately to reinforce one main point which the adaptation is meant to illustrate: the futility of patriotism. In Shakespeare's play, Titus, despite his initial foolishness and brutality, is now usually seen as a tragic character, more sinned against than sinning, deserving of our empathy. Yet in the adaptation, Titus grotesquely clings to his flawed beliefs about Rome, the 'fatherland', and about the 'justice' meted out by those in power. Dürrenmatt misses no opportunity to highlight these issues. For instance, Titus's first speech ends on 'Schlaf friedlich, Sohn! Du starbst fürs Vaterland' (120), Baudissin's translation of 'And sleep in peace, slain in your country's wars' (1.1.94). The word 'Vaterland', 'fatherland', has of course rather different connotations from the more general 'country' in the original. Dürrenmatt preserves Baudissin's word, but gives it further prominence by placing it at the very end of Titus's opening speech. Throughout the adaptation, Dürrenmatt's changes in fact serve to stress the absurdity of Titus's lofty ideal of dying for one's country.

The futility of patriotism which Dürrenmatt is at pains to stress leads us back to the question of how his adaptation constitutes a *local* response to Shakespeare, a response that is embedded in the cultural position from which Shakespeare was approached and adapted. And it leads us to understand to what extent Dürrenmatt's position is specifically Swiss rather than German or, more generally, Germanic. Whatever the lingering sympathies for the aspirations of the Third Reich may have been, patriotism, in the decades immediately following World War II, was not a common topic of public debate in Germany. In Switzerland, the situation was altogether different. Having emerged more or less unscathed from the ravages of the war in which the surrounding countries had been involved, Switzerland, in the eyes of many, had profited more from the war than it had suffered. In such a situation, the judgement posterity passed on the role Switzerland had played during the war was bound to be politically explosive. Judgements were multiple but can, for the sake of the present purpose, be grouped around two opposing poles. The political establishment, on the one hand, engaged in various degrees of retrospective mystification and glorification, imputing the country's escape to the quality of its politics and Germany's failure to invade Switzerland at least partly to the dissuasive effect of the Swiss army. The anti-establishment, by contrast, accused the Swiss government of opportunism and full-scale collaboration with Nazi Germany.[14]

Now for Dürrenmatt, defenders and critics of Swiss politics during World War II represented the two sides of the same coin as both depended on the ideological constructions of patriotism and fatherland to which he objected. One side did so by claiming that Switzerland had lived up to the standards of these ideological constructions, the other side by holding that it had failed to do so. In other words, the standards the two sides employed were identical. In his non-fictional writings as well as in interviews, Dürrenmatt touches on this subject on several occasions,[15] but it emerges most clearly in an interview he gave four years before completing *Titus Andronicus*:

> Retrospectively, Switzerland no longer dared to adhere to its former self; it thought of the plight in which it had found itself during the war as shameful and reconceived of itself no longer as human but as either heroic or diabolic. The truth is that we had no choice. We certainly made many mistakes during the war, but essentially our politics were human. Politicians cannot be expected to be heroic. We have no right to cast stones at our former politicians. They achieved their political aim, keeping Switzerland out of war. They often achieved it with morally insufficient and even alarming means. ... In unworthy times, an entirely worthy attitude is impossible. To ask retrospectively for heroism from our politicians is inappropriate.[16]

Dürrenmatt holds that the ideology of patriotism and fatherland is dangerous, indeed potentially destructive, in that it is in its name that innocent people get killed. This applies both to recent history – World War II – and to fictionalized history as in his *Titus Andronicus*. What motivates Dürrenmatt's writing is therefore the unmasking of these insidious ideological concepts. From this perspective, the raped and mutilated Lavinia is no more than another illustration of the point that Titus's patriotism is flawed.

And what Dürrenmatt's Titus is deprived of in the course of the play are not dearly beloved relatives, but ideological concepts, belief in justice and the fatherland which, Dürrenmatt holds, serve to establish and perpetuate power. As he put it in his 'Notes on *Titus Andronicus*', 'patriotism is only believed in by those who profit from it, the powerful, and justice serves to legitimate their power'.[17]

What emerges from the above is the extent to which Dürrenmatt's dramatic adaptation constitutes in fact a 'readerly' response to *Titus Andronicus*. Arguably, few of Shakespeare's plays and none of his tragedies need performance as badly as *Titus Andronicus* to achieve their true impact. Pageantry pervades the play from the beginning as Titus and his army enter, an aspect of Shakespeare's play that is all but lost on the page. Moreover, even though a reader can be intellectually aware of Lavinia's presence on stage after her rape and dismemberment, this awareness is no substitute for the effect her glaring, albeit silent, presence on stage has on a spectator. One of the most eloquent 'speaking pictures' in all of Shakespeare, the mutilated Lavinia, a 'map of woe' (3.2.12), can move spectators, move them to emotions and tears as perhaps no earlier play had done, with the exception of Thomas Kyd's *Spanish Tragedy*. The predominantly intellectual activity of readers does not expose them to the same emotions. Significantly, Dürrenmatt heavily abridges the role of Lavinia. A 'reading' of *Titus Andronicus* can thus easily result in the view that the play is absurd or grotesque. As Kott (1965: 281) put it, 'In reading, the cruelties of *Titus* seem childish. I have recently re-read it, and found it ridiculous'. Even though responding to *Titus* by means of a dramatic adaptation, Dürrenmatt's view of Shakespeare's play is very much that of a reader, a fact that may at least partly account for the lack of success Dürrenmatt's adaptation has hitherto had on stage.

Turning Shakespeare's 'lamentable tragedy' into a grotesque comedy, Dürrenmatt arguably tries to legitimate the views his play advances – notably that of the futility of patriotism – by means of the label 'Shakespeare' of which neither spectators nor readers could possibly have remained unaware. While Dürrenmatt's adaptation can be shown to conform in significant ways to the critical reception history of *Titus Andronicus*, he participates in this history not by writing criticism but by means of an adaptation which can serve to diagnose the nature of the reception of which it is a part. Ironically, reading *Titus* with Dürrenmatt and his understanding of the absurd and the grotesque in mind can help us perceive both Dürrenmatt's adaptation and certain critical interpretations as fascinating misreadings of the Shakespearean original that are profoundly and inevitably local.

12 Subjection and redemption in Pasolini's *Othello*

Sonia Massai

Pier Paolo Pasolini adapted and directed a short cinematic version of Shakespeare's *Othello* in 1967. *Che Cosa Sono Le Nuvole?* (*What Are Clouds Like?* henceforth *Nuvole*) was initially conceived as one of the episodes of a feature film called *Capriccio all' Italiana* (1968) but has since been shown as a short film in its own right and is often included in retrospectives on Pasolini's career as a film-maker.[1] Pasolini's work is better known abroad than in Italy, where his sexuality, his uncompromising political views and the controversial circumstances of his death in 1975 still overshadow his artistic stature. However, *Nuvole* is still largely unknown even among Shakespearean scholars, partly because a long and unresolved copyright dispute has prevented it from being re-released, and partly because Pasolini himself may have regarded it as a fragment of a larger project, a sequence of short films which he never completed. And yet, even as a fragment, *Nuvole* represents a groundbreaking appropriation of *Othello* and deserves more visibility than it has been accorded so far. Like the other local Shakespeares discussed in this volume *Nuvole* represents a significant 'new position' within the field, which, as Bourdieu puts it, 'by asserting itself … determines a displacement of [its] structure' (1993: 58).

Since Pasolini shot *Nuvole* in 1967, the critical reception of *Othello* has been dominated by issues of gender, sexuality and race.[2] Pasolini's appropriation is worth critical attention because it anticipated in interesting ways the work of later critics, directors and adapters, by exposing the patriarchal and racist views associated with the play and its reception. Even more crucially, though, roughly thirteen years before Stephen Greenblatt focused on Iago's ability to turn the other characters into recognizable (or stereotypical) subject-positions (1980: 222–54), Pasolini established a connection between Iago's fashioning powers and the impact of discursive formations, including the works of canonical authors like Shakespeare's *Othello*, on their recipients. While Greenblatt glamorized Iago by identifying him as 'the principle of narrativity itself' (1980: 236) and by comparing his improvisational skills to Shakespeare's own 'limitless talent for entering into the consciousness of another, perceiving its deepest structures as a manipulable fiction, [and] reinscribing it into his own narrative form' (1980: 252), Pasolini used meta-theatrical and meta-cinematic devices to show his audience how to resist the influence of familiar patriarchal and racist narratives embedded both in Iago's improvisational strategies *and* in the play as a whole.

Pasolini's exploration of the ideological power associated with the legacy of canonical authors is not confined to *Nuvole*. Adaptation was his favourite mode of artistic expression. Most of his better-known films rework seminal texts at the heart of Western culture, including *The Gospel according to Saint Matthew* (1964), *Oedipus Rex* (1967), *Medea*

(1970), *The Decameron* (1971), *The Canterbury Tales* (1972) and *Thousand and One Nights* (1974). Adaptation embodied Pasolini's ideal of a reflective and self-conscious art, which would promote a constructive resistance to the values of a bourgeois, post-capitalist, consumerist society. As the black crow in *Uccellacci Uccellini* (*Hawkes and Sparrows*) explains to its human disciples, who then dutifully proceed to eat it, 'masters are meant to be eaten in a spicy sauce'.[3] David Ward effectively captures the spirit of Pasolini's creative impulse when he claims that his 'aim [was] to elaborate forms which [would] stimulate enquiry but at the same time avoid the sedimentation of thought to which rigidly held ideological positions are prone' (1999: 331). Also helpful is Ward's definition of Pasolini's 'cinema di poesia' (poetic cinema) as the 'process by which an unreflective consciousness develops into a reflective one' (1994: 128). According to Pasolini, the artist should avoid mimetic realism in favour of forms which can effectively expose the constructed quality of a cultural artefact. As Keala Jewell observes, 'Pasolini rejected mimetic models in favor of a complex literary technique that textualizes reality through a *contaminatio*, a plurality of superimposed styles' (1992: 24). Adaptation, resting by definition on multiple perspectives, helped Pasolini achieve critical distance from the literary tradition. The title of an earlier film, *La Terra Vista dalla Luna* (*The Earth Seen from the Moon*), epitomizes his efforts to defamiliarize canonical texts.

Shakespeare's *Othello* was not a fortuitous choice for Pasolini. In a poem called 'Religione del mio Tempo' ('The Religion of my Time' 1957), Pasolini recalls that Shakespeare, along with Tommaseo and Carducci, had been one of his main sources of inspiration. On 6 November 1960 he rejected Luciano Lucignani and Vittorio Gassman's proposal to adapt *Romeo and Juliet*, but shortly afterwards he wrote a poem called 'Poema per un Verso di Shakespeare' ('Poem on a line by Shakespeare').[4] The line alluded to in the title – 'ciò che hai saputo, hai saputo, il resto non lo saprai' – is a free rendition of Iago's final words, 'Demand me nothing, what you know, you know./From this time forth I never will speak word'. (5.2.300–1).[5] In this poem, Shakespeare's line becomes a black bird that pretends to be white[6] and comes back to haunt the poet from faraway lands.[7] The poet fights forcibly against the bird, but he is also obsessively attracted to it. The conclusion of the poem commits the verse and the mystery of evil associated with it to the past, to history, to experience, thus allowing the poet to preserve his right to future innocence.[8] Apart from spelling out Pasolini's attitude to the literary tradition, in general, and to Shakespeare's *Othello*, in particular, this poem can be read as a prelude to *Nuvole*, where Pasolini finally exorcizes both Iago's cryptic line and the play's influence on his artistic development. The result of the poet's struggle with the black bird is Pasolini's imaginative revision of Shakespeare's *Othello*.

In *Nuvole*, Pasolini turns *Othello* into a puppet show, thus lowering the register of the Shakespearean original. The text is heavily cut, Shakespearean verse is translated into Roman and Neapolitan dialects, and the characters are played by full-sized human puppets before a working-class audience. The theatrically illiterate audience get increasingly frustrated as they watch Iago's evil plan unfold. They shout alarmed warnings during Pasolini's shortened version of Shakespeare's eavesdropping scene in 4.1: 'Othello, watch out!'; 'It was Iago who gave Cassio the handkerchief!'; 'Cassio wasn't talking about Desdemona. He was talking about Bianca! You're as bad as he [Iago] is! If you lay a finger on Desdemona, we'll teach you' (958)[9] (Siti and Zabagli 2001: 958). During the murder scene, the audience storm the stage to rescue Desdemona from Othello's grip as he tries to smother her. While the women in the audience revive

Desdemona, the men kill Othello and Iago and hail Cassio in triumph. Pasolini's wish to popularize Shakespeare is emphasized by his cast. Totò, a famous Neapolitan comic actor, plays Iago alongside another popular comic duo, Franco Franchi (Cassio) and Ciccio Ingrassia (Roderigo). Domenico Modugno, singer and song-writer, is cast as 'l'Immondezzaro', the rubbish collector, who takes away the dead – Othello and Iago – and dumps them in a nearby open-air tip as the film draws to the end.

Despite its unassuming register, *Nuvole* offers interesting insights into Shakespeare's representation of femininity in *Othello*. Pasolini's Desdemona is childish and her child-ishness acquires erotic connotations when she teasingly offers her cherry earrings to Othello just before their wedding night. This trait in Desdemona's character re-emerges in a later sequence, when Cassio asks her to try and persuade Othello to reinstate him. As Cassio enters the stage, Desdemona is rocking a doll in her arms and singing a lullaby. The lullaby betrays the morbid nature of her innermost fantasies: 'Poor child,/She died of love/Poor child,/She died of love./Passers-by will drop/a beautiful flower [on her grave]'[10] (Siti and Zabagli 2001: 951). When Othello smacks her, she screams like a child, but her words suggest that she derives masochistic pleasure from Othello's sudden display of brutality: 'Yes, my lord ... (*being smacked has increased her love and respect for him*) ... what a slap, though! Nobody had slapped me before! Would you want to slap me again ... (*she has an ambiguous expression of submission on her face*)'.[11] (Siti and Zabagli 2001: 961). These lines, along with Desdemona's lullaby, support the puppeteer's view that Desdemona craves to be killed by Othello:

PUPPETEER: Maybe ... you want to kill her.
OTHELLO: What? Do I enjoy murder? Why?
PUPPETEER: Maybe ... because Desdemona likes to be murdered.
OTHELLO: Oh, is that it? (*his face betrays terror and wonder*).[12]

(Siti and Zabagli 2001: 959)

Since the puppets are forced to re-enact the Shakespearean script by the puppeteer who pulls their strings, Pasolini suggests that Desdemona's unconscious drives are at least already implicit in Shakespeare. Pasolini's intimation that Desdemona's sexuality manifests itself in Shakespeare primarily as masochistic subjection anticipates Anne-Marie MacDonald's reworking of *Othello* in *Goodnight Desdemona, Good Morning Juliet* (1980).

Othello's racial otherness is also interestingly handled. Pasolini exposes the brutal logic of racism by turning Cassio into a victim of racist intolerance and discrimination. In a new, sexually suggestive sequence, Cassio and Bianca are shown holding a stuffed bird and a nest. Bianca looks invitingly at Cassio and tries to get him to put his bird into her nest. Cassio teases her several times by pretending to respond to her advances only to disappoint her by suddenly retracting his bird. Cassio and Bianca's pantomimic wooing ritual is brought to an abrupt end by a group of Cypriots led by Roderigo in disguise. Roderigo eggs the Cypriots on by shouting: '*Marrano*, how dare you harass our women?'[13] (Siti and Zabagli 2001: 949). Othello, as in Shakespeare, is attracted by the noise of the ensuing brawl, and when he demands an explanation, the Cypriots complain: 'He injures the honour of our women, Lord Governor! What a scandal! What a scandal!'[14] (Siti and Zabagli 2001: 950). Ironically blind to the implications of the Cypriots' complaints against an outsider, Othello demotes Cassio. Once again, by shifting the motif of racial hatred from Iago, the 'insider', to the Cypriots, the 'outsiders', Pasolini anticipates the strategies of revision employed by later adapters. In *Harlem Duet*, for example, Djanet Sears shows how Othello's former black partner, Billie, is caught up in a web of detrimental feelings of racial hatred against the white, which eventually drive her mad.

Pasolini did not only rewrite *Othello*. He framed it, both literally, by turning it into a play-within-a-film, and metaphorically, by resorting to a rich web of visual and verbal citations. Pasolini's decision to turn *Othello* into a play-within-a-film may have been inspired by French films, like Marcel Carné and Jacques Prévert's *Les Enfants du Paradis* (1945) and Jean-Paul Sartre's *Kean* (1956), where the main characters obsessively replicate in 'real' life the tragic plot they re-enact or watch in stage performances of Shakespeare's tragedy.[15] Pasolini's use of semi-human puppets stems instead from a popular theatrical tradition, *L'Opera dei Pupi* (Sicilian Marionettes). The device of the play-within-the-film reduces the fictive world of Shakespeare's characters to 'a dream within a dream'[16] (Siti and Zabagli 2001: 956). This line recalls the title of Calderon's play, *La Vida es Sueño*, the main source of inspiration for a play called *Calderon*, which Pasolini started in 1966 and then completed in 1973. Other visual and verbal citations frame *Othello* metaphorically and suggest that while Iago shapes Othello's responses within the fictive world of the play-within-the-film, powerful authorial discourses, like Shakespeare's *Othello*, shape both the fictive and the real audience's responses within *and* without Pasolini's film. A few minutes into the film, before the play-within-the-film starts, the camera cuts from the back room, where the puppets are stored, to the outer wall of the theatre, where four posters advertise recent and future productions. The four posters are reproductions of four famous paintings by Velasquez. The portrait of Don Diego de Acedo is used to advertise *La Terra Vista dalla Luna* and is lying on the ground, possibly to suggest that Pasolini had already completed this short film. The titles of two short films, which Pasolini meant to shoot shortly after *Nuvole*, *Le Avventure del Re Magio Randagio* and *Mandolini*, are printed on Velasquez's portraits of Philip IV and Baltasar Carlos.[17] The poster advertising *Nuvole* is *Las Meninas*, the painting which Michel Foucault analyses in the first chapter of his book, *The Order of Things* (1966).[18] Through this visual citation Pasolini acknowledges Velasquez and Foucault as further sources of inspiration besides Shakespeare and gives his audience a powerful interpretative key for the film as a whole.

In his analysis of Velasquez's *Las Meninas*, Foucault identifies several aspects of this peculiar painting, which forcibly turn the onlooker into the object, rather than the recipient, of representation. The first element is the painter's gaze, who painted himself standing next to a large canvas. The painter stares at his models, who stand outside the painting. Foucault argues that this invisible point outside the painting coincides with the onlooker's point of view and explains the implications of this peculiar visual arrangement as follows:

> From the eyes of the painter to what he is observing there runs a compelling line that we, the onlookers, have no power of evading: it runs through the real picture and emerges form its surface to join the place from which we see the painter observing us; this dotted line reaches out to us ineluctably, and links us to the representation of the picture.

(1989: 4)

The power of the painter's gaze is emphasized by the fact that the onlooker has no control over representation, because the big canvas faces the painter, showing the onlooker its blank side. As Foucault continues:

> As soon as they place the spectator in the field of their gaze, the painter's eyes seize hold of him, force him to enter the picture, assign him a place at once privileged and inescapable, levy their luminous and visible tribute from him, and project it upon the inaccessible surface of the canvas within the picture. He sees his invisibility made visible to the painter and transposed into an image forever invisible to himself.
>
> (1989: 4–5)

Another element in Velasquez's painting leads Foucault to stress the formidable power of the painter's gaze. Although inconspicuous, the onlooker soon becomes aware of a round mirror hanging from the back wall. Unlike Dutch painters, who introduced mirrors in their paintings to emphasize the mimetic power of their art, Velasquez's mirror has a murky surface that gives no additional perspectives on the characters *in* the painting, but captures a glimpse of the models standing *outside* it. While the onlooker is led to believe that those models might be King Philip IV and his wife Mariana, the mirror's indefinite reflection also suggests that its surface might be capturing the onlookers' own reflections. In Foucault's words:

> [The mirror's] motionless gaze extends out in front of the picture, into that necessarily invisible region which forms its exterior face, to apprehend the figures arranged in that space. ... The unexpected mirror holds in its glow the figures that the painter is looking at ... but also the figures that are looking at the painter. ... For the function of that reflection is to draw into the interior of the picture what is intimately foreign to it: the gaze which has organised it and the gaze for which it is displayed.
>
> (1989: 8, 9, 17)

Foucault's startling conclusion is that the figures standing outside the painting are *just* figures arranged by the painter's and by the mirror's gaze into objects of representation.

The visual citations used by Pasolini at the beginning of *Nuvole* are more than passing references to either Velasquez or to Foucault. As Alberto Marchesini remarked:

> [t]here is another audience beside those who become involved with the theatrical event, a for-ever-changing audience who, far off and detached, watch the film. We are that audience. We also coincide with the audience who watch a production of *Othello* in the little theatre, and, as a result, Iago's winks are addressed simultaneously to two different audiences. ... Iago's gaze, which is clearly aware of our complicity, has the same ensnaring power as the painter's gaze in the painting, which we fall captives to.[19]
>
> (1994: 100–1)

Pasolini's double reference to Velasquez and Foucault suggests that if Shakespeare's characters are puppets tied to strings that force them to re-enact a predetermined set of actions as envisaged by the artist's imagination, the audience are also fashioned and ideologically constructed by the Shakespearean script. The real audience and the fictive audience, collapsed into one entity by Iago's gaze, are therefore to share the puppets' destiny, which is to be just 'a dream within a dream'.

Like Foucault, Pasolini regards representation as a powerful discourse that imprisons and reifies. In an interview about his later film *Salò*, Pasolini echoes Foucault's early theories on power almost literally: 'Power reifies the body, by reducing it to an object, and never was this process made as visible, palpable and physical as under the Nazi-Fascist regime. I believe that power today manipulates conscience more profoundly'.[20] (Borgna 1995: 53) Although Pasolini's views on power were also affected by Crocian and Gramscian notions of cultural hegemony and by the disappointing outcome of the students' uprising in Rome in 1968, parallels with Foucault's theories are hard to avoid. As Ward explains:

> Pasolini sees ... Power [as] a system of control that has reached such a stage of sophistication that its effects go almost unnoticed. It has succeeded in masking its true oppressive nature so successfully that it no longer needs to exercise its domination through outright coercive means like violence or military threat. Rather, it dominates through consent, a kind of non-coercive coercion which is at its most powerful when at its most invisible.
>
> (1999: 223)

Nowhere is the collusion between power and authorial discourse more explicit than in Pasolini's *Calderon*. The setting of the second episode is Velasquez's studio in the Escurial as represented in *Las Meninas*. In this episode, the king and queen address the other characters in the painting from the mirror. They point out that the painter 'is himself involved in our world of wealth and patrimony,/and although he looks out of the painting he is inside it!'[21] (Bonino 1973: 55).In the eighth episode, Pablo claims that 'Velasquez is in prison because he has a body'[22] (Bonino 1973: 97). What Pasolini seems to suggest in *Calderon* is that the painter, despite being the origin of representation and partaking in the process through which representation contributes to reify the subject, is himself at the same time contained by it.

Unlike recent Anglo-American critics, who have thoroughly absorbed Foucauldian theories on the power of discursive formations to fashion individuals into subjects, the thick web of citations which Pasolini used in his reworking of *Othello* granted him critical distance from all his sources of inspiration, including Shakespeare and Foucault. *Nuvole* is radically different from *Calderon* and, more crucially, from recent approaches to *Othello*, which, by focusing on Iago's meta-dramatic strategies of subjection, find no scope for resistance within the play (cf. Greenblatt 1980: 222–54). Unlike *Calderon*, *Nuvole* makes clear that representation, discourse and the author function can become vital sites of resistance. As early as 1967, Pasolini challenged Foucault's theories on power and discourse by problematizing Shakespeare's status as a canonical author. Pasolini's choice to cast his friend and poet Francesco Leonetti as the puppeteer, for example, suggests a degree of ambiguity towards Shakespeare. If Shakespeare's legacy is visualized through the strings that force the puppets to re-enact the original script, Leonetti's stature as a poet and his personal friendship with Pasolini confirm the latter's investment in Shakespeare as a source of inspiration. More importantly, Shakespeare is not made to appear solely responsible for the artistic (and ideological) 'dream' which entraps the puppets. Pasolini, like Velasquez, puts himself 'in the picture'. His name, not Shakespeare's, appears on the poster hanging on the outer wall of the theatre. Also crucial is the fact that, by storming the stage, Pasolini's popular audience claim the right to rewrite the plot and to free the characters from its foregone, tragic resolution. The fictive audience, in other words, claim authorial agency for themselves and deny representation of any single authorizing point of origin.

Paradoxically, reviewers of *Nuvole* have often regarded Pasolini's fictive audience as illiterate and violent because unable to fathom the intricacies of meaning and the moral complexity of the Shakespearean source. According to B. D. Schwartz, for example, 'the common people ... cannot tell the difference between a play and the truth, between actors and real people, between the content of art and the morality of artists who create it' (1992: 500). Similarly, Serafino Murri blames the audience for overlooking the difference between reality and fiction and for selfishly rearranging the ending so as to please their unsophisticated urge for a comic resolution:

> The audience's narrow, sordid world, within which one is expected to act according to a pre-determined code of action ... is truly hellish. The audience's violent reaction is triggered off by a superficial perception of what happens. The audience enters the world of the puppets and shatters it. Their reaction can only be explained as the result of their social dejection, of their blindness, which depend on ignoring what one is encouraged to consume. Because they have paid, they expect to see their bourgeois "ethical" expectations fulfilled.[23]
>
> (Murri 1995: 82)

Both Schwartz's and Murri's arguments are blatantly flawed. Schwartz is clearly misled when he claims that Pasolini's audience storm the stage because they cannot relate to the moral complexities envisaged by the artist's imagination. The audience is in fact the closest fictional counterpart to the adapter who eats his master to absorb his creative power while exorcizing it, as preached by the speaking crow in *Hawkes and Sparrows*. Proving Marchesini equally wrong when he claims that the real audience is captivated by the trajectory of Iago's gaze (p. 99), Pasolini's audience breaks the spell of representation, and 'rearranges' it. Inexplicably, Murri refers to Pasolini's working-class audience as middle-class. Visually, Pasolini's audience belong to the same world as the marginalized urban poor who people his early prose works, *Ragazzi di Vita* (*The Ragazzi* 1955) and *Una Vita Violenta* (*A Violent Life* 1959), where they retain their primitive purity and dignity in the face of poverty and marginalization. But even more bewildering is Murri's claim that Pasolini's audience act according to a predetermined code of action. In fact, the history of the reception of Shakespeare's *Othello* on stage and on film emphatically suggests that Pasolini's audience is radically innovative.

Audiences have traditionally found Shakespeare's *Othello* a disquieting and upsetting play. Marvin Rosenberg reports how Pepys's 'pretty lady cried out' when she saw Desdemona smothered (1961: 216). Rosenberg also reports 'a rare "review" from 1610 which tells us that when Shakespeare's company performed *Othello* in Oxford, the actors ... "drew tears not only from their speech, but also from their action" ' (1961: 5). Given the strong reactions elicited by the play since Shakespeare's own days, it is surprising that the ending was not altered during the Restoration. Rosenberg is proudly relieved that 'no English actors agreed to such a defacement of the play' (1961: 33) and praises French adapter Jean-François Ducis, who 'had at first the temerity to let the heroine be killed'. The fact that 'the prettiest women in Paris fainted in the most conspicuous boxes and were publicly carried out of the house' convinced Ducis to spare Desdemona, although the actor playing Othello demanded the original back to the 'peculiar agonies of the most obviously handsome and fashionable' (1961: 32). No real audience, though, has ever been granted the degree of agency enjoyed by Pasolini's fictive audience. Once again, Pasolini's departure from Shakespeare's play *and* from its theatrical tradition was probably suggested by yet another local source of inspiration, the Neapolitan episode in Roberto Rossellini's *Paisà* (1946), where a black American military policeman joins the stage fight between the white paladin Orlando and the Moor, both impersonated by Sicilian marionettes (*pupi*).[24]

An even greater degree of agency is granted to Pasolini's puppets. To some extent, the puppets seem to find redemption only in death. Only when lying on their back, on heaps of rubbish in the open-air tip, are Othello and Iago allowed out of the enclosed space of representation, the decrepit theatre, with its mobile stage, dirty walls and dusty courtyard, all sealed off from the 'real' world. However, the ontological status of the puppets in Pasolini's film is never diminutive. Pasolini's puppets do not partake of the spiritual qualities which Heinrich von Kleist famously ascribed to marionettes. Kleist's marionettes have more natural grace than human beings, because they have a natural centre of gravity and their movements are perfectly natural and unimpeded by the all-too-human consciousness of sin (Kleist 1989). Pasolini's puppets, on the contrary, *are* all-too human, and if they are fashioned by the Shakespearean script while on stage, they are endowed with agency, stoical strength and self-awareness when they linger in the wings. Despite his green face and bright-red tongue, Iago becomes 'earnest and kind, as an old, patient philosopher'[25] (Siti and Zabagli 2001: 955) when he is off-stage. In a short note within the opening stage direction, Pasolini employs quasi-biblical language to describes the puppets, who are said to be 'one and bifold' (Siti and Zabagli 2001: 935), as if their nature constituted a mystery similar to that of the Holy Trinity. The Pirandellian motif of the unstable distance between actor and character becomes a crucial site of resistance in *Nuvole*. Going back once more to Velasquez's *Las Meninas*, one could argue that the back of the canvas, as much as the wings in Pasolini's theatre, provide a site of resistance because both the canvas and the wings are suggestively outside the site of official representation. Marchesini endorses a similar view when he claims that 'Velasquez's mirror and Pasolini's dream, by abandoning a mimetic intent, add to the motif of vision the far more disquieting one of elision, of the untold, which represent the most authentic feature of the puppets' world'[26] (1994: 105).

Nuvole is misrepresented by those who reduce it to mere escapism or to a pessimistic parable about life (Ferrero 1977: 94). Naomi Greene, for example, has argued that '[t]he sad end that greets the marionettes suggests that, even in his most light-hearted work, Pasolini could not escape the tragic view of the world so deeply rooted within him' (1990: 91). Greene overlooks the fact that Iago and Othello, who are neither conquered by death nor beyond it, greet their initiation into the 'real' world with a profound sense of joy and wonder. The film ends on their final words: 'O marvellous and heart-rending beauty of creation'[27] (Siti and Zabagli 2001: 966). The religious undertone in this final line, along with the explicit association between Desdemona's cherry earings and Eve's apple[28] (Siti and Zabagli 2001: 946), might suggest a reading of the 'happy' ending in Biblical terms. Accordingly, one could argue that the puppet impersonating Othello, whose head is screwed onto his body at the very beginning of the film, is first born, then falls on discovering his sexuality, only to be re-admitted to God's presence at the end of the film. Allusions to Plato's 'myth of the cave' – the stuffy, enclosed space of the theatre, as the *locus* of illusion, is tellingly sealed off from the 'real' world except for 'a single window, as narrow as a slit'[29] (Siti and Zabagli 2001: 935) – may similarly suggest that the puppets have ultimately gained access to a higher level of existence. On the contrary, the most radical element in Pasolini's 'happy' ending is that what might be regarded as a Christian paradise or as a Platonic world of ideas is in fact, very clearly, this world, in all its beauty (the clouds) and all its ugliness (the rubbish dump).

Nuvole is a complex, genuinely intercultural appropriation, within which Shakespeare functions as just one of the many models which Pasolini challenges to signify anew. Pasolini's neglected appropriation of *Othello* invites its viewers to reconsider the Shakespearean original not only in relation to issues of gender, sexuality and race, but also in relation to wider concerns, such as the potential for resistance in the face of powerful discursive formations. While critics like Stephen Greenblatt glamorize Iago's powers by extending his colonization of the other characters' subjectivities to the audience, *Nuvole* offers radically alternative insights into *Othello* which can help us overcome what Thomas Cartelli describes as 'the damaging and distorting effects of [this play's] "afterlife" on both sides of the colonial divide' (1999: 169).

13 'Meaning by Shakespeare' south of the border

Alfredo Michel Modenessi

Al principio creyó que todas las personas eran como él, pero la extrañeza de un compañero con el que había empezado a comentar esa vacuidad le reveló su error ... .

Jorge Luis Borges[1]

'I'll make thee think thy swan a crow'

The Complete Works of William Shakespeare (Abridged) must be the most successful of current world-wide appropriations of Shakespeare. It has certainly been so over the last three years in Mexico, where productions involving Shakespeare hardly ever run longer than a few months. However slim its artistic merits as yet another parodic take on the iconic value of the Bard, the implications of its world-wide popularity deserve attention. The success of the Reduced Shakespeare Company might suggest, for example, that Gary Taylor was right in prophesying the 'shrinking of the bard' (1999: 205). However, despite its healthy scepticism and playfulness, Taylor's prophecy is somewhat unpersuasive. For a start, his assessment of Shakespeare's 'size' focuses on 'reputation', a category that is appropriate to gauge little else but the shrinking of bardolatry. A fine day it will be when the immortal Bard finally goes out the window and theatre practitioners and academics relate more freely to the superb textual legacy of this mortal and refashionable *playwright*. And therein hangs a tale of more significant objections. A major one is that hardly any of the evidence Taylor provides stretches outside the English-speaking world. For all the reverence that he may command anywhere, it is precisely *outside* the English-speaking world that Shakespeare thrives from living in the company of many 'others' who perform and transform his texts – not only writers, directors and players but *translators, dramaturgs and audiences*.

What's missing from Taylor's analysis, therefore, is a better understanding of Shakespeare as a global phenomenon. Too often are world-wide Shakespeares misleadingly discussed in oppositional terms, if they are discussed at all.[2] Nevertheless, Shakespeare continues to invite complex responses from 'foreign' artists and cultures. Although to many of them Shakespeare stands tall – sometimes very tall indeed – he *doesn't stand alone* nor is he uncritically or exclusively taken to do so. So many attempts to do Shakespeare 'straight' seem to have become a 'wild-swan chase', that it now seems best to opt for the crow – that is, to try out angles unseen, dismissed, ignored or impossible, made feasible or merely made up, by Shakespeare's interaction with other languages and cultures. Unlike 'straight' attempts to mean by Shakespeare – whatever *that* may mean – *local* versions of Shakespeare, always provisional *ab ovo*, resist the temptations of universalist truisms.

'The quarrel is between our masters and us their men'

The world-wide success of *The Complete Works* also suggests that the word 'Shakespeare' in its title functions as the key concept of an international franchise, consistent with current practices of corporate business management and marketing. In other words, this show tellingly exemplifies how a stimulating dramatic tradition can also function as a 'global' brand. However, one should also be reminded that 'it makes no good sense to define the global as if the global excludes the local' (Robertson 1995: 34). *The Complete Works* couldn't have succeeded in Mexico without the tactical transformations interpolated by its local operators.[3] The Mexican production – directed by Antonio Castro and adapted by Flavio González Mello – didn't simply cater to the uncritical expectations of audiences that pack a playhouse solely because the show is imported or internationally acclaimed. On the contrary, the Mexican ensemble rightly assumed that the key concept would be of greater use as a *vehicle* for locally meaningful, mostly political, satire. Every sketch in the show was adapted to incorporate local references, and ample room was provided for close-range improvisation between the players and the audience. In short, *The* (Mexican) *Complete Works* is an oblique example of what has happened to Shakespeare 'south of the border' in recent times: the local transformation of a foreign but not alien cultural icon where a tradition of admiration – whether sincere or merely a matter of course – combines with an equally old inclination to cultural poaching and cannibalization[4] as legitimate tactics of self-invention. In Mexico, Shakespeare is seldom associated with hegemony or imperialism – those categories rather apply to other kinds of global brands, mostly from the USA, the imperative reference for the locative 'south of the border'[5]– and is much more often viewed as either an indifferent given of 'high culture' or an artist of the greatest worth, regardless of his national origin. Here, Shakespeare is 'global' only inasmuch as globalization may be understood as a 'heterogenetic' and not a 'homogenizing' process (Ashcroft 2001: 214).

In its hegemonic sense, 'globalization is the radical *transformation* of imperialism, continually reconstituted' (Ashcroft 2001: 213) in the attempt to maximize its homogenizing effects upon multiple markets. A high degree of conformity to ideological, cultural and political inputs of globalization from identifiably 'homogenized' social groups in Mexico and the rest of Latin America may be readily granted – I am mostly referring to our small but powerful upper and upper-middle classes, of course. During the emergence of the highly heterogeneous Latin American nations (de Alva 1995: 270), those sectors of our 'post-colonial'/'neo-colonial' societies retained a hegemonic role of Eurocentric persuasion. As a result, a strong subservience to global practices is imposed upon national culture from the top of our financial, administrative and educational institutions. In other words, many cultural endeavours in Latin America are inevitably 'grounded in the social, economic being of a ruling class so conditioned by the extreme "social duality" of "its" national formation that it cannot generate "ruling ideas" of its own' (Larsen 2001: 80). These groups and their representative products operate at once as agents of neo-colonization and promoters of a 'national' identity often anchored in whatever global trends are at hand, which they seek to spread as homogeneously as possible throughout the social spectrum.[6]

Nonetheless, although the intensive marketing of global products testifies to the levelling *aims* that are intrinsic to globalization, an assessment of the *outcome* of such aims cannot proceed exclusively from the limited perceptions afforded by the fields from which they originate. Richard Burt, for instance, seeking to provide an alternative to the term 'globalization' in his recent discussion of Shakespeare's 'decanonization and decolonization via film, television, advertising, and other media in the US and the UK' (2003: 17), argues that

> As glo-cali-zation collapses the local into the global, cultural centers and margins are no longer opposed as high to low culture, authentic to inauthentic, serious to parody, sacred to profane, and so *Shakespeare cannot rightly be placed squarely on the side of the hegemonic, dominant culture or counter-hegemonic resistant subculture.*
>
> (16, my emphasis)

The last statement is true enough, but it can hardly be called a new insight, nor can it be attributed to a 'collapse' of the 'local into the global' entailing a domino effect upon other binaries of the kind Burt enumerates: 'The dominant and the subaltern do not exist in a simple and incontrovertibly oppositional mode' (Ashcroft 2001: 215), nor do they seem to have ever done so.

Inside the heterogeneous and ever-provisional national formations of Latin America, then, disempowered communities remain colonized; consciously or not, however, they are 'more than simply the objects of imperialism' (Ashcroft 2001: 212) and retain significant agency within constrained, *sub-national* fields in ways consistent with Bill Ashcroft's definition of the 'local':

> When we speak of the local, we speak of a community that operates transversely to, or below the level of, those state apparatuses which organize representation in the interests of national identification. It might be one identified with a spatial location, but it might also be identified with an ethnic, gendered or cultural 'location'. It is a community small enough not to be 'imagined' as the nation, or any wider community of identification.
>
> (2001: 215)

The very imbalanced economic and cultural configuration of our societies makes local cultural energies, often *without an outspoken agenda*, inhabit and transform global inputs into transculturally operative products that resist homogenization and, concomitantly, generate 'ruling ideas' of *their* own. While Burt's evaluation of Shakespeare's status seems generally justified in connection to the English-speaking world, and to the impact that the media he discusses have therein, it implies a relativistic homogenization of current uses and receptions of Shakespeare, and his proposition that the local and the global have 'collapsed' into the 'glocal' remains as flat as a binary opposition, mindless of the dialectics whereby 'local' and 'global' interact to mutually transformative effects. His 'neologism' 'glo-cali-zation' (Burt 2003: 15), then, looks faint and over-reaching, insofar as it implies that a blanketing and undynamic levelling of cultural fields is actually possible.[7]

Conversely, the notion of 'glocalization' proposed by Roland Robertson (1995) 'more adequately describes the relationship between the local and the global as one of interaction and interpenetration rather than of binary opposites' (Ashcroft 2001: 215). Products of global cultural circulation cannot effect an actual levelling of local cultural fields: 'As "globalization" does not automatically lead to the breaking down of all cultural and intellectual "trade" barriers and disparities, ... neither does it necessarily equalize or de-center the particularities of national or regional intellectual cultures' (Larsen 2001: 76–7). Local energies have the tactical advantage not only of knowing but of *inhabiting* the targeted field (see Ashcroft 2001: 157–82). Thus, far from levelling out, 'cultural communication grows as one considers the variety of group, family and ethnic contexts wherein standardized messages are received and made to interact with local modes of understanding' (García Canclini 2002: 23, my translation). The fact that Latin America represents a peculiar cultural field cannot be overstressed. Although art and literature in subordinate cultures enjoy international attention mostly through the endorsement of external cultural centres, the extraordinary quality and reach of Latin-American arts have instead been the outcome of complex negotiations more often founded on headstrong resilience than on theoretical awareness. Latin-American artists and intellectuals aren't native to either the 'old' or the 'new' world, and therefore inevitably make 'European' and 'American' models at once collide and collude. Neither model is perceived as dominant, however; in fact, a dialectical tension between them gives rise to a third, ever-shifting 'self' capable of radically contradictory cultural transactions.

'Th'attempt and not the deed confounds us'

In Latin America, 'categories shaped by European experience function in a space with a *different but not an alien* sociological conjunction in which they neither apply properly nor can help but be applied; better, they circulate in counterfeit but are an obligatory reference' (Schwarz 1999: 95).[8] 'South of the border' Shakespeare is a highly prestigious but *distinctly foreign* reference that can almost exclusively circulate in translation and adaptation.[9] Whatever 'Shakespeare' may mean here, must mean through practices radically removed from his own. The reception of Shakespeare's works and by-products is further complicated by the intervention of local dramaturgs, players and directors rendering translations apt for consumption by local audiences who, in turn, receive and recirculate them in ways just as strongly transformative but far less controllable or pre-dictable. Valuable 'meaning by Shakespeare' 'south of the border' is thus frequently vehicular and at its best challenges lingering notions of 'authenticity'.

Many Mexican directors over the last twenty years have opted for what some might call radical, disruptive or dissident approaches, which are distinctly local in the sense outlined above. Local appropriations of Shakespeare were virtually unknown between 1950 and 1980, when the Mexican theatre reached a peak of innovation and experi-mentation informed by, and consistent with, contemporary European trends.[10] The flourishing of experimental theatre was partly due to the relative stability of our econ-omy between the post-war years and the politically restless 1960s and 1970s. During this period of relative prosperity, Shakespeare would be played either in 'traditional' or 'kottian' and 'experimental' ways. Political theatre was also popular – the 1960s and 1970s brought about a great amount of productions with overtly political purposes – but, overall, Shakespeare remained the preserve of more 'cosmopolitan' endeavours and spaces. Even when approached 'experimentally', Shakespeare served mainly the agenda of 'existential exploration'.

Since the early 1980s, however, Mexican cultural markets have steadily declined. This ongoing crisis has had severe consequences for the theatre. A drastic reduction in the number of playhouses, the growing appeal of cinema and the chaotic growth of Mexico City have contributed to a lack of interest from the younger generations. To make matters worse, the upper classes gravitate towards a pseudo-Broadway market;[11] as a result, private companies often apply Broadway-style criteria of staging, casting and box-office appeal to their productions. However, since the 1988 electoral fraud, through the crash of 1994, and on to the present day there have also been more locally oriented productions involving Shakespeare. 'Straight' Shakespeare still exists, of course, but it has proven generally unimaginative, ineffectual or irrelevant.

Two productions illustrate conventional approaches and the driving forces behind them. One is the National Theatre Company production of *Othello* by José Solé (1995), who directed more imaginative Shakespearean productions in the 1960s and 1970s. Perhaps constrained by the highly subsidized institution to which he belonged, Solé's *Othello* was a jumble of sub-par acting by reliable veterans (Othello, Cassio) and young-sters ironically performing in the worst 'grand old style' (Desdemona, Emilia), counter-pointed by an outstanding but isolated Iago who looked lost in a meaningless setting. Even more worryingly, the translation was unprofessional and uninformed – a typical recycling of the standard prose version by the Spaniard Luis Astrana Marín.[12] This pro-duction ran in one of our best playhouses for more than seven months regardless of attendance figures – a harmful trait of Mexico's cultural policy making is the die-hard vice of subsidizing artistic endeavours, which in turn enables state control over cultural production, criticism and, eventually, education, as well as the creation of cliques that monopolize decisions, playhouses and allocations.

The second production is a representative example of medium-budget commercial proj-ects which aim to exploit a modish need for 'high culture' and are often poorly acted and directed but well publicized, if ultimately worthless. *The Merchant of Venice* by Héctor Ortega (1997), featuring a former Miss Mexico runner-up as Portia, typically relied on a poorly translated old text for which no credits were given, no rights or royalties paid, and little effort made, if at all, by way of adaptation. The producers of such shows regard Shakespeare as the ultimate challenge in 'serious' theatre-making, and therefore opt for ludicrous imitations of old (colonial, perhaps) Spanish standards in acting and directing. Sometimes the actors involved in this type of productions will even go as far as putting on a slightly 'Spanish' accent to sound more in keeping with their understanding of Shakespeare as a holy relic.

Fortunately, other directors have used Shakespeare as a vehicle to explore locally relevant, and often highly political, agendas. One example is Jesusa Rodríguez – a fiercely critical lesbian artist who significantly prefers to be known by her first name.[13] In the early 1980s Jesusa stunned her less agressive if equally talented colleagues by staging a fantastic *Don Giovanni* with an all-female and multiethnic cast who would exchange and sing all parts in a disruptive combination of languages that she called *Itañol antiguo* ('old Italspanish'), frequently interacting with the piano player, cabaret-style. A little later, she staged her first Shakespeare-based show, *¿Cómo va la noche, Macbeth?* ('How goes the night, Macbeth?'), a high-handed minimalist gignol explo-ration of sleeplessness as a political metaphor. Where others had tried the worn-out 'erotic' approach to the 'dead butcher and his wife',[14] Jesusa focused on the bed – dead centre, impossible to move – as a desert of sexual, cultural and political confrontations.

Her Weird Sisters were sharply humorous puppets, 'hags' (literally interpreted as nightmares), serving as the only link between the sleepless, uncoupled, 'unsexed', spouses. Since then, Jesusa has remained one of our most provocative and imaginative stage-artists.

Since 1990 Shakespearean productions have consistently deconstructed Shakespeare's assumed 'timelessness, humanity and universality'. Some directors have used the Shakespearean text without overtly relocating it,[15] while others have incorporated explicit topical references.[16] More radical appropriations include productions where the Shakespearean text has been used as a platform for authorial/directorial intervention[17] and pastiches.[18] Hereafter I shall focus on two productions that clearly illustrate the motivations, risks, merits and flaws involved in appropriating Shakespeare as a vehicle of local relevance in Mexico. The first one is a transparent instance of opportunistic cannibalization; the second incorporates global strategies in heterogenetic fashion.

'Two truths are told'

Despite the image of democratic and economic progress promoted internationally by the Salinas regime since its inception in 1988, Mexico continued to be ruled in authoritarian ways leading to increasing poverty, violence and lawlessness. The extent of Mexico's decline became evident to the rest of the world only in 1994, after the *Zapatista* uprise and the murder of the ruling party's presidential candidate Luis Donaldo Colosio, which took place in the city of Tijuana, the northenmost point of our republic, the most important town in Baja California, and a Mexican sub-version of the 'supermodern non-place' (see Augé 1995: 94–115). In 1995 Ángel Norzagaray, while based in Baja California – a border state more than geographically closer to the USA than to the Mexican capital – was quick to bring Shakespeare's plays of power to bear upon Mexico's political, economical and cultural deterioration.

¿Tú también, Macbeth? ('*Et tu*, Macbeth?', 1995) was a roughly produced and performed, topical and short-lived, one-act show based on scenes from the first three acts of *Julius Caesar*, the first two of *Macbeth*, and two key speeches from *Richard II* and *Henry V*. These extracts were adapted to focus directly on the 'prologue to the swelling act' and obliquely on its immediate consequences, underlining nothing 'beyond this ignorant present'. A narrator started the show by reciting a transformed version of the Chorus' opening speech in *Henry V*. Then another actor, playing a combination of Caesar and Duncan, delivered lines originally spoken by Richard II in his speech on 'the death of kings', and afterwards sat motionless on a pedestal centre-stage. This stony figure presided over the ensuing array of multiple variations on the scenes preceding the murders of Caesar and Duncan against a backdrop of plain black curtains, neutral lighting, and more importantly, a *crescendo* of 'sound and fury', consisting of night-bird cries and metallic noises. At the peak of such chaos, the actors playing Macbeth and Brutus came on to do 'the deed' together, the former using a dagger, the latter a handgun in what looked like a re-enactment of the infamously graphic filmed sequence of the assassination of Colosio. After the assassination, Macbeth briefly took over Duncan/ Caesar's place only to be killed in exactly the same way before the narrator redelivered his opening speech in blatantly circular fashion.

Norzagaray's adaptation constituted an irreverent and avowedly opportunistic use of Shakespeare as source and vehicle. As parts of a script that stressed image and sound over linguistic semiosis, the texts related juxtapositionally, increasingly obliterating each other. Some of the speeches were paired off because of evident connections between them (e.g. Macbeth and Lady Macbeth's exchange in *Macbeth* 1.7 with Brutus and Portia's conversation in *Julius Caesar* 2.1, or Caesar and Calphurnia's in 2.2), but instead of making their words match or combine, Norzagaray's blocking – obsessive and circular – and the deliberately simultaneous performance of these scenes had the effect of making them monochromatic and pointless. Their senselessness grew more disturbing as textuality became increasingly immaterial. Indeed, for audiences who have become all-too familiar with political duplicity and conspiracy, and hence deeply distrustful of speech, particularly *political* speech, the poetic representation of doubt or conflict leading to politically motivated violence mattered less than the crude quality of the act.

The murdered Caesar/Duncan and the murderer/murdered Macbeth were thus finally interchangeable not because of an explicitly formulated connection between early modern text and contemporary context, but as an act of local indifference towards 'meaning'. Within the thoroughly neutral scenery and costumes, the gun became the only conspicuously significant prop and presence. But it wasn't meant to disrupt the picture of sameness and repetition conveyed by Norzagary's production; instead, it epitomized how and why the identity of those who fired the gun no longer makes any difference in the mind of a Mexican. The opening and closing speech, which in either case sounded hollow, stressed the impossibility of evoking the extraordinary under present circumstances. The transformation of poetic discourse into a relentless reiteration of raw, intense violence and confusion succeeded precisely because Shakespeare was thoroughly overwritten, (ab)used, as a vehicle for extremely crude, unliterary but literal signifiers.

Jesusa's *King Lear* (1996) – which was never fully performed[19] – was instead the result of an interesting experiment in linguistic and cultural translation. Jesusa needed both a new text in Spanish to suit her agenda and a locally identifiable situation within which to reinscribe the text. During pre-production, she came to the conclusion that tragic sense would be impossible to convey beyond the level of a moral fiction without resorting to a contemporary frame. She therefore decided that the translated text would be delivered as if it was happening inside the mind of a retired actress living in a sordid nursing home as she projected her growing insanity unto a world of recurrent abuse disguised as professional care. The old actress' imaginary version of a play and a part she never performed but presently experienced could be interpreted as a critique of her literal exclusion from the *drama* of Lear and, at the same time, of her forcible inscription within a transliteration of that drama into institutionalized violence. Jesusa's choice to frame the universal tragedy thus was prompted as much by her decision to employ an all-female cast as by her wish to foreground the conditions frequently accompanying old age and madness in our midst, on the one hand, and theatricality as a major element of *King Lear*, on the other. Thus, the nursing home was at once also an asylum and a theatre. Meta-theatrical devices were used to suggest the overlapping of the 'real' and the fictive worlds. Lear's male guardians were represented by nineteenth-century wooden puppets, while other wooden objects served as Lear's sceptre, her heart and her crown. Several scenes (the torturing of Gloucester, for instance) were performed by the puppets and included the projection of videotaped images against the 'actual' 'sanitized' walls of the asylum, the screen of the Actress/Lear's imagination. Subtitles from Shakespeare's text were interspersed with projections of magnified reproductions of

Giotto's Padova frescoes depicting the vices of *Ira, Invidia, Stultitia* and *Desperatio*, and his allegory of *Caritas*. During the closing sequence 'play' and 'reality' became inseparable.

Ironically, Jesusa's *King Lear* was never staged but became a book, an imaginary performance locked inside pages, a mere projection. This paradoxical book includes a translation of Shakespeare's text[20] and the playscript, with Jesusa's detailed staging notes and the new material added by dramaturg Malú Huacuja to bridge the gap between the nursing home and the Actress/Lear's imagination. These texts are introduced by a prologue by Luz Aurora Pimentel, Jesusa's textual adviser and co-translator, describing the process of textual preparation and adaptation, as well as the fundamental principles informing Jesusa's projected staging. The truly impressive scenes that Jesusa managed to rehearse before this project collapsed did manage to convey her keen views on madness in locally relevant ways, because she and her collaborators largely succeeded in transforming *King Lear* past 'the deaf, inert equation of two dead tongues' (Benjamin 1968: 82). Although never staged, Jesusa's *King Lear*, aptly subtitled *una (a)puesta en escena*,[21] remains a provocative (textual) performance of great local relevance.

Norzagaray and Jesusa represent a new breed of directors who understand intercultural appropriation as a 'heterogenetic' and not a 'homogenizing' process. Norzagaray's accomplishment, his dissolution of Shakespeare's texts into an effective *ostinato* of action and sound, was due as much to his keen grasp of local politics as to his ability to exploit the transcultural potential of his chosen sources. Norzagaray managed to transform Shakespeare into a rough outflow of local anxieties unlikely to be actualized at any other time than his own 'ignorant present'. Alternatively, Jesusa's finally unstaged 'bet' envisioned a transformation of *King Lear* into a *new* work of global relevance but local specificity. Her approach was highly articulate: well-informed, refined, nuanced, but at once just as domestic and locally political as her own plays. Her efforts ultimately reflected how 'the relationship between the local and the global' can be 'one of interaction and interpenetration' (Ashcroft 2001: 215; see Robertson 1995: 30–1), capable of generating an 'infinite variety' of opportunities for artistic realization instead of dreary homogeneous repetitions. Both these productions offered local, provisional alternatives to a Shakespeare too frequently assumed to speak directly past economic, cultural and historical boundaries. Both productions, in other words, showed that 'universal' Shakespeare is the least relevant and productive of all the names behind that name.

14 Dreams of England

Robert Shaughnessy

Dreamlands

A Midsummer Night's Dream remains Shakespeare's most frequently produced play on the British (and, especially, the English) stage. Between 1990 and 2003, there were 180 professional productions of various kinds; if we add to this total the undocumented amateur, school and university versions, the statistical evidence suggests that the *Dream* represents the kind of Shakespeare that English culture holds closest to its heart. The key factors in the play's appeal as national folktale can be readily isolated: its naïve and nostalgic connections with the world of childhood, where it is still just possible to believe in fairies, and the atavistic lure of woodland, a scene of fantasy and desire which traces the contours of an ideal England best glimpsed by looking backwards. But these qualities are equally capable of provoking reactions of ennui, embarrassment, exasperation and nausea. Such feelings may be alleviated by the introduction of a third perspective: rather than a child-friendly pastoral fantasy, the play is, thanks to Jan Kott, Peter Brook and a succession of 'dark', cynical and emphatically non-literal stage and film versions, imagined as an adult entertainment steeped in brutality and eroticism, its magic metaphorical, secular or illusory. As Barbara Hodgdon has compellingly argued, relations between these variant *Dream* scenarios have, in the English theatrical and cultural context, generally been reduced to an antagonistic binary, between the 'traditional' (both 'innocent' and pictorially elaborate) and the 'modernist' (represented pre-eminently by Brook's landmark RSC production of 1970, obsessively re-engaged in subsequent productions); and this division has been defined, in part, through a sense of nationhood. Thus 'the binary not only marks out a history of *Dream*'s theatrical formations but tropes a nexus of its supposed cultural functions in constructing a perfected national community', by means of 'a geography that no longer exists and an imaginative space riddled with desire'; in the end, though, the 'magical, enraptured, and quintessentially *English* wood and the Athenian patriarchy offer locales where a late twentieth-century spectator (even one who has read Jan Kott) may still come away refreshed' (Hodgdon 1998: 175). This essay traces some of the ways in which, in recent performance, refreshment has been imbibed as guilty or anxious pleasure: focusing upon the English theatre, I examine how its culture continues to dream the *Dream*, through a scrutiny, first, of the historic legacy of imperial and colonial discourse, then of some key moments in the post-modern era that was effectively inaugurated by Brook's production (in many ways, the first recognizably 'global' stage Shakespeare), and finally of two productions in 2002 (mounted by the Royal Shakespeare Company and Shakespeare's Globe) which, in different ways, articulate the ambiguities, and the nervousness, of contemporary 'English' Shakespeare, in the cultural and economic context of globalization. I am concerned, in particular, with the relationship between the historic legacies of nationhood, and performance's engagements with, and constructions of, race and ethnicity. If globalization has, at once, rendered Englishness both more tenacious and more precarious, it has also created a hugely expanded and diversified context of reception for the internationalized Shakespeares of the twenty-first century.

Within the setting of British culture, the stage *Dream* has, of course, long been shadowed by preoccupations and anxieties about race and nation, gender, sexuality and class, although for a long time these were rarely explicitly articulated as such. As Gary Jay Williams has demonstrated in a valuable cultural history of the play in performance, its *mise en scène* has, especially since the early nineteenth century, been inflected with the nation's trading relations and imperial ambitions (Williams 1997). The 1840s marked the emergence of the production vocabulary which would hold sway for the rest of the century: elaborate, romanticized scenery, Mendelssohn's overture and incidental music, *corps de ballet* fairies, including children. In terms of its intervention into the culture of British imperialism, the nineteenth-century *Dream* operated on a number of ideological fronts: within the wider setting of theatrical production, the labour- and material-intensive, conspicuous excess of pictorial Shakespeare was a product of an imperial economy, while the homologies between Athens and Britain promoted national self-confidence in classical, heroic and legendary terms, complementing and extending the contemporaneous cultural work of theatrical archaeology in the staging of the history plays (Schoch 1998). The upright Athenian columns of Theseus's palace, as viewed in the theatres of the metropolitan centre between 1816 and 1900 (the year of Sir Herbert Beerbohm Tree's production at Her Majesty's), represented a monumental, masculine rationality as well as period grandeur; they also reproduced the architectural style of British imperialism, as witnessed throughout its colonies and in London itself, not least in the frontages of the theatres in which these visions were performed (Covent Garden, Williams points out, was modelled 'after Athenian acropolis temples' [1997: 84]). But it was in the combination of this framework of rationality and order with the lush, dark space of the forest, a zone of transformation, sexuality and magic, that defined the play's unique appeal as imperial *fantasy*, and that enabled it to work upon the racial and sexual imaginary of Victorian colonialism.[1] As a gendered space, the nineteenth-century Athenian forest was simultaneously a well-choreographed matriarchy and, potentially, a wild, predatory, Amazonian domain of sexual licence and display; but it was also a realm where female sexuality could be displaced or even erased, along with the corporeality of its fairy inhabitants. If the ethereal nature of the fairy corresponded to aspects of the Victorian ideal of femininity, the introduction of child performers, 'consistent with the frequent images in late Victorian art of children as angelic and semidivine' (Williams 1997: 134), reinforced the axis of innocence that connected spirituality to purity. The costuming and choreography of fairies tended to emphasize wispy, delicate, gauzy whiteness aspiring towards immateriality; importantly, the interconnections between spirituality, asexuality and purity were racially as well as sexually marked. In this respect the Victorian fairies belonged to what Richard Dyer, in his analysis of the cultural construction of whiteness, has identified as the cult of the 'white woman as angel', which he reads as 'both the symbol of white virtuousness and the last word in the claim that what made whites special as a race was their non-physical, spiritual,

indeed ethereal qualities' (1997: 127). And it was this capacity to dematerialize, to transcend the body and its corruptions, that made such fairies ideally equipped for their environment: while ancient Greek and deeply English, the woods of the Victorian *Dream*,
reproducing the specular economies of botanical display at Kew Gardens, and in hot-
houses and conservatories, also evoked – and tamed and domesticated – the colonial
jungle, whose rights and duties of rule fell to the English.

It was this ideological dimension, rather than the specific theatrical means of articu-
lating it, that proved to be the play's most enduring cultural legacy. The notion that the
advent of modernism represented a revolutionary break with theatrical tradition is
qualified by the play's continued entanglement within the discourses of race and
empire. Harley Granville Barker's production at the Savoy Theatre in 1914 famously
lifted the heavy hand of Victorian literalism through its post-impressionist scenic innovations, with brilliant white light, emblematic gauzes and curtains in place of live
rabbits and lush greenery, and a relatively uncut text. Barker's attempt to delocalize the
space of representation implicitly distanced his version from the brasher territorial
claims of nineteenth-century imperialism. Nonetheless, the tendency towards abstrac-
tion needs also to be read as itself a response to the accelerating modernization of the
colonial economy; as Fredric Jameson argues, 'the emergence of a properly modernist
"style"' is prompted by 'the representational dilemmas of the new imperial world
system', produced by the 'spatial disjunction' inherent in colonialism, whereby 'a significant structural segment of the economic system as a whole is now located elsewhere,
beyond the metropolis, outside of the daily life and existential experience of the home
country', a world which is 'unknown and unimaginable for the subjects of the imperial
power' (1990: 50–1, 59). Barker's key means of negotiating the unimaginable alterity
of the world elsewhere lay in his reinvention of the fairies. Covered in gold leaf,
prescribed formalized and mechanized moves, wielding scimitars, wearing 'masks,
Indian head-dresses, or wigs of ravelled rope and metallic curls' (Halio 1994: 34), these
were, controversially, not the white nymphs of popular cliché; for many observers, they
originated from the world of Orientalist fantasy: 'Cambodian idols' (Walkley 1914), 'a
quaint little golden idol from an Indian temple' (*The Referee*, 8 February, quoted in
Kennedy 1985: 160), 'ormolu fairies, looking as though they had been detached from
some fantastic, bristling old clock' (MacCarthy 1914). Barker's method of rendering the
fairies as something other than mortal was to racialize them, fashioning yellow bodies,
in a glittering, Orientalist variant of the stage convention of blackface, that also performed
the work of humanoid machinery. Uncanny but servile, these 'quaintly gorgeous metallic
creatures' could appear and disappear without recourse to illusionistic literalism: the
New Statesman reported that as they froze in place on stage, 'the lovers move past and
between them as casually as though they were stocks or stones'. As a theatrical device
this was generally commended; as representation of the alien it participated in what
Homi Bhabha identifies as 'the particular regime of visibility employed in colonial
discourse', switching between exotic specularity and docile invisibility, these fairies occupied the place of the subaltern within the colonial imaginary, wherein 'the visibility of
the racial/colonial Other is at once a *point* of identity… and at the same time a *problem*
for the attempted closure within discourse' (1994: 81). There was, nonetheless, a racial
and administrative hierarchy within the spirit world: understanding Puck to be 'stage
manager', Barker conceived him, in contrast to other fairies hailing 'from the farthest
steppe of India', as a figure of 'pure English folklore' (Granville-Barker 1993: 36).

Set against the raced bodies of his fairy subordinates, Puck was a flame-haired Caucasian in a livid red, Elizabethan-style doublet. Barker was similarly in no doubt that the music and dance in the play should be English, and the domestic element was reinforced by Cecil Sharp's score, which ditched Mendelssohn for arrangements of traditional English airs and folk tunes.

Barker's innovations were more than enough for some critics, but in truth he favoured an even more radical clearance; 'what is really needed', he asserted in a 1915 interview, 'is a great white box. That's what our theatre really is' (quoted in Williams 1997: 152). A half-century later, this is, famously, what the *Dream* got in Sally Jacobs's design for Peter Brook's 1970 RSC production. So familiar is this production, from critical commentary and theatre history, from the recirculation of images of its iconic moments, and from its reiteration in later productions, that it is hardly necessary here to labour its detail. The show's extensive citation of 'Eastern' performance practices (the baggy silks and primary colours of the fairy costumes, modelled on Chinese circus acrobats, 'Asian' chanting and percussion), however radical it appeared in Stratford in 1970, perpetuates a history of Western avant-garde appropriation that can be traced back to Artaud and Craig. Reflecting upon his discovery of the solution to the 'problem' of the fairies – the key to the production's aesthetic – Brook cites an intercultural epiphany prompted by the figure of the Chinese circus artist: 'a human being who, by pure skill, demonstrates joyfully that he can transcend his natural constraints, become a reflection of pure energy' (1987: 97). Like Artaud's fabled Balinese dancers, the acrobats of the Orient provided both a limit and a lesson for a reinvigorated Western performance practice (and in turn Brook's synthesis would itself prove exemplary, instructive and influential); in Brook's and Jacobs's white-box setting (ostensibly a version of the director's 'empty space'), the vibrant, energetic, colourful fairies inverted the traditional *Dream* relationship between figure and ground, the whiteness that had marked the *corps de ballet* now constituting a would-be neutral, universal environment. But, as Dyer argues, there is nothing at all neutral about white when it is read as racial ideology: as 'both a colour and, at once, not a colour', white is 'the sign of that which is colourless because it cannot be seen: the soul, the mind, and also emptiness, non-existence and death, all of which form part of what makes white people socially white' (1997: 45). The playground of the imagination defined by Brook's white box accommodated the signs of the Orient, for sure, but assumed an invisible and universal white ethnicity as its normative framework. Nonetheless, for Brook (and many others) the *Dream* supplied the initial template (subsequently much elaborated in the multi-ethnic work at the Bouffes du Nord) for an intercultural Shakespeare, which, as the experience of touring over the next three years would demonstrate, was as readable in New York and Tokyo as in Stratford.

If Brook's *Dream* indisputably changed the face of Shakespeare performance both in the United Kingdom and internationally, it did so by renegotiating the theatrical vocabulary of English Shakespearean nationalism (although without altogether abandoning a Eurocentric worldview); and as such it was as disliked by a few as it was admired by many. And, in 1977, the next Stratford *Dream*, directed by John Barton and designed by John Napier, was a determined, and, for the most part, warmly welcomed, attempt to reclaim the play for England through a self-consciously retrograde and anti-modernist scenography, in which 'leaves drift down through moonlight, carpeting John Napier's forest of crystalline trees', creating an environment 'inhabited by a horde of bark-skinned, frond-waving earth sprites that freeze into stumps and exotic foliage when mortals approach' (Barber 1997). Although Barton's scenography seemed consciously retrograde and anti-modernist in relation to Brook, his treatment of the fairies – albeit unwittingly – engaged (in a way that Brook's did not) with concerns which were to become central to *Dream* performance in England during the next three decades. Although his decision to present the fairies as, according to a programme note, 'a curious mixture of wood spirits … household gods, pagan deities' advertised the recovery of a properly Elizabethan, indigenous spirit world, the fairies were generally perceived as exotic and alien: as *The Daily Telegraph* commented, 'they swarm over their gaunt conifer forest like refugees from a surrealist Bedlam. Blue-haired, shock-haired, or with no hair at all, waving long finger-nails like Struwelpeter, or galumping grossly like Caliban, these eerie grotesques are a world away from Shakespeare's delicate elves and sprites'. The references to refugees and to Caliban, together with *The Times*'s allusion to 'bark-skinned' (a slip for dark-skinned?) fairies (Wardle 1977) suggest a racial component which was confirmed by the portrayal of Oberon (not, here, doubled with Theseus). Played by Patrick Stewart, clad in a loincloth and reddish-brown body paint, long dreadlocked hair bound by a tight headband, Oberon was a curious composite of racial signifiers, variously described as 'a dusky faun, loin-clothed and combining the attributes of a Greek athlete and a Hindu temple dancer' (Wardle 1977), 'lithe and muscular, bird-faced like the Quetzal the Aztecs worshipped' (O'Connor 1977), 'a fugitive from *Royal Hunt of the Sun* or *Tarzan of the Apes* ('RNC' 1977), and 'a magnificent Indian Brave' (Lloyd Evans 1977), who had 'just strayed off the set of *Bury My Heart at Wounded Knee*' ('VJD' 1977). What is significant about these responses, in addition to their apparently gratuitous, geographically arbitrary and queasily fetishistic positioning of the racial other, is that they were articulated in the historic context of a Britain whose experience of post-imperial immigration was rapidly transforming both political discourse and cultural practice. By putting a white actor with what *The Observer* called 'a considerable flair for the exotic' in full-body quasi-blackface at the centre of his production (which costumed the courtiers all in white, like Elizabethan cricketers), Barton seemed to be calling attention to contemporary racial anxieties without quite knowing why (or even that) he was doing so.

We shadows

This was not the first time Barton had played with racial stereotyping on the Stratford stage, but it would prove increasingly difficult to do so in the future, and in this respect, the British culture of *Dream* performance after Barton participated in changes in the wider culture of raced Shakespearean performance, as manifested at the RSC by, for example, the end of the practice of playing *Othello* in blackface (Donald Sinden was the last twentieth-century actor to do this at Stratford, in 1979), and the adoption of integrated and colour-blind casting policies, starting with the casting of Hugh Quarshie as Hostpur in the 1982 *Henry IV* (Daileader 2000). Throughout the 1980s and 1990s, the *Dream* figured in English theatre as a play where race, according to the liberal utopianism of colour-blind casting, could be both visible and unmarked; operating within a stylistic context dominated by the retro-aesthetics of post-modern pastiche, the non-white performer could find him or herself deployed to more or less pointed effect alongside production choices which left other aspects of racial representation curiously unproblematized.[2]

The casting of black actor Nikki Amuka-Bird as Helena in the 2002 RSC *Dream* was not read by the reviewers as particularly pointed.[3] And yet, ironically, this was an emphatically – and for most critics, relentlessly – colour-coded production, designed (like so many previous productions at Stratford and elsewhere) both to invoke Brook's scenography and to invert it. Quoting Freud in the programme ('At bottom, dreams are nothing other than a particular form of thinking'), the show's *mise en scène* suggested a monochrome realm of international avant-gardist performance and art cinema: within a Brook-homage white box set, the lovers, costumed in white, shed their clothes in the third act to reveal white and off-white designer underwear (which, Dyer observes, has assumed an iconic significance in contemporary consumer culture by focusing the white body's purity, integrity and cleanliness [1997: 76–7]); the fairies, a close-knit Complicite-Le Coq physical theatre ensemble in rehearsal blacks, were given to co-ordinated hissing, tics, twitches and mime gestures alternating between the extravagant and the microscopic, and led by a bare-chested Puck 'with black trousers melding into his body paint' (Coveney 2002); throughout the entirety of the forest scenes a single black-clad actor stood, with Noh-like discipline, motionless centre stage, sporting a headpiece of stunted and tangled branches, briefly coming to life in 3.2 to attempt to grope the hapless Hermia. Jones and Cadle's white box décor is as liable as Brook's to the charge that it presumes as neutral ground a whiteness grounded in 'a system of thought and affect whereby white people are both particular and nothing in particular, are both something and nothing'; we might also note that the deployment of a monochrome scheme directly derived from classic cinematography draws upon a representational system which has, historically, served to construct and privilege white identity, endlessly reiterating 'the assumption that the normal face is a white face' (Dyer 1997: 47, 94).

Rather than pursuing the implications of these observations here, however, we can record that the imposition of the black and white scheme, characterized by a number of critics as a form of directorial totalitarianism, not only dehumanized the play but also delocalized it. Although the passage from forest back to Athens at the end of the fourth act was marked by insects turning to butterflies, birdsong, and the distant tolling of village church bells, this *Dream* was positioned in an indeterminate cultural space, which, wherever it was, certainly wasn't England. And in this respect, it is possible to read the studied weightlessness of the scenography as very precisely attuned to its conditions of articulation, appropriate to a production designed for a national (and limited international) touring circuit, in accordance with the RSC's millennial role as peripatetic national theatre. When it opened at Stratford, newspaper reviewers heavily criticized what they saw as art-house perversity, elitism and pretentiousness ('As a flagship production, which is going on a major regional tour, it is a disgrace, the kind of smug, knowingly perverse show which will leave audiences feeling angry, stupid or ripped off' [Spencer 2002]), but by the time it reached London's Barbican Theatre in London at the end of April, it was evident to more than one reviewer that the show's style drew on an internationalized media vocabulary that unsettled convenient divisions between high-concept art and junk culture; and, as far as its target audiences (weaned on Branagh and Luhrmann rather than Brook) were concerned, very readable indeed.

At Stratford, reviewers had glumly documented the show's reference points in contemporary popular – and youth – culture, including 'the Gossard and Calvin Klein underwear show' (Coveney 2002), a Titania 'resembling a debauched Hamburg night-club queen' (Billington 2002) and (along with Oberon) 'washed up Seventies rock stars in urgent need of a trip to the rehab clinic' (Spencer 2002), and 'scruffy and loutish' fairies, 'like teenage thugs trying to imitate Slipknot' (Peter 2002a). But it was the production's embrace of the cinematic American gothic mode of the modern horror movie that provoked most comment – and that marked it, for all its apparent idiosyncrasies, both as a representative instance of RSC post-modernism and as symptomatic of the current configuration of the English national Shakespeare. The range of cinematic intertexts baffled the high art/low art divide, combining popcorn and arthouse (*Friday the Thirteenth, A Nightmare on Elm Street, Halloween, Edward Scissorhands, Repulsion, The Addams Family, Nosferatu, The Evil Dead*); operating in the placeless eternal present of Americanized media culture, it also virtually eradicated England and Englishness as reference points. And it was this tactic of disaffiliation, so irksome to the first-night reviewers, which appealed to 'the teenage school groups' who were observed by one London critic during the interval 'giggling … re-enacting their favourite bits of rudery' (Thaxter 2002), and by another as 'bewitched … start[ing] out giggling in all the wrong places and finish[ing] up captivated and laughing at the right ones', and who at the end 'gave it a hearty cheer, which it richly deserved' (Espiner 2002).

If English culture was a subordinate element in this production, it retained a small but telling presence in the treatment of the mechanicals; symptomatically, this production's version of Englishness was framed in its mobilization of the contemporary comic archetype of the average white guy as loser. An oddball blend, remarked one critic, of 'Soviet convicts and British hikers' (Nightingale 2002), Peter Quince's men planned the rehearsals of *Pyramus and Thisbe* while sitting on a bench of a third-class railway compartment, telegraph poles whizzing past behind frosted glass. Emphatically internationalist elsewhere, the show was in this aspect at its most defiantly parochial, and in its citation of a more localized order of media reference, its most opaque. Here was a crew of klutzes, nerds and misfits, with thick horn-rimmed specs, poor dentistry, badly fitting suits and daft hats (beret, knitted cap, trilby) a parade of icons of comic failure drawn from the Ealing Comedies, the *Carry On* and *Confessions* films, and 1960s and 1970s British television situation comedy: Benny from *Crossroads*, Michael Crawford's Frank Spencer (figures familiar from one of the prime cultural zones of loserdom, nostalgia-channel cable TV). As Bottom, Darrell D'Silva, reminded the *Independent*'s critic of cricket commentator Fred Trueman (Myerson 2002), but with his loud checked jacket, bad hair, concertedly fastidious delivery and perpetual air of wounded superiority, he was also a note for note copy of the classic petit-bourgeois, perpetually disappointed, little England aesthete, Tony Hancock. Translated, he acquired a grotesque slasher-movie warty grey mask with elongated Mr Spock ears, simultaneously suggesting an ass, a pig and *A Nightmare on Elm Street*'s Freddie Kruger. Like the lovers, he was stripped to his underwear for his sex scene, but, in contrast to the athletically sexy chic of their detergent-white Calvin Kleins, he was a paunchy figure in saggy off-white Y-fronts, a knee bandage, school shoes and grey socks, a hopeless dancer mauled by a mascara'd Titania, sucking and pulling vigorously at his ears while accompanied by a derisive, choric farmyard cacophony of animal noises, snorts and cockerel cries. This was the stuff of pornographic nightmare, a gross-out comedy of wretchedness, humiliation and failure. It was also a departure from what has become a standard feature of English productions since Brook, the treatment of the Bottom–Titania liaison as a Lady Chatterley-style fantasy of sex across class boundaries. Often, the combination of sexual frankness and the sympathetic handling of the mechanicals as serious and committed artisans, who are eventually afforded a certain dignity in the labour of performance, has led to the invest-ment in Bottom of a fabulous sexual potency (iconically depicted in the famous shot of the actor's fist punching between David Waller's thighs in the Brook production, which is generally read for its festive celebration rather than its sexual aggression): equipped with the mythical phallic bravado of the white English working-class male, as seen from the main stage at Stratford, he is usually more than capable of seeing to the needs of an upper-class fairy queen. In the place of a distinctively English sexual fantasy, and one of the few components of the national mythology that is conventionally neither interna-tionalized nor treated ironically (we may have lost an empire, but not yet our capacity to please the ladies), this was an altogether limper sex comedy, haunted by the pathos of an Englishness identified in terms of disappointment, false hopes and inevitable failure.

No place like home

The 2002 Globe *Dream* opened on 5 June, the Wednesday following the Bank Holiday weekend that marked the climax of the Royal Golden Jubilee celebrations. A 'modern practices' production, this set the action in the world of bedtime and slumber, which began with pyjama-clad actors settling down under duvets 'for a good night's sleep', coming to life like somnabulists as they made their entrances into the play; and all props derived from the bedroom and bathroom, so that Lysander and Demetrius duelled with the extended aerials of miniature radios, Puck's magical flower was fashioned from tissue paper, Bottom (John Ramm) acquired ass's ears made from a pair of fluffy women's slippers, and a Pyramus beard from hastily applied shaving foam, and Lion's mane was supplied by a bathmat. The improvisational vocabulary suited a production which worked a small cast hard by doubling mechanicals with fairies (a switch effected by the activation of fairy lights embedded in their pyjamas). Most reviewers found the conceptual framework acceptable (if not too rigorous: as one reviewer tartly observed, '"sleep, dream" seems to have been the complex thought process here' [Mountford 2002]), and in keeping with the generally undemanding, consensual spirit of the show. That the aesthetic (like that of the majority of 'modern practices' in Globe productions) worked against the environmental logic of the building accommodating it is obvious, but there was a particular tension here between the sense of the Globe as open space, monumental façade and public forum, and the poignantly everyday, domestic intimacy of the staging. Under the grey skies of the English summer of 2002, the slap of bare feet on boards, the flap of cotton and winceyette, and the prickling of gooseflesh manifested a rare vulnerability in the performers that was all the more marked in a production determined to emphasize its pre-Freudian innocence ('Don't expect ids and egos at play here' [Johns 2002]). Comparing the *mise en scène* to a slumber party, review-ers located the show in the realms of pre-adolescence: the pyjama- game costuming (more *Peter Pan* than Alan Ayckbourn) and larks-in-the-dorm ethos not only de-eroticized the performers and the action but also infantilized them (during the pre-show bedding-down sequence, a performer was glimpsed cuddling a stuffed toy donkey, antic-ipating the transformation of Bottom), and if some reviewers found this 'delightful' (Taylor 2002) or 'amiable and open-hearted' (Gross 2002), others were unimpressed by 'schoolboy jokes' (Peter 2002b) or by a Puck (played by Simon Trinder) projecting 'all the menace of a children's TV presenter' (Cavendish 2002); as Michael Dobson wearily concluded, 'it certainly proved that it is possible to direct all of *A Midsummer Night's*

Dream at the mentality of a twelve-year-old boy, but it seems a bit of a waste to do so' (2003: 264).

By positioning the play in a childhood world that attempted to be as warm, inclusive and innocent as the RSC version was cool, dark and self-consciously adult, the Globe *Dream* reflected the predominant values of its institutional location, of course; but it can also be read as a – largely defensive – response to its cultural moment. The flavour of the *unheimlich* so evident in Jones' production was replaced here by an emphasis on the child as, in a multiple sense, an emblem of unworldliness. The pyjamas and duvets, and the mundane props of everyday intimacy, might have been variously seen as charming, banal or puerile, but they were unmistakably, and nostalgically, English ('mostly of the early-1960s Marks & Spencer style', or 'Selfridges, circa 1970' [Peter 2002b]); moreover, in its homely repudiation of the post-modern ethos of placelessness that has shaped *Dream* performance for a quarter of a century, the show referenced the familial and the domestic, the mythical, securely bordered space of originary safety, which, Gaston Bachelard has proposed, provides our most enduring psychic structure, and which he characterizes as the maternal memory zone of the house, whereby 'through dreams, the various dwelling-places of our lives co-penetrate and retain the treasures of former days...we live fixations, fixations of happiness. We comfort ourselves by reliving memories of protection' (1994: 5–6). Amidst the general anxiety generated by the events of 9/11 and its aftermath, which had not only brutally revealed the less benign aspects of globalization but also severely tested the claims of contemporary multiculturalism, this *Dream*'s dive beneath the homeland security of the comfort-blanket should not surprise us. And, sadly perhaps, it is not likely to persuade us either: inadvertently, the open-air setting (which allows the intrusion into its acoustic space of jet planes, now all too obviously capable of being turned into bombs) reveal the vulnerability of props and bodies, emphasizing the fragility of their offer to cradle memories of childhood and home; even less intentionally, the very image of a supposedly inviolable interior world turned inside out, the contents of the bedroom and bathroom disgorged into the streets, is shadowed by modern media memories of the effects of war and terror, of the death of innocence as the heart of the home is explosively ripped out, exposed and desecrated.

In terms of the *longue durée* of British *Dream* performance, the 2002 RSC and Globe productions will doubtless soon count as little more than minor contributions to a production tradition that, at the beginning of the twenty-first century, still operates within a formal dialectic whose thesis was established in the nineteenth century and antithesis in the final quarter of the twentieth; geared respectively towards the demands of a small-scale national tour and an international summer tourist season, these were in their own ways localized instances of a national cultural investment in a play which continues to act as both testing ground and safe haven for hopes and fears of belonging and exclusion, and for fantasies of incorporation, integration and transformation. Viewed from outside the English theatrical and cultural context, these productions, and perhaps the larger history of which they form a part, may themselves seem like examples of what Sonia Massai in the Introduction to this volume aptly refers to as local appropriations. If so, this account might be considered as making a modest contribution to the work of, as Ania Loomba and Martin Orkin put it, 'provincialising Europe' (1998: 19). Divergent as they were in terms of style, context, tone and mood, the productions' chief claim to representativeness lay in a common nexus of national sentiment characterized by thwarted hopes, disappointment, shame and failure, and in this respect they articulated some of the current ambivalences of being English. As a comic resolution of the prolonged mourning that has accompanied the end of empire, the occupation of the space of the loser (whose icon in this play is Nick Bottom himself) yet proves a pragmatic, perhaps ultimately constructive, response to the waning of the influence and prestige of the British nation-state. One way or another, it seems that the English *Dream* could be about to enter one of its more uncertain, but also more interesting, phases.

15 The cultural logic of 'correcting' *The Merchant of Venice*

Maria Jones

Reviewing Shakespeare on stage in 1993, Alan C. Dessen (1994: 6) referred to the 'devious' and 'suspect' route by which the Royal Shakespeare Company's production, directed by David Thacker, achieved a more sympathetic portrait of Shylock, in part by 'the major rewriting' of 3.1.[1] Dessen remarked that the director 'took the refashioning of Shylock farther than any other production I have ever seen'. When the play was performed at the Barbican in London, the *Guardian* critic, Claire Armitstead chaired a discussion between the playwright, Arnold Wesker and the RSC director. Wesker (Armitstead 1994) argued that his own strategy of writing a new play, *The Merchant* (in stages of rewriting and production between 1976 and 1978, and later called *Shylock*) was 'a more honest approach to the problems than rejigging and imposing on the play'. His play appealed to questions of historical record in order to *correct* the stereotyped account of Jews and Jewish history that he found in Shakespeare's play. My essay examines the influence of local contexts on our understanding of what constitutes a 'genuinely Shakespearean' appropriation of *The Merchant of Venice* and the geo-politics of Thacker's heavily cut production of *The Merchant of Venice* at Stratford-upon-Avon and London, and the British premiere of Wesker's play at Birmingham.

Thacker's 'rejigging' began in Act 1, significantly by having Tubal (Nick Simons) present when Shylock (David Calder) agreed the bond with Antonio (Clifford Rose). His presence as a skull-capped rabbinical scholar contrasted with a Shylock in shirt-sleeves and fashionable bracers, working on a laptop computer. Benedict Nightingale commented in *The Times* that Shelagh Keegan's split-level set of 'steel stairs, walkways and vast slanting tubes', was 'hardly a Venice of gondolas and guitars or, for that matter, palazzos and Doges'. This Shylock looked at ease in a high-tech world of computers, mobile 'phones, faxes and credit cards. The contemporary context could make little sense of Shylock's historic hatred of Christians so Tubal supplied a cultural memory of Judaic tradition. Shakespeare's play did not have Tubal in this scene and the device opened up a divide that would widen between a historicized Judaic tradition and Shylock's eventual misconceived path of 'Jewish' vengeance. Peter Holland (1994: 197) commented on Thacker's 'careful use of Tubal to place and define the audience's attitude to Shylock'. In effect, Thacker gave Shylock an *alter ego* who would prevent the stage villain from becoming synonymous with the representative Jew. Tubal stood in as the true representative Jew who expressed horror when Shylock manifested increased signs of maniacal revenge, associated with a stereotyped 'Jewishness'. This was a clever way of having Shylock and not having Shylock. Individual psychology – his treatment by bigots and the loss of his daughter – would explain his ill-chosen path, while theatre audiences would be helped to sympathize with Shylock, while accepting the law's judgement as morally right.

The production established Shylock as a private, cultured man who enjoyed quiet moments at home, sitting in a smoking jacket, listening to classical music and thinking of his wife, Leah. At work, he succeeded by seeking a strategy of co-existence, evidenced in his ability to make jokes at his own expense, assuming a mock 'Yiddish' accent with business associates. However, 'co-existence' was always threatened by less overt forms of prejudice, simmering under the surface. David Calder commented of the role:

> You can't do the play that is on the page. It has attitudes of its time which are not acceptable today. You have to look at the nature of intolerance. The play contains an historical intolerance which Shylock experiences. It is the intolerance of the society in which he lives. In our 1993 version it is not so overt. It is a more insidious racial prejudice.
>
> (RSC Education 1993: 12)

Calder and Thacker (RSC Education 1993: 11) agreed that Shakespeare's play had unacceptable 'attitudes of its time' that would need to be cut, and both were anxious that the character of Shylock should not 'be handicapped from the start by the hidden agenda of a man who was vengeful and harbouring grudges'. By cutting the line, 'If I can catch him once upon the hip,/I will feed fat the ancient grudge I bear him' (1.3.43–4), they removed any evidence that might suggest premeditated murder.[2] Thacker (RSC Education 1993: 11) commented that he 'needed an actor who would accommodate cuts or alterations for the success of the production as the play that is on the page had to be looked at in great and sensitive detail'. Although directors have often cut offensive lines to soften our view of Shylock, the changes to 3.1, notably a reversal of the two halves of the scene, produced far-reaching effects.

The scene began as usual with Salerio and Solanio discussing Antonio's misfortune, thus imparting the news to the theatre audience. However, Shylock entered as at line 75, greeting Tubal with desperate pleas for information about Jessica, 'Hast thou found my daughter?' The effect of Shylock's immediate callous reaction to Antonio's losses, 'Let him look to his bond' (1.44) was therefore removed at this point. In the exchanges with Tubal, the repeated references to his 'ducats', 'jewels' and 'gold' were cut. On hearing of Antonio's losses, Shylock's reaction 'I will have the heart of him if he forfeit' (116–7) sounded like misjudged bravado and this was immediately checked by Tubal. The prompt book indicates that Tubal 'stands' at the word 'forfeit', turns back to look at Shylock at the word 'synagogue' before exiting on the second reference to 'synagogue'.[3] By cutting the previous line, 'go Tubal, fee me an officer, bespeak him a fortnight before' (115–6), the production partly steered thoughts away from the execution of the law relating to the bond. Given the emphasis on Jessica, Shylock could have been seeking spiritual consolation and community support at the synagogue. On Tubal's exit, the rearranged scene brought Solanio and Salerio to taunt him. Shylock's outburst, 'You knew, none so well, none so well as you, of my daughter's flight' (lines 22–3) reinforced the idea that Shylock's key concern was for Jessica. The changed effect of this can be compared with the usual sequence of the scene, which ends with Shylock's unfeeling response:

TUBAL: But Antonio is certainly undone.
SHYLOCK: Nay, that's true, that's very true. Go, Tubal, fee me an officer. Bespeak him
a fortnight before. I will have the heart of him if he forfeit, for were he out of
Venice I can make what merchandise I will. Go, Tubal, and meet me at our synagogue. Go, good Tubal; at our synagogue, Tubal.

(3.1.117–23)

Here, Shylock's hasty decision to have Antonio arrested changes the effect of the reference to '*our* synagogue', possibly implicating Tubal in Shylock's desire to make a ritual-
istic oath of vengeance.

In Thacker's production, Solanio and Salerio baited Shylock at his emotional low
point. Distressed at the loss of Leah's ring, he rounded on them, 'You knew, none so
well, none so well as you, of my daughter's flight' (23–4). When Salerio repeated the
rumours of Antonio's losses, Shylock's line, 'Let him look to his bond' took on a different emphasis. The production positioned the 'Hath not a Jew eyes?' speech at line 50
just before the interval. Shylock's final line, 'The villainy you teach me I will execute,
and it shall go hard but I will better the instruction' (65–6) suggested the remorseless
path now taken. As Shylock took on the mantle of a stereotyped 'Jewishness', he and
Tubal would part company. Peter Holland (1994: 196) commented:

> I have always preferred to believe that *The Merchant of Venice* is not anti-semitic but
> directors have usually lacked the perceptive ability to show how it is not. Thacker's
> production was the most coherent and convincing demonstration that the play
> need not be.

Arnold Wesker (1997: xvi) agrees that 'it was not that Shakespeare's *intentions* were anti-
Semitic. Not at all. His genius is a generous one. But the *effects* were anti-Semitic'.
However, it can be argued that 'the most coherent and convincing demonstration' of
this was made possible only by 'rejigging and imposing upon the play'. The problem
with Thacker's version for Wesker was not that it didn't work. Most patently, it did – but
that it was dishonest. It claimed to be Shakespeare's play while deliberately misremembering
the original text. This is not an argument about failing to be faithful to an original play
but conversely, about seeking to hide the historical record of the cultural transmission
and the bad effects it can produce. The play is frequently performed, and the performance will (unless the director is careful) create a stage villain and an audience primed to
laugh at his come-uppance.

Thacker's production was careful to humanize Shylock, and, through the imaginative
use of Tubal, to suggest that Shylock was a good man who had sadly pursued his own path
to destruction. In the trial scene the modern-day businessman was costumed in a gabar-
dine suit, yarmulke and 'Star of David' pendant. However, Tubal's growing disapproval
of Shylock alerted the theatre audience to view the guise of Judaic tradition as wilful
misuse. Nevertheless, such was the powerful effect of the first half of the production
that playgoers might understand and forgive this Shylock. A terrifying trial scene
brought a climactic moment when Shylock drew a line around the heart of Antonio
(Clifford Rose) with a felt pen. Portia (Penny Downie) was decisive and relentless in her

legal pursuit of the 'alien' Jew who had conspired against the state. Towards the end of the trial scene, Shylock was knocked to the ground. Left on his own, he drew himself up by clutching the chair that, moments earlier, held a shaking Antonio. Shylock pulled himself round and turned abruptly to confront the audience. The moment was held before the lights dimmed bringing spontaneous applause. In an article in *The Sunday Times* (1993), Wesker argues:

> Anti-Semites feel comfortable with Shylock because he conforms to the myth they love and to help assuage any guilt they might be experiencing while watching the play, he is given lines of redemption. An audience can breathe freely as he utters his apologia. They can feel merciful and generous while enjoying their cherished image of the cruel Jew.

Wesker criticizes the play's strategy of humanizing Shylock through the famous 'Hath not a Jew eyes' speech and attacks the sentiments in this speech in his own play. He asserts: 'Jews do not want apologies to be made for their humanity ... Their humanity is their right' (Wesker 1993). Thacker (Armitstead 1994) defended his production on the ground that it tackled contemporary anti-Semitism:

> I wasn't interested in some academic exercise in trying to turn a play that I thought was dodgy into a production that I thought was good. It was born out of a passionate desire to put this event on the stage in relation to what I perceive to be our needs of the moment. The rise in anti-Semitism is an issue which is resurging in a very dangerous way.

However, Wesker's counter-argument (Armitstead 1994) suggests that Thacker's contemporary slant is guilty of erasing history: 'A young audience who may not know what the Holocaust is would not know that the Holocaust happened from your production'. In Wesker's argument the 'Holocaust' functions as part of what Hodgdon (1991: 3) refers to as part of a 'larger intertext', that is, a dialogue between the original play text and textuality past and present. Wesker is arguing that Holocaust knowledge should travel with Shakespeare's play. However, Holocaust knowledge is not an overt feature in Wesker's solution. Instead his 'new' play appeals to a sixteenth-century historical record. Wesker recontextualizes Shylock's Venice and reappropriates it to tell another story, a story featuring actual Jewish history. He gives Shylock a history in the Jewish ghetto of Venice in 1563 and presents him as an enlightened bibliophile whose books are his real treasures. Antonio and Shylock are friends who would gladly loan each other money but are forced to make a ludicrous bond in order to keep within the law.

Sally Aire (1978) reviewed the Birmingham production in *Plays and Players*: 'Wesker has not only created a play in its own right, but has also given us, inevitably, a critique of Shakespeare's.' Aire identifies the exploration of the past from the present and refers to 'topics which we think of as belonging more to the twentieth century (such as Marxism, property, the role of women)', while at the same time noting 'Wesker's exploration of his own Jewish inheritance: an examination of what being a Jew *means*'. As Aire notes, 'Wesker's Shylock shows us the action from inside the ghetto, inside the man, inside the experience of being an *alien*'.

In Wesker's play, Shylock is a 'loan banker' fulfilling a role that is vital to the prosperity of Venice but which gives him little pleasure. Tubal, his business partner, observes:

> Trade is trade and they know it also, and we pay! An annual tribute of twenty thousand ducats; another twenty thousand for renting these squalid walls; fifteen thousand more to the Navy Board – for God knows what; another hundred for the upkeep of the canals, which stink! And, on top of all that, ten thousand more in time of war which, since our beloved and righteous republic seems constantly fighting with someone or other, ensures that sum too as a regular payment. Why, sometimes there's barely pennies in the Ghetto. For days we're all borrowing off each other, till new funds flow in. Only fourteen hundred souls, remember. We're no more than that, trapped in an oppressive circus with three water wells and a proclivity for fires.
>
> (*Shylock*, 1.4)[4]

While Shylock seeks riches from an intellectual life (prizing his books above all), it is his friend Antonio, the merchant, who voices the emptiness of mercantilism:

> Those books. Look at them. How they remind me what I am, what I've done. Nothing! A merchant! A purchaser of this to sell there. A buyer-up and seller-off. And do you know, I hardly ever see my trade. I have an office, a room of ledgers and a table, and behind it I sit and wait till someone comes in to ask have I wool from Spain, cloth from England, cotton from Syria, wine from Crete . . . I travel neither to England to check cloth, nor Syria to check cotton, or Corfu to see that the olive oil is cleanly corked.
>
> (*Shylock*, 1.1)

Wesker places the developments of proto-capitalism in the context of the decline of aristocratic wealth as Portia inherits a neglected estate and purposes to leave behind the 'speculating days' of her father and move into agriculture: 'What an inheritance! Ten estates in ruin, and a foolish philosophic whim for to find me an idiot husband' (1.2). Portia and Shylock are unlikely soulmates in that both read avidly, are survivors and yet are ready for new interests and fresh ideas. Portia describes herself as 'a new woman', telling Nerissa, 'There is a woman on the English throne. Anything can happen' (1.2). In an interview with Stuart Ward, Wesker commented, 'I think that the roles of Portia and Jessica are underplayed in current Shakespearian production. You will notice how we show the strength of Jewish women when you see the play.' In the context of 1970s feminism, Wesker's emphasis on strong, free-thinking women is notable. Portia is not taken in by Bassanio and agrees the match purely in honour of her father. Her feelings are revealed in an exchange with Nerissa:

NERISSA: You should not love someone you don't like.
PORTIA: What a ridiculous carrier of passion – a casket. I'm uncertain all right. What if I should tire of him? . . . Of his vanities and little faults which always, always, magnify with time. He has such a blindness for his image, such an incredible satisfaction with his long-considered thimbleful of thoughts.

> (*Shylock*, 2.1)

Jessica is a strong, educated woman, similarly frustrated by her father's inability to recognize her need for autonomy. She flees with the anti-Semitic Lorenzo but realizes her mistake, refuses to marry him and defends her father: 'You misrepresent the bond. Whatever my father's flaws you know the bond had mockery not malice in it' (2.4). Shylock has an older sister, Rivka, who is not afraid to tell him home truths: 'Mean! Mean! To withhold praise from your daughter, mean' (1.6). Portia's role in the trial scene is not romanticized. She simply comes up with a commonsense idea. Shylock is delighted at the irony of this outcome, 'No blood, no flesh. Oh, Antonio, how could such a simple fact escape us?' (2.5). Finally, it is not Portia but the Doge who spells out 'an old Venetian law' against aliens, and pronounces, 'the State must take your goods' (2.5).

Besides his revision of the female roles, Wesker's radical reworking of Shakespeare's play features two specific areas of concern: the representations of Judaism and Jewish history. In the theatre programme, Wesker explains the genesis of the adaptation:

> The impulse for the play came to him while watching Jonathan Miller's production of the Elizabethan version at the National, London 1973; when Portia announced her interpretation of the bond for a pound of flesh, saying that it couldn't be carried out because the bond didn't call for blood, only flesh, it struck Wesker that the real Shylock would have said "thank God" – he'd been relieved of the burden of taking life which is anathema to Jewish teaching.[5]

Rabbi Gabriel Maza (Wesker 1997: 381) from the Suffolk Jewish Center in New York saw Wesker's production in 1977 and referred to it as 'a logical and brilliant correction', but one that failed at the end 'religiously and dramatically'. It was unclear how a man 'so enlightened and humane', who understood an unequivocal Jewish law, could feel impelled to endanger his friend's life. David Nathan's review in the *Jewish Chronicle* (1978) questioned Shylock's decision to uphold Venetian law in order to safeguard the Jewish community:

> If there is a flaw in the logic of the play it is that Wesker does not explore the possibility of what would happen to the Ghetto Jews if Shylock had been allowed to use the knife. Would the Venetian mob have the same respect for the law as the Venetian patricians? Or rather would they have rampaged through the ghetto as they have done throughout history even on the merest suspicion of Jewish involvement in a Christian death?

Responses to the British premiere, with David Swift in the role of Shylock, were generally positive. Michael Coveney referred in *The Financial Times* (1978) to 'a play of considerable merit'. Reviewers were in broad agreement on the success of the imaginative set designs by Christopher Morley. Nathan describes the 'central, low-walled square bounded by brilliant back projected slides of the Ghetto, the Doge's Palace and Belmont', that located the action both geographically and historically.

Clearly Wesker's re-appropriation of Jewish history was a dominant theme of the play and the issue of appropriation surfaces in some reviews. Robert Thornber confided to readers of *The Guardian* (1978):

I was dreading the British premiere of Arnold Wesker's *The Merchant* at Birmingham Repertory Theatre. Given his track record of passionate commitment to the sufferings and sub culture of his people, a people who are not strangers to racial discrimination, I expected a tedious attempt to rehabilitate those of the Hebrew persuasion and demonstrate that Shylock was really the good guy. But that is not what the play is about.

A reviewer for *Punch* (1978) observed that Wesker had delivered:

A massive teach-in on historical and literary attitudes to the Jews. Thus we have a learned, bookish, academic evening of dispute and discussion which never quite lifts off into a play but which nevertheless I'd not have missed.

The reviewers recognized that Wesker's 'teach-in' started from a *contemporary* view of Jewish history so that Thornber's reference to 'the play's wealth of Renaissance learning', was framed by post-Holocaust understanding. Thus, Shylock's readiness to help sixteenth-century Portuguese Jews flee persecution has a post-Holocaust resonance:

USQUE: An entire family burnt.
REBECCA: Facing each other. [*Silence*]
        But there are survivors. It's to those we must attend. Signor Shylock, we're
          among friends?
SHYLOCK: Everyone, inseparable.

                              (*Shylock*, 1.4)

At a fundamental level, Wesker's adaptation, which was variously described as a 'correction', a 're-write', 'a thoroughly original work' and 'the play that eluded Shakespeare', is an argument about ownership of knowledge.[6] Wesker resists the hegemonic use of Shakespeare's play to tell Jewish history – and insists on retelling the past from the long viewpoint of the present.[7]

I want to conclude by reflecting on Wesker's impression that 'vested interests' prevented his play from being performed in London. Wesker's play received its world premiere at the Royal Dramaten-theater, Stockholm, on 8 October 1976 and its English-speaking premiere at the Plymouth Theater, New York, on 16 November 1977 (Wesker 1990: 184–5). Tragically, Zero Mostel who was originally cast as Shylock died after the first night out of town in Philadelphia on 8 September 1977. After the play's success on Broadway, Wesker attempted to persuade a major London theatre to stage it. The National Theatre turned it down, and Peter Farago, associate director of the Birmingham Repertory Theatre mounted the British premiere on 12 October 1978. Wesker accused major state theatres in London of thwarting his attempts to stage his alternative play. He argued that a perverse adulation of the original text, continued to keep Shakespeare's play in circulation:

The play has been tried, proven, well received. Its subject is an internationally notorious theatrical character; Shylock has a curiosity value, controversy encircles Shakespeare's portrait of this Jew; a British playwright of no mean international reputation has essayed an alternative portrait. Why is there such resistance? I am beginning to suspect it is other than artistic. 'Leave us the Jew,' the theatre establishment seems to be saying, 'we need to be allowed the pleasure of forgiving the Bard's Semitic villain whom we hate. Tamper with him not.'

(Wesker 1997: 358)

David Nathan remarked on 'the many other dimensions' to Wesker's play that 'qualifies it for a wider audience than it will get if it is confined to Birmingham'. After good local and national reviews, Wesker tried again to persuade the National Theatre to stage it in London but without success.

As other contributors to this volume have laboured to show, 'locality' is a complex cultural construct that exceeds mere geographical boundaries. As Doreen Massey (1995: 134) argues, 'the identities of places are a product of social actions' and there may be 'rival claims to define the meaning of places'. The Royal Shakespeare Company's 'home' is Stratford-upon-Avon but, arguably, it is not really a local or regional theatre. Colin Chambers (2004: 171) has remarked on the fact that Stratford 'did not have an audience drawn from the local community with whom the theatre could build a relationship'. Historically, the Royal Shakespeare Company and the National Theatre have often been described as dominant and hegemonic institutions.

Accordingly, when Chambers (1978) reviewed Wesker's play for *The Morning Star*, he observed that the Birmingham Rep had 'rushed in where National Theatre angels feared to tread'. His remark suggested the triumph of regional independence over national hegemony. However, the role of the Birmingham Rep in bringing Wesker's play to British audiences is a contradictory one. The play is not about local or regional Jews in Birmingham. It is a play that is both autonomous and is also dependent on there being a play by Shakespeare of canonical status, which it critiques. The Rep staged Wesker's *Roots* in 1961 and invited the playwright to bring *The Merchant* to Birmingham, in keeping with the theatre's reputation for staging exciting new work from contemporary writers. In a sense, the Birmingham Rep claimed a 'thirdspace' identity, taking the lead on behalf of the nation in staging a radical but marginalized play.[8] This is a position that the National Theatre claims currently. Jude Kelly, former artistic director of the West Yorkshire Playhouse argues that Nick Hytner, artistic director, 'is forcing The National to consider how ideology relates to contemporary theatre-making':

It's no longer about having only one beacon that everyone flocks to, it's about creating many beacons – British artists shaping a landscape of alliances and oppositions that will lead us into the future.

(Costa 2004: 5)

In October 1989, Wesker (1997: 358) invited commercial producers and artistic directors of subsidized theatres to a workshop production at The Riverside Studios in London, with Oded Teomi, from Israel, as Shylock. He hoped the workshop might create enthusiasm for a full-scale production, but he was disappointed. Wesker recalls, 'the critics were impressed' with the play, one of them remarking that it would be 'a travesty if it does not reach the West End stage'. Perhaps, there is still time.

Part Three

Local Shakespeares for international audiences

16 Dancing with art: Robert Lepage's *Elsinore*

Margaret Jane Kidnie

Shakespeare's drama has long functioned as an import/export commodity, and a volume entitled *World-wide Shakespeares* raises the question of how one might understand the politics of such an exchange within and across geographical and cultural borders. In the case of *Elsinore*, a one-man production of *Hamlet* devised and directed by the Québécois actor–director, Robert Lepage, familiar models of subversion, appropriation, hybridization and dialogic interaction seem unable to capture, quite, this show's peculiar engagement with the canon. It is difficult, for example, to see how *Elsinore* 'writes back' to Shakespeare, nor does Lepage appropriate *Hamlet* to speak to a national or ideological agenda. The production does not draw on local or intercultural theatre traditions in the manner of a Peter Brook or Ariane Mnouchkine, and one struggles to identify anything about the performance style of *Elsinore* recognizably French-Canadian, or even Canadian (whatever that might be). A one-man show, realized in its earliest touring life by Lepage himself – a white French-Canadian man speaking the lines, when performed in English, with an assumed British accent – *Elsinore* does not even incorporate the sort of linguistic, racial and ethnic multivalences so fundamental to the interpretation of other Lepage productions such as *Tectonic Plates* or *A Midsummer Night's Dream* (Hunt 1989: 111–17; Hodgdon 1996: 68–91). And yet *Elsinore* undoubtedly constitutes a 'world-wide' Shakespeare event, not just from an Anglocentric perspective that marks the show's origin in a nation other than Britain, the home of Shakespeare, but also from a Canadian perspective that notes that the vast majority of the show's dates (twenty-three out of twenty-nine, not including a cancelled Edinburgh engagement) were scheduled for venues outside of Canada. Is home something Shakespeare returns *to*, or that Lepage departs *from*? Or is the idea of 'local' best represented by a set of relations that exceeds both Britain and Canada?

The production was devised at La Caserne Dalhousie, the multi-media creative centre built in Québec City for Lepage and his company, Ex Machina. As Ric Knowles reminds us, however, this laboratory lacks a full-scale performance space; perhaps for this reason, despite Lepage's French-Canadian base, 'no reviewer has noticed … *any* immediate social or cultural signification' to his treatment of *Hamlet* (1998a: 205). *Elseneur*, the French language version, premiered in Montréal in November, 1995, before transferring to Québec City, and then to Sherbrooke in December; the English language version, *Elsinore*, was the one most often staged over the next two years at theatres in Toronto and Ottawa, the United States, Britain and continental Europe. Paradoxically, the idea of 'local' in such a mobile geographical context breaks free of national boundaries associated with author (Shakespeare) or auteur (Lepage) to attach itself instead to the particular *locales* at which *Elseneur*/*Elsinore* played during the course of its international tour. Jennifer Harvie and Erin Hurley, attending to the financial circumstances imposed by Ex Machina's touring mandate, perceptively argue that 'world-wide', in this context, 'is more accurately Western, Northern, and metropolitan': 'Ex Machina's shows may travel extensively…but the destinations of their pilgrimages are remarkably homogeneous: major metropolitan international festivals, mainly in Europe' (1999: 307–8). To try to interpret *Elsinore* as rehearsing a post-colonial dynamic between (French-Canadian) margin and (British) centre would be to neglect the peculiar and rarified tension between 'international' and 'local' that lies at the heart of this production. Lepage's one-man version of *Hamlet* can be read as an innovative engagement with Shakespeare, not because it was a peculiarly Canadian rendering of a – perhaps *the* – classic British drama, but because of the way it played with the ability of privileged, even élite, North American and European audiences simultaneously to recognize, and fail to recognize, this most canonical of plays.

   Studying Lepage's devised pieces involves some of the same textual uncertainties associated with Shakespeare's drama. What is it that we call *Hamlet*? The text as printed in the Folio of 1623(F), the second quarto of 1604(Q2), or the early, so-called 'bad' quarto of 1603(Q1)? Or does our idea of Shakespeare's play somehow extend beyond its earliest surviving documentary witnesses to include, for example, landmark theatrical interpretations, portraiture, even comic books?[1] While *Elsinore* lacks the multiple textual and theatrical layers that have attached themselves to *Hamlet* over the course of four hundred years, Lepage's insistence that theatre is a process of play – always evolving in response to input offered by collaborators and spectators – makes it likewise difficult to locate a fixed script behind *Elsinore*. In its earliest form, the performance had a running time of three hours (Donnelly 1995); by the time it reached London, England, it was half the length; when it toured to the Brooklyn Academy of Art in New York a year later with Peter Darling, rather than Lepage, at its centre, the sequence of the scenes (and some of the stage business) had been rearranged yet again. Tellingly, the script of *Elsinore* printed in *Canadian Theatre Review* as the 'revised' Darling version is the script as performed in Ottawa in September 1997; as scripts and recordings archived at Ex Machina indicate, the opening scenes had been rearranged yet again by the time *Elsinore* arrived to New York the following month, the show no longer opening with the 'To be or not to be' soliloquy (Lepage 2002: 89–99). A conception of theatre as a never-completed work in progress, fundamental to Lepage's dramaturgy, is particularly relevant to a treatment of *Hamlet* which he describes in his 'Director's Note' as 'a sketch', a 'solo show based on themes from *Hamlet*' (Lepage 1997).[2] Textual instability comes as standard with Lepage's theatrical creations, even when talking about pieces such as *Elsinore* based on literary drama, and therefore to analyse the production is necessarily to focus on one or more synchronic moments in its life in the theatre. This chapter will consider the dynamic between international and local, performance and audience in relation to one stage in the touring schedule of *Elsinore*, its run at London's Royal National Theatre (4–11 January 1997). My concern is to understand better the contribution this production of *Hamlet* made to an ongoing debate about Shakespeare, performance, and the canon in a global context.

   London spectators entered the Lyttleton Theatre to see three contiguous floor-to-ceiling screens, onto which was projected an image of the night sky. The show opened with the faint sound of howling wind. An impassive male voice, accompanied in the darkened theatre by a vibrating blue sound wave projected onto the screens on either side of the central screen, began speaking:

> The castle at Elsinore. A platform before the battlements. Enter Hamlet. The air bites shrewdly. It is very cold. It is a nipping and an eager air. What hour now? Horatio. I think it lacks of twelve. [*Bell tolls.*] No, 'tis struck. [*Central screen rises into flies.*] It then draws near the season wherein the spirit held his walk. Look, my Lord, it comes! Enter Ghost. Ghost. I am thy father's spirit …

As the disembodied voice began to deliver the Ghost's message of murder and revenge, a white spot picked out a golden breastplate of armour fixed to the middle of a wall, now positioned in place of the central screen. With the final lines of the scene ('Exit Ghost. Exit Hamlet'), the wall was lowered backwards to the floor. When it slowly returned to the vertical, one discerned a central aperture resembling a doorway in which was suspended a figure seated in a throne. Chic in a pair of sunglasses, and framed in a projected playing-card border that alternated between the King of Spades and Queen of Hearts, Lepage played Claudius and Gertrude welcoming Rosencrantz and Guildenstern. His voice was electronically modified to distinguish between the two roles, a shift further underscored by body movement and gesture. When the courtiers (inferred, not seen) were sent to seek out Hamlet, the wall fell back again, descending around the still seated Lepage, to form a level platform. As Robert Caux's music swelled, the wall, now detached from the throne and with the doorway closed off, rose to meet the two side screens. Onto this flat expanse was projected the impassive bricks of the castle's exterior, production credits on the left and right screens, and the title 'ELSINORE'.

Projected images, electronically rendered voice and sound effects, doubling techniques, and an ever-transforming machine at the centre of the stage foregrounded, meta-theatrically, the play's non-representational staging. One's absorption in plot and character was at best intermittent, checked by a constant awareness of technological process as the wall/floor/ceiling on and around which Lepage moved was raised, lowered, and revolved. British audiences had been primed for a hi-tech *Hamlet* not just through familiarity with Lepage and his oeuvre (this was his fourth production in seven years staged at the National), but also by the huge advance publicity generated by the non-appearance of *Elsinore* at the Edinburgh Festival the previous August due to a faulty rivet.[3] If London theatre-goers knew nothing else about the show, they knew about its set: the machine at the heart of the performance that had failed, spectacularly, five months earlier at an estimated cost of £100,000 in lost revenue.[4] A rhetorical opposition between spectacle and text evident in media coverage at that time – that a definition of theatre as 'two planks and a passion' is betrayed when 'computerised sets and electronic wonders' take over from 'living actors delivering the words, sometimes the music, of human writers' – became even more entrenched after the London press night (Spencer 1996b). Reviewers complained that *Elsinore's* one-hundred minute treatment of *Hamlet* foregrounded Lepage's spectacle at the expense of Shakespeare's words. Michael Billington, who saw the production in Oslo before it arrived in Britain, argued in *The Guardian* that this 'hi-tech version of *Hamlet* reduces the play to a box of tricks in which the human dilemma is upstaged by LePage's [*sic*] visual ingenuity … Text is subordinated to image, idea to effect and the chemistry of interplay between actors to the faint narcissism of solo display' (1996). Alastair Macaulay for *The Financial Times* lamented that 'the poor old Danish play has been skewered, laid out on the slab, cut up, reordered, and turned into a flashy one-man show, a cold array of theatrical effects' (1997).

These reviews criticize Lepage's 'images' as self-indulgent showmanship; spectacle has its place in Shakespearean theatre, but only if it is in the service of the words, and not the other way around. Ironically, a tension between text and visuals was likewise a concern for Lepage. In conversation with Andy Lavender, he comments that

> I'm a bit burdened by people coming to see Lepage play Hamlet – and of course there's absolutely no interest in seeing me perform Hamlet. What's interesting is to see how I cut up the story and devised theatrics out of that [...] how does it change the story, how does it bring insight to some parts of the story? So it's ... an experiment.
>
> (Lavender 2001: 108)

An experiment in story-telling, then, in two distinct parts: script and theatrics. The controversy and media attention in Britain surrounding Lepage's technological 'boldness' obscured a significant part of what he himself considers interesting about the play, 'how [he] cut up the story' (Curtis 1997). Christopher Innes, in a thoughtful discussion of Lepage's complex links to mainstream and alternative theatre, argues that *Elsinore* is '[d]irectly comparable' to Charles Marowitz's 'Collage Hamlet' (1996: 67). While comparisons are perhaps available in terms of running time, or the challenge to expectations these two performances of *Hamlet* presented to their respective spectators, *Elsinore* is anything but a collage. It cuts lines, and sometimes whole scenes, but the overall shape of the story played in London offered only minor disruptions to the sequential action of Q2 and F *Hamlet*.[5] Indeed, what surprises about the way Lepage shaped the script is not the radicalism of what remains, but its utter familiarity.

Polonius' famous precepts to his son were gone, as were his instructions to Reynaldo about how to take a 'carp of truth' with a 'bait of falsehood', yet Lepage's interplay of words and images preserved a view of this senior counsellor as a meddling fool. We first encounter him when he informs the King and Queen that their son is mad for love of Ophelia. Costumed in a heavy robe, wearing glasses and an obviously fake beard attached with a band around the back of the actor's head, Polonius delivers his circumlutory speech all the time trying to keep his balance and position steady while the platform on which he is standing, with an open rectangular trap in the centre, spins beneath him. The image – his character note – is that Polonius endeavours busily to get nowhere. Hamlet's letter, projected in oversized colour behind him, and to which he directs our attention with the aid of a wooden pointer, completes the image of a bustling, pedantic schoolteacher lecturing his silent listeners. The flat platform rises, lifting Polonius with it, to create a wall, leaving the counsellor standing in the open central aperture. As the doorway, previously the trap around which he was stepping, turns counter-clockwise one final time, Polonius 'falls' out of one scene and into the next, where he finds himself looking up at Hamlet's legs, as the prince reads on a ladder in the library.

The production's treatment of Claudius likewise combined an unexceptional interpretation with extraordinary theatrics. The vision of Claudius as a powerful gamesman/politician, suggested by an early visual identification with the King of Spades, was enhanced in his scene with Hamlet after the murder of Polonius. This meeting between prince and king was staged as a confrontation at opposite ends of a table. The effect of dialogue was created by Lepage, seated facing the audience, spinning the table hard through 180 degrees while simultaneously transforming his body language and voice to paint in turn a stern Claudius and ironically bitter Hamlet. The revolving table punctuated the cut and thrust of their exchange, while the playfulness of Lepage's solution to the problem of dialogue in a one-man show intensified a reading of their struggle for power as a tense and deadly game. Spectators were left with this image of male competition as they went into intermission, but returned at the top of the second half to a composite vision of female frailty: Lepage as the Queen incorporating into his/ her narration of Ophelia's 'muddy death' fragments of the young woman's songs. As Gertrude finishes her monologue and sings the first stanza of 'Saint Valentine's day', Lepage removes the Queen's heavy dress to reveal Ophelia's white shift below. Ophelia moves centre stage to lie on a large sheet, bathed in blue light; while the machine, its aperture open (in which empty space she is lying), slowly rises around her, she struggles with the billowing sheet but is finally engulfed by it as the set completes its transformation from floor to wall.

In her four short scenes in *Elsinore*, Ophelia is portrayed as emotionally confused and physically abused. Scene 9 spliced together Ophelia's account to her father of Hamlet's erratic behaviour with Hamlet's verbal attack on her in the 'nunnery' scene, and Lepage shifted fluidly between Ophelia's vulnerability and Hamlet's brutality with the aid of lighting and voice effects. This stunning counterpoint concluded with Ophelia's 'O, what a noble mind' lament, after which she collapsed to the floor. As a swelling, heavily modified, and repetitive electronic treatment of Hamlet's misogynist 'you jig, you amble' speech filled the theatre as a coda to the scene, Lepage slowly stepped away from the female 'dress' (the effect of a dress was created with a dappled screen) to pull on a male shirt in full view of the audience, only then exiting the stage to re-enter as Hamlet. *Elsinore* offered provocative gender shifts within and between scenes, as Ric Knowles has noted (1998b). And yet Lepage's shape-shifting performance also powerfully reinforced a metaphorical reading of Ophelia-the-character, and a literal reading of Ophelia-the-role, as consumed by Hamlet. His presentation of Ophelia, like his portrayal of Polonius and Claudius, combined innovative staging with a conventionalized interpretation of character. Her mimed drowning, in particular, drew on a visual life that has grown up quite apart from Shakespeare's tragedy. Painters such as Arthur Hughes, John Waterhouse, and most famously, John Everett Millais, were fascinated by Ophelia's suicide, interpreting it as an exquisite moment of female fragility, madness, and beauty. Lepage has noted *Elsinore*'s indebtedness to painting, explaining that he became 'interested in this play [*Hamlet*] mainly through people who painted. It's a play that has been painted a lot' (Lavender 2001: 133). Lepage's haunting and solitary death scene thus brought to life in performance a familiar, even iconographic, off-stage moment, with the sight of Ophelia's drowning doubled and tripled through the explicit verbal frame and implicit pictorial allusions provided by Shakespeare's words and Pre-Raphaelite painting.

An attention here to the palimpsest-like quality of *Hamlet* – one's experience of Ophelia's death, in other words, not just as words on a page but as layers of theatrical, interpretive, and cultural history traced one on top of the other – ran throughout *Elsinore*. The narrative introduction, locating the action at 'The castle at Elsinore. A platform before the battlements', rephrases a description of place for 1.1 first introduced by Capell, elaborated on by Malone, and conventional well into the twentieth century

('Elsinore. A platform before the castle'), thus overtly situating *Elsinore* in relation to the sort of mediated and modernized editions through which readers typically come to *Hamlet*.[6] Lepage's treatment of Rosencrantz and Guildenstern was likewise wittily attentive to the stage history of these two bit parts. Simultaneously alluding to their lack of individuating features, and citing a piece of traditional comic business that transfers that inability to distinguish them to Claudius and Gertrude, Lepage's Queen in her first scene pointed the line 'Thanks, *Guildenstern* and gentle *Rosencrantz*' to correct her husband's previous misidentification of the courtiers. Playful echoes of a Stoppard-like identity crisis with respect to Hamlet's schoolfriends might be discerned elsewhere in *Elsinore*. Unlike Fortinbras who – in another example of traditional stage practice – was cut entirely from the play, Rosencrantz and Guildenstern were part of the action, but always 'appeared' off-stage. In the second scene, welcomed to Elsinore by the King and Queen, their silent presence was implicitly located downstage, among the spectators. In the next scene, when they encountered Gertrude's 'too much changèd son', Lepage as Hamlet stood in the doorway in the centre of the wall while live video projections of his head and shoulders captured on fixed cameras stage left and right were fed to the screens on either side of him. The audience had access, in other words, not to the two courtiers, but to how they, separately, saw Hamlet, two slightly different perspectives to which Lepage comically called attention as he turned his head quickly from one friend to the other, seeking, but failing to get, an explanation for their visit.

The way Lepage 'cut up the story' and developed theatrics out of what remained shaped a performance of *Hamlet* as seen through its cultural history; by necessity, this created a conventionalized, even clichéd, interpretation of character and narrative. Reviewers who saw Elsinore at different stages of its development in the theatre note the familiarity of its perspective on *Hamlet*. Ian Shuttleworth, after the Nottingham press night, described the piece as having 'surprisingly little to say about Hamlet', while Lavender, who saw the show in London and witnessed in Québec City the process of rehearsing Peter Darling in the role, comments that 'Hamlet is pictured, still, as the brooding malcontent, Ophelia as the fragile victim of male fantasy. The staging erodes some boundary lines, but still depends upon stereotypical images…which it sustains almost as archetypes' (Shuttleworth 1996; Lavender 2001: 129). Ric Knowles, quipping in his introduction to the published script of *Elsinore* that 'to read the play is to be reminded of the old joke about a student's dismissal of Shakespeare's *Hamlet* itself as nothing but a pastiche of familiar quotations', glances at my argument by tentatively suggesting that 'Lepage in *Elsinore* is less concerned with adapting, interpreting or producing *Hamlet*' than 'in the ways that play's words and iconography have entered contemporary discourse' (2002: 87). *Elsinore* tells a tale of true and betrayed friendships; of troubled relationships to women and sex; of suicide and mortality; of power struggles between men. The direction in which the production developed over the course of its two-year tour, foregrounding Hamlet's trauma and his efforts to trap his uncle, only further strengthened a dominant narrative of filial loss and revenge.[7] Significantly, the final image before Hamlet's death in the New York staging was of the prince erasing his uncle's presence by seeming to wipe clean a floor to ceiling screen on which appeared a frozen still of the dead King's face.

Elsinore, then, is an experiment in deploying innovative theatrical form to convey, not necessarily, and certainly not in their entirety, the words on the page, but the play as it has slowly taken imaginative shape over time in response to a reception history which might embrace, for instance, art, print editions, criticism, stage adaptation, and theatrical performance. To assume that Lepage is playing Hamlet is to misidentify the project; Lepage is playing *Hamlet*. It is not the *character*, but the *play*, the canonical work of art, that is filtered through his solo performance, accompanied by the machine he called the play's other 'dancer' (Glaister 1996). The piece missing from *Elsinore*, however, the gap in Lepage's performance that left spectators unable to find Hamlet in the *Hamlet*, was the effect of interiority. Lepage's voice, filtered through microphones and fed through computers, and delivered in a flat, understated tone with something approaching a Royal Shakespeare Company, rather than his own, Québécois-inflected English, accent, was criticized as disengaged, drained of energy. Commenting on a moment where the live actor faces, in profile, a reversed and enlarged projected image of himself to create the multi-media effect of Hamlet in dialogue with Hamlet/Horatio, Nick Curtis of *The Evening Standard* writes that it is 'as if the multiplied image were giving a deeper insight into Hamlet's psyche. Well, it doesn't' (1997). Jane Edwardes admits that there is 'technical wizardry galore ... But if there is a heart to this piece, it is not one that beats with any vigour' (1997). Billington likewise argued that the show's form made for an 'emotionally cold' performance: '[Lepage's] work on Shakespeare...always seems emotionally underpowered. In *Elsinore*, for all the breathtaking skill of Carl Fillion's design, he seems to be holding the mirror up to art rather than to Nature' (1996).

The London reviewers insisted that a performance of *Hamlet* had to get beyond surface effects. They wanted 'deeper insight', to feel the production's beating 'heart', to see, as Michael Coveney put it after seeing the show in November at the Nottingham Playhouse, 'the soul beneath the skin' (1996). It is Lepage's emotional detachment, his failure to get into the head and psyche of Hamlet the character, that was criticized as bad acting, weak interpretation. Although the 'two planks' missing from Spencer's theatrical formula were not mentioned explicitly, the production's lack of passion was. *Hamlet* in the late-twentieth century, it would seem, necessarily requires Hamlet's passion. Not encouraged to identify with the suffering of the central character – not given, as it were, a piece of Hamlet – these spectators objected that the show had no heart, no soul, no centre.

But this, one could argue, and to appropriate Benedict Nightingale's review headline, is 'Missing the point' (1997). Lepage did, and did not, deliver the 'universal' dimension for which this play is typically prized so highly. A close analysis of Lepage's performance within the context of this volume furthers an understanding of how Shakespeare signifies within a self-referencing and profoundly local, cultural tradition. *Elsinore*'s ability to speak 'to' and 'for' the world (or at least that small, Northern corner of the world to which the production toured) rested not on a supposed 'humanity' at the heart of the story, but on a self-conscious manipulation of the situation of *Hamlet* at the heart of the Shakespearean canon, and the circulation of the play in popular culture – the skull, the madness, the voice from beyond the grave – *as* art.

Lepage's performance drew attention to his protean changeability from man to woman, from prince to king to counsellor, and back again. Curiously, though, the body beneath the vaguely Elizabethan costuming always displayed the same neat moustache, picke-devant beard, and high forehead accentuated by a wispy, dark, receding hairline. These choices seem especially remarkable given that due to a childhood injury Lepage, himself, has no hair. Playing all of the characters in *Elsinore*, Lepage oddly resembled, not himself, or even the usual portrayal of a blond Danish prince, but Hamlet's

author, Shakespeare. The effect of the London performance was of watching the like-
ness of an image, known to us only through engraving and portraiture, perform acrobatics across and within a constantly changing space that represented the castle at
Elsinore. *Elsinore*, by this light, is less about releasing or revealing the passion of Hamlet
(an emotion, Lepage argues, this character lacks[8]), than it is about watching an actor
grapple with a monolithic, yet unstable, cultural icon: Shakespeare's *Hamlet*.

'Hamlet' (both play and character) consisted in this production of surfaces and images
that Lepage explored and displayed by means of what he calls 'theatrics': actorly technique
and the visual effects enabled by a uniquely responsive set. The performance event – each
irreproducible performance of *Elsinore* – thus physicalized the experience in the late-
twentieth century of ranging across the many and shifting contours of a canonical text,
a canonical character, a canonical author. We never got the sense that we could know
Hamlet; instead, we were witness to, and vicariously took part in, one performer's experi-
ential encounter with 'Hamlet'. To splice together Billington's paraphrase and Lepage's
metaphor for the machine at the heart of the production, Lepage was not holding the
mirror up to art – he was dancing with art.

17 Hekepia? The *Mana*[1] of the Maori Merchant[2]

Mark Houlahan

We often take the global to be the multinational and the corporate, blandly disseminating sameness throughout the world; and the local to be the heroic, small-scale attempts to sustain specific difference, holding out for all 'things counter, original, spare, strange' (Hopkins 1974: 31), believing that 'Reality must be local and special at the point where we pick up the traces' (Curnow 1960: 17)[3]. However, the intersection of 'global' Shakespeare with 'local' New Zealand cultural traditions shows that a rigid, essentialist understanding of these categories is fundamentally reductive and does little justice to the complexity of recent appropriations. Many of these are irrevocably local, and would not readily travel beyond New Zealand. Conversely, Don Selwyn's filmed version of *The Merchant of Venice* (*Te Tangata Whai-Rawa o Weniti*), first released in New Zealand early in 2002 and subsequently screened to global Shakespearean audiences and at festivals of indigenous film making,[4] strikingly negotiates the distance between the 'local' and the 'global'. Selwyn freely draws on aspects of traditional Maori culture and language for the sound and look of his film; these are then blended with signifiers of high 'European' culture (especially in terms of costuming and setting). As a result, his film is a cultural product at once uniquely from and of New Zealand (since this is the only location where the Maori are indigenous) and one which is designed to resonate beyond these shores. The film is crafted to make sense simply as a version of *The Merchant,* and is thus readable by any audience interested in Shakespeare. At the same time Selwyn's detailing, as this chapter shows, creates a specifically local frame of references which is only accessible to New Zealand audiences. In creating such a suggestive future for Shakespeare appropriations in New Zealand, Selwyn draws on the *longue durée* of Shakespeare's texts here in the South Pacific.

The opening of Aotearoa/New Zealand to the wider British world began on the morning of 6 October, 1769 when Captain James Cook sighted the land mass of the North Island of New Zealand, calling the bluff first seen from offshore 'Young Nick's Head' after the far-sighted young sailor who first saw land (Salmond 1991: 117). The arrival of the 'Endeavour' brought the many trappings of European civilization to New Zealand, Shakespeare among them. For a copy of Shakespeare's *Collected Works* was on board in the luggage of the ship's artist, Sydney Parkinson. The records of the voyage do not tell us whether this Shakespeare was actually read in New Zealand waters. Let it stand rather as the symbolic beginning of the enveloping of New Zealand inside British culture. Cook's voyage of course coincides with Garrick's famous jubilee and the subsequent global dissemination of Shakespeare's works. In New Zealand this dramatically accelerated from the 1840s onwards, when large numbers of British settlers arrived bearing their Shakespeares along with their Bibles.

For most of the time since then, New Zealand Shakespeares have been more global than local; imperial and colonial, as Dennis Kennedy terms them (2001a: 258). The 1990s though, have seen a series of energetically local appropriations, including Selwyn's film, which have sought to acknowledge the Pacific locale of New Zealand, 19,000 kilometres from the London where Shakespeare's plays were first performed. Viewers of Nicky Caro's film *The Whale Rider*, or those who watched the parade of New Zealanders accepting Oscars in 2004 for their work on *The Lord of the Rings* trilogy, could be forgiven for thinking that film making in New Zealand was in good heart, with highly skilled local film makers producing resonantly local films to acclaim in New Zealand and throughout the world. In fact here, as elsewhere in the English-speaking world, local films struggle against the massive predominance of Hollywood products. Most New Zealanders who work in film practice their craft on 'Hollywood' vehicles, made in New Zealand but which strive by all means possible to occlude their location. In the Tom Cruise vehicle *The Last Samurai*, for example, a New Zealand mountain, Taranaki, does double duty as Mount Fujiyama. The green fields of the film are mocked up to look like rural Japan.

Making a truly indigenous film within the context of such a film industry inevitably presents a challenge. In fact it took Don Selwyn ten years to persuade people that his Maori film of *The Merchant of Venice* would be viable. Making a New Zealand Shakespeare film would be seen as literally eccentric, an activity more apt for those closer to the 'centres' of Shakespeare production of London and Stratford. Moreover, Selwyn's would be the first feature length film entirely in Maori. Two developments were necessary for the film to come about at all. First, Selwyn needed a cast and crew fluent in *te reo*, the Maori language. The use of Maori languished from 1945 until the 1970s. A generation of Maori were brought up to believe that fluency in English was the only way to survive in an urban, post-industrial world. As the language decayed, so too did the traditions the language preserved. Since the 1970s, however, there has been a renaissance in the speaking and reading of Maori, along with the greater dissemination of Maori protocol (*tikanga*) into mainstream New Zealand society. That society has also undergone massive change in the last twenty years, acquiring its own level of post-colonial confidence, boosted by international cultural success, such as the awarding of the 1985 Booker prize to Keri Hulme for her bicultural epic *The Bone People* and the international art house success of films like *The Piano* and *Once Were Warriors*.

Selwyn's address to Shakespeare capitalizes on both these trends. He adapts a translation of the play in Maori completed by Pei Te Hurinui Jones in the 1940s. Jones' birth father was Jewish, and he also translated *Julius Caesar* into Maori. With the success of Selwyn's film, plans have been made to publish this translation also. Selwyn staged Jones' *Merchant* in 1990, so he knew that the translation would provide a viable script. The great set-piece speeches, in the 'formal, poetic classical Maori' (Jackson 2002: 156) Jones deploys, have the resonance of oratory in Maori protocol, where richness of figuration and elaborateness of argument are highly prized. The poet Merimeri Penfold's recent version of nine of Shakespeare's Sonnets also draws on the similarity between Shakespeare's verse and *te reo*. She finds that both languages share a 'fascination with highly wrought intricacies of language, [and] feeling for the rhythmic energies of the spoken word' (Penfold 2000: 7). When the film was first released in Hamilton, New Zealand, the actors playing Portia, Antonio and Shylock in the film performed their big speeches live in Maori in a public park. They recited with great brio, adopting many of the mannerisms New Zealand audiences would identify as part of the world of traditional Maori oratory.[5]

To make Shakespeare speak in an indigenous, proudly non-English voice would suggest to many an aggressively post-colonial production, alive with contemporary issues. Indeed, the film is redolent with local concerns. But, overall, Selwyn combines sustained attention to racial, colonial and religious issues in relation to local Maori history and traditions with his flair for international art-house conventions. Within the confines of their tiny budgets, his designers have striven to produce as sumptuous a *mise en scène* as possible. Rich fabrics and stunning neo-Renaissance façades abound throughout. Every possible location in Auckland has been used to produce a syncretic version of sixteenth century Venice, a Venice which just happens to be populated entirely by Maori actors, who live and dress like Renaissance Europeans, yet who talk with the richness of the Maori language, and who treasure also the material objects (*taonga*) prized in traditional Maori culture.

This is seen most clearly in the opening titles of the film, in prologue sequences using visuals and an arresting sound track before Antonio's familiar opening speech is heard. The sound track morphs from the lush romantic score composed by Clive Cockburn, relying heavily on the sounds of violins to the Maori *waiata*, traditional songs composed by the late Hirini Melbourne. The orchestration underlines the striking procession we see as, by moonlight, suitors travel to Portia's Belmont ('Perimoni').[6] These suitors are the only non-Maori actors on screen. In Selwyn's film Belmont is not a coastal estate, somewhere near Venice, but rather a romantic retreat in the New Zealand bush, which gleams in the moonlight. Fairy-like figures peer through shadows at the procession. Overhead figures perform Hong Kong style acrobatics. A global audience would perhaps understand this sequence as adding to the exotic gloss of Portia's realm. New Zealanders would instead read these as 'turehu', children of the mist, haunting parts of New Zealand far from the giddy world of commerce of the film's Venice (Jackson 2002: 158).

Here, in this fastness, we find Portia in a palace with a central courtyard, with lush vegetation and cooling fountains, a southern extrapolation from Moorish Spain. Portia's attendants dance formally to a Maori love song, while Portia and Nerissa drily dissect the waiting suitors. In cut-away shots they look especially ridiculous and out of place in this Maori environment. For, despite the women's Renaissance costumes, Portia is emphatically presented as a high-born 'ariki tapairu' or princess. Her fondness for European clothing is akin to that adopted in formal nineteenth-century portraits of Maori aristocrats. But she signals a dual allegiance, for her Maori inheritance is all about her. Carved Maori faces adorn the walls of her house; she sits meanwhile robed in the kind of feather cloak prized in traditional Maori society (Starzecka 1996: 141–3). These are now highly treasured, for the birds from which they are made are either protected, like the kiwi, or extinct, like the huia. In Portia's courtyard loom two imposing statues. One, in white stone, represents the koru (the frond of the New Zealand fern palm tree) a traditional emblem for life. Opposite stands a wooden figure who seems to represent an imposing male ancestor, one of the tipuna who watches over Portia and in whose interests she must administer the will. Such figures guard the entrance ways of Maori meeting houses, a visual means by which a culture with no writing technology could record its ancestors (Starzecka 1996: 85). Once again, global audiences are bound to read this figure differently, or rather exclusively as some sign of her dead father, who perpetuates his *mana* into the present. The quest to sustain *mana* does become a thematic leitmotif of the film as a whole. For this Maori décor becomes a visual equivalent of the Maori soundtrack. The *mana* of *te reo* is given new Shakespearean life. Selwyn effectively pays triple homage to the *mana* of Maori language and culture; of Shakespeare; and of Jones as a bicultural pioneer, striving through his Maori translations to bring the two cultures of Aotearoa together.

From Portia's palace the film then cuts to a version of the first scene of the play, Antonio's evocation of his nautical melancholy. Selwyn makes this literal: we see a model ship tossing in a special-effects sea, one of Antonio's missing argosies. Then we cut to a peaceful coastline, a grey–green bush-clad shore, down which proceeds Antonio's barque, bearing Antonio, Solerio and Solanio. As the scene unfolds they dock and continue talking through the market of Venice. The vessel is a deliberate anachronism, an early twentieth-century sailing boat, on loan from New Zealand's National Maritime Museum. The light on the water, the colours of the bush, even the wooden planking on the dock give the scene a New Zealand air. The process of establishing landings, coastal ports and harbours was the inevitable end point of the voyages out made by early European settlers; and most New Zealanders still live in coastal settlements. As in Belmont, Selwyn's Venice is syncretic. The townsfolk are of course all Maori (for only outsiders here are white), busily engaged in the street trading which still marks Venice – Selwyn's city is notably a place where fish is in ample supply, as it remains in Venice's famous fish market in the district of San Polo on the Grand Canal. This kind of commerce in produce was taken up energetically by Maori traders in the nineteenth century also, as they sought to convert local produce into the clothing and arms imported from England by early settlers. Yet here we are not in the nineteenth century. Rather, all the townspeople are clad in Renaissance costumes, with starched ruff collars and rich tunics for the main actors in the story. Had sixteenth-century Maori had access to European finance, clothing and lifestyles, the film suggests, this is how they might have lived. Of course Shakespeare's England considered the Pacific an as yet empty 'south sea of discovery' (*As You Like It* 3.2.193) and in 1600 Maori knew nothing of a world beyond the Hawaiki from which they had come to New Zealand.[7] Selwyn's film then evokes in its setting a beguiling parallel universe, fantastical and glamorous, a lovingly burnished tribute to a great playwright, a great scholar and a powerful language.

Yet the film does not simply wallow in nostalgia for a world which never was. Viewers are not encouraged merely to revel in its luxury, forgetful of the racism which the history of the play's reception has registered. No modern adaptation of the play, still less one set in New Zealand, could overlook the racial issues which underpin the play. The first words spoken in the film make that plain. Preceding the magic of the Belmont parade we see a lonely, squat, powerful figure. Clad in simple black he descends concrete steps. Against a louring sky of storm clouds Shylock speaks Shakespeare's famous plea for humane tolerance: 'Hath not a Jew eyes...' (3.1.154). For the meantime, Selwyn suspends the issue of revenge around which the story hinges, and allows Shylock's words to sound as a plea for tolerance. They are emphasized by the power of Waihoroi Shortland's widely praised incarnation of Shylock. Implicitly these words reveal the main purpose of the film. For the words spoken are not Shakespeare's English but Jones and Selwyn's adaptation of them in Maori. The global audience for the film may thereby be hearing Maori on screen for the first time. And even New Zealand audiences hear the words as prologue to a first feature entirely in Maori, by far the longest continuous stretch of spoken Maori yet made available in the media of film, television or DVD. Forcefully the film wears its Shakespearean plea for difference 'with a difference' (*Hamlet* 4.5.182).

One of the film's most striking settings makes this point, drawing again on resonances available to global and local audiences. Selwyn films 1.3, where famously Antonio contracts a pound of flesh in return for three thousand ducats, in an artist's working studio. An artist is seen painting while Christians and Jews negotiate. Frequently of course the scene is staged as if in a public Venetian piazza. Here, Selwyn draws on Venice's fame not just as a great commercial centre but, as well, as a city which prized and, in Shakespeare's lifetime, paid handsomely for art in public spaces and Churches as well as in private houses. The taste for visual, representational art is also the mark of a Christian elite. It's the filmic equivalent of a scene from the torrid meditations on art, commerce and politics in Howard Barker's *Scenes of an Execution*. Barker, Shakespeare and Selwyn all grasp the chance to use Venice as a metaphorical as much as a literal location. Using an artist's studio frees the actors to roam amongst the canvases. Shylock delivers 'I hate him for he is a Christian' (1.3.40) directly to the camera, isolating him from Antonio and Bassanio, and making the viewer his confidant. The roaming camera shows other patrons seeking paintings to purchase and shows an artist painting. Here again Selwyn fuses the time in which his film is set and the times in which (and for which) his film has been made, anachronistically alluding to contemporary New Zealand inside his neo-Renaissance Venice. Selwyn achieves this effect by casting a real (and distinguished) New Zealand painter, Selwyn Muru, one of the most prominent Maori painters of the last decades, to play the aforementioned artist at work in his studio. He is not, like some, a strict adherent of traditional Maori forms, like the many who weave flax or carve wood for canoes or meeting houses, producing figures like the tipuna in Portia's palace. Rather Muru paints in contemporary styles which he uses to reflect on Maori themes. Here we see him at work on such a painting. New Zealanders will quickly register that Muru is painting an expressionist version of Mt. Taranaki, the beautiful cone-shaped, snow-covered mountain Cook named Egmont and which *The Last Samurai* shows as Mt. Fuji. But Muru is not strictly a landscape painter. The sequence he is working on centres on events which happened at the base of the mountain.

The volcanic soils in the Taranaki province of New Zealand are fertile, now home to some of the best dairy farms in New Zealand. In the nineteenth century, new settlers sought to acquire this land from the Maori tribes who had lived there for hundreds of years before Cook's sighting of the peak which dominates the province. A fierce short war was fought for control of this territory in the 1860s. In 1881 local Maori adopted a different tactic. On a slope facing out from the mountain and down to the Tasman Sea a local chief Te Whiti established a community at Parihaka. He encouraged people to sustain themselves by farming together and offering only passive resistance and non-violence to the English army which eventually came to arrest him on 5 November, 1881 (Scott 1975: 111). The community was disbanded and Te Whiti and many of his followers imprisoned. To this day he is venerated as a prophet and leader, and people gather yearly at his tomb to commemorate his heroism and continue his mission. Muru is clearly at work on paintings showing the mountain and the tragic events below it. The year the film was made an exhibition of paintings, archival records and songs devoted to *Parihaka* brought these events to new light. Te Whiti's *mana* attracted Maori and

Pakeha celebrants of his peaceful ideals, and the exhibition drew large crowds. Effectively the studio in Selwyn's Venice is preparing a major contribution to just such an exhibition.

Such local readings will pass by non-New Zealanders. Yet none would miss the resonance of the final canvas over which the camera lingers. As Shylock leaves the studio Antonio prophesies to Bassanio: 'The Hebrew will turn Christian; he grows kind' (1.3.177) where 'kind' is drawn into the intricate labyrinth in the play around kinship and 'human' kindness. Bassanio, less forgiving, underlines the hatred that prevails, despite Antonio's optimism: 'I like not fair terms and a villain's mind' (1.3.178). As we see these words (and hear their Maori equivalents) the camera closes in on a canvas across the top of which is painted 'HOLOCAUST'. It's a telling, brief reminder to the global audience of the eventual outcome of Europe's anti-Semitism, to which the fate of the play in performance has been inextricably linked. The gesture reads locally as well. Muru is in part a follower of Colin McCahon, New Zealand's greatest painter, who famously painted words into his canvases, and who intermingles Old and New Testament themes with Maori history and mythology. Selwyn and Muru use the McCahon style to make a bitter joke about New Zealand's racial politics. As the film was being made a Maori Cabinet Minister, Tariana Turia, was being excoriated for suggesting that the dispossession of land in Taranaki in the nineteenth century, with its attendant legacies of economic poverty, alongside psychological, physical and spiritual malaise, was itself a kind of 'holocaust'. This sparked a flurry in the media. Could there only ever be one Holocaust? Or could one describe forced evictions and massacres as a kind of holocaust? The film makers' local wit suggests of course that they take Turia's side in the debate. Early in 2004, Turia left the Government and resigned from Parliament over the issue of land rights for Maori, forming her own party to advance the cause.[8] If she has seen the film, her conclusion would surely be that, in Selwyn's hands Shakespeare has effectively become her contemporary.

Drawing attention to local, current issues became an integral part of Selwyn's larger task, which was to make an engaging Maori version of the play, which could draw different audiences into the story as well as into its local agenda. Selwyn was mindful that his primary audience would be more versed in *te reo* than in Shakespeare and would bring to the film a set of cultural referents quite different from those shared by global audiences. An early screening helped me reflect on the interesting issue of how even strategies of appropriation which privilege the local over the global are affected by the desirable prospect of world-wide distribution. Dutiful New Zealand Shakespearean that I am, I was taking notes on the film in the dark. Around me a group of students from a Maori polytechnic were in fits of laughter, responding to the story-line for the first time. They did not know the outcome of the trial, so followed it as eagerly as Selwyn's extras do. Jackson reports similar reactions in Auckland where 'a largely Maori audience was engrossed by the production, reacting with the spontaneity of the men and women who crowded the theatres of Shakespeare's Elizabethan London' (2002: 163). Here, Shylock makes the trial credible. He is passionate, grave yet gleeful; his massive shoulders carry the weight of his defeats. At the same time they make his threats quite plausible. When he wields the sacrificing knife in the trial scene, you know you're watching a Shylock who really could do the business, the opposite say of the effetely assimilated gentlemen Olivier depicts in Jonathan Miller's television *Merchant*. Shylock's glee is palpable: unlike Lady Macbeth he would be keen to see the wound his knife could make. This stern drive for vengeance helps make Selwyn's trial scene a triumph, one of the great set pieces of the film.

For the exterior approach shots, Selwyn films outside the District Court in Auckland, with a colonnaded walkway with an art deco façade. The colours and shape of the arches lend the exterior a Venetian look. For the interior of the court, Selwyn makes another of his time leaps, filming overtly inside St. Mary's Cathedral, one of the most beautiful of the wooden churches built in nineteenth-century New Zealand. This Anglican space is unaltered. Rather the camera roams around the main actors, taking delight in the glorious stained glass, the ornately carved pulpit, and the golden cross on the high altar behind where the judge sits presiding. This striking setting underlines the sectarian nature of the victory wielded over Shylock, defeated by a Christian conspiracy, complete with the cross-dressing Portia's quick-witted manipulation of the law. Shylock is worn down by sharp practice dressed up as the triumph of truth. Here, Antonio has a change of costume, dressed for the trial in a brown tunic on which is emblazoned the large red cross of martyrdom. The dock in which he stands as potential victim is the pulpit, visually the highest point to stand on the ground floor of the church. Awaiting sentence he looms over the court, already, it seems, half-way to heaven. Like his adversary Shylock he is unbowed and comparatively unemotional, leaving his supporters like Gratiano to conduct rhetorical warfare. These outbursts in Maori are extraordinary, deep guttural outcries, evoking the rituals of pre-battle manoeuvres, resonant and ominous. Each side here rallies its supporters in this way. Selwyn films equal numbers of Jews and Christians barracking for each side. This creates a strikingly different impression from most stage versions, where Christian extras far outnumber Jewish ones. It is across the uproar created by the large crowd that Portia speaks, winning the day for Christianity and her husband's best friend. The ethnically homogeneous nature of the public serves to emphasize the importance in the play of sectarian and cultural differences on which so much of the mutual hatred in Shakespeare's Venice is based. Quietly Shylock begs leave to go: 'I am not well'. A crane shot shows him slowly walking down the aisle of the church, watched by all. As he proceeds along the colonnade outside, the violins Cockburn uses to mark the sound of the ghetto swell up. From this point in the play Shylock has no more to say. Here, the sound track has something in reserve. As he walks away we hear Shylock thinking the final lines of his 'hath not a Jew' speech, picking up where we left them at the very beginning of the film. Thus, though defeated by the story, the last words Shylock is seen to think are 'why, revenge'. Despite the sinking of Shortland's ample shoulders, this Shylock is unvanquished.

Memories of Shylock then linger in the comic confusion of the final scenes. Here, Selwyn returns to his Belmont hidden in the lush fastness of the New Zealand bush. The community here affirms its commitment to traditional values, its central prop Portia with her traditions and grace. As at the beginning of the film the camera lingers on the flax tukutuku panels adorning the walls (Starzecka 1996: 162) and the ancestral carvings. This is a world steeped in old ways. Even Jessica reluctantly accepts the defeat of her father. She enters her new world gravely, reluctantly, as if she were exchanging one Maori tribe (or *iwi*) for another. The double wooden door closes: on the outside we see the fern-frond spiral design which Maori carvers made their own. For the meantime the *mana* of this realm is secure.

The cinematic confidence of this moment underlines again the daring quality of Selwyn's achievement, brought about against the odds that attend financing such an unusual film. Despite such odds he has succeeded. A character in a recent New Zealand novel grasps the paradox of South Seas Shakespeare this way: 'I don't know why we have to do this Shakespeare. Who in New Zealand likes Shakespeare? Why are we doing this Shakespeare? That's what I want to know' (Trim 2000: 19). Cultural logic suggests that New Zealanders will be 'doing' Shakespeare for some time yet. What kind of Shakespeare they should read, study or perform remains moot. Whether Selwyn's double action, of enhancing the *mana* of Maori by giving it to Shakespeare audiences worldwide while enhancing Shakespeare's *mana* by giving him in Maori to Maori viewers is the start of a trend or a uniquely splendid stunt, it is too soon to say. 'New Zealand Shakespeare?', commented Ian Mune, at a forum on 'Shakespeare in the Pacific' held in Auckland in the year 2000: 'Not yet'.[9] Selwyn's film is one luminous example of what yet might be. 'If it be not now, it will come'.

18 The Haiku *Macbeth*: Shakespearean antithetical minimalism in Kurosawa's *Kumonosu-jo*

Saviour Catania

'We are in a Mist'
John Keats[1]

More in less: the Shakespearean Zen

A distinctive feature of *Kumonosu-jo* is Akira Kurosawa's tendency to 'purposely restrict ... himself' (Richie 1973: 120). According to Donald Richie, the result is filmic minimalism of an extraordinary kind: 'visually, the film is a marvel because it is made of so little: fog, wind, trees, mist – the forest and the castle' (1973: 120). Strangely, however, Richie does not associate such filmic terseness with Zen influences on Japanese artists who 'tend to use the fewest words or strokes of the brush to express their feelings' (Suzuki 1973: 257). The Zen principle of concision is undoubtedly fundamental to Japanese aesthetics. Hence, the seventeen-syllable brevity of haiku poetry and the visual sparseness of monochrome ink painting. As Stryk points out, 'the appeal of *haiku* is not unlike that of a *sumie* (ink-wash) scroll by Sesshu, and many *haiku* poets, like Buson, were also outstanding painters' (Stryk and Ikemoto 1981: 21). Quite possibly, *Kumonosu-jo* owes its visual style to such artists, for not only did Kurosawa receive his 'early training [...] in painting' (Zambrano 1974: 262) but, more importantly, he found in haiku poetry a constant source of inspiration. Significantly, besides recalling his wartime habit of 'construct[ing] *haiku* poems', Kurosawa also confesses his ardent belief that 'the only way to make a successful film is to apply the same kind of very concentrated interest' that is absolutely necessary to haiku poetry.[2] What *Kumonosu-jo* offers is intense haiku minimalism. It is also worth pointing out that Kurosawa was attracted not only by the essential concision of the haiku lyric but also, and more crucially, by its tendency to collapse condensation into antithesis, whereby something becomes simultaneously both itself and its opposite. For instance, Basho's haiku – 'Spring night,/cherry-/blossom dawn' (Stryk 1985: 26)[3] – rests on a spatio-temporal disjunction which intermeshes darkness and light in a flash of insight. Such antithetical concision is not only a defining feature in Kurosawa's cinematic reworking of *Macbeth*, but it also reflects 'one of the predominant characteristics of the general style of the play, which consists of multitudinous antitheses'.[4]

Recent critics, such as Goodwin and Richie, have also usefully pointed out that 'the film draws from traditions of *suiboku-ga* (ink-painting)' (Goodwin 1994: 174), a visual genre to which Yoshiro Muraki, Kurosawa's art director, also refers as a key source of stylistic influence (Richie 1973: 122). *Suiboku-ga* consists in the intermeshing of 'empty expanses of white separating intense black brushstrokes' (Goodwin 1994: 174) – that 'empty/full dichotomy' (Richie 1994: 159), which neither critic associates with the haiku self that is paradoxically 'selfless' (Suzuki 1973: 262), nor with Kurosawa's visual reworking of the paradoxical language in *Macbeth*. Other critics, including Stephen Prince, have commented on Kurosawa's fondness for Noh drama, and, more specifically, for the Zeami[5] principle of theatrical restraint based on the 'dialectical combinations of its elements' (1991: 146). A typical example is the Noh actor's integration of 'violent bodily movements and gentle foot movements or the reverse' (Prince 1991: 146). Kurosawa shares this antithetical notion of Noh performance for he defines it as a theatre where 'both quietness and vehemence co-exist together'.[6] However, once again, although Prince establishes a connection between haiku and Noh theatre when referring to the Japanese 'delight in the juxtaposition of contrary values' (1991: 47), he, like Richie and Goodwin, fails to consider how Kurosawa appropriates such an aesthetic to recreate his Shakespearean source in terms of its central paradoxical vision where 'nothing is, but what is not' (1.3.142)[7] – arguably the most minimal of paradoxes in *Macbeth*. My essay consequently aims to reconsider the impact which local traditions have had on *Kumonosu-jo* and which earlier critics have either underestimated or overlooked. A better understanding of the visual and poetic conventions which affected Kurosawa's cinematic reworking of Shakespeare's *Macbeth* in turn provides fresh insight into one of the play's central paradoxes, which has haunted its critical reception: mankind's predestined freedom to fall.

Misting *Macbeth*: the timelessness of space-less space

Cobweb Forest, 'a place of contradiction' (Donaldson 1990: 75), offers a congenial starting point for a close analysis of Kurosawa's reworking of *Macbeth*'s antithetical language. In fact, the film's forest, which Donaldson describes as 'sunlight streaming down through rain' (1990: 75), epitomizes the play's interest in antithesis and paradox even more effectively than Shakespeare's Scottish heath. Evocative of Gyodai's haiku 'Slowly/over cedars,/sunshine, showers' (Stryk and Ikemoto 1981: 121), Kurosawa's sylvan scene intensifies the Japanese lyric's sense of *yugen*, or mystery, by intermeshing the contradictory atmospheric conditions of Malcolm's statement: 'The night is long that never finds the day' (4.3.240). As in Shakespeare, where night and day coalesce to puzzle Macbeth – 'So foul and fair a day I have not seen' (1.3.38) – so in Kurosawa the forest baffles Washizu by casting an 'immense darkness in daytime' (Goodwin 1994: 179). Since such daylight darkness constitutes the same antithetical weather witnessed after Duncan's murder, Ross's words ring as true of Cobweb Forest as of Inverness: ' ... by th' clock 'tis day,/And yet dark night strangles the travelling lamp' (2.4.6–7) Like Macbeth, Washizu enters the 'blasted heath' (1.3.77) where 'Light thickens' (3.2.50). The telephoto panning shots of Washizu's furious ride remarkably reinforce the impression that Cobweb Forest is 'more a state of mind than a place' (Hapgood 1994: 238). Through the blurring of foreground and background the horse's movements are accelerated to such an extent that Washizu's galloping seems unhinged in time and space. As Blumenthal has argued, 'for Washizu this first encounter with the forest is nothing less than a headlong plunge into the self' (1965: 191).

That Cobweb Forest functions like the dark penumbra of Washizu's psyche is further stressed by its antithetical state of blooming decay. A veritable tangle of intertwining branches reminiscent of the 'twisting, curving forms' of Yamato-e pine trees in Heian picture scrolls (Stanley-Baker 1995: 147), Cobweb Forest visualizes Washizu's twisted path to power – its gnarled, withered trees eroding his sense of direction in an ironic reversal of Duncan's image of Macbeth as some kind of seedling-friend: 'I have begun to plant thee, and will labour/To make thee full of growing' (1.4.28–9). Far from being 'an image that is not wholly integral to the play' (Gerlach 1973: 352), Kurosawa's forest enhances Shakespeare's own use of metaphor. Typical of Kurosawa's use of antithetical images is his decision to embed the birth of Washizu's ambition in images of wooded decadence, thereby unmistakably hinting at its withering, as does Macbeth when he compares himself to the autumn-stricken tree: ' [...] my way of life/Is fall'n into the sere, the yellow leaf' (5.3.22–3). Such intimations of Washizu's vernal shrivelling imbue the forest sequence with an acute sense of impermanence which is so characteristic of ambivalent seasonal haiku lyrics like Joso's lines: 'These branches/were the first to bud-/falling blossoms' (Stryk and Ikemoto 1981: 113). Like Joso's cherry tree, Washizu seems to be in the autumn of his spring. Hence, Washizu's accelerated galloping in an ambiguous forest where time is minimized and compressed to such an extent that discrete events occupy the same temporal frame. Cobweb Forest is more than just a place where it simultaneously shines and rains. Since Kurosawa invests it with 'deep moral meaning' (Blumenthal 1965: 191), it attains the classical status of a nether region where the beginning is the end and where, as in Dante's dark wood, hope droops the moment that it blooms.

In Cobweb Forest, however, both time *and* space are antithetically minimized. Washizu cannot penetrate this thicket of dense minimalism – and the more he gallops and bolts, the more he rides in the same sylvan spot. In fact, Miki (Banquo) realizes that they have been riding in circles and, like Macbeth, they are 'cabin'd, cribb'd, confin'd' (3.4.23). Moreover, Washizu's circular riding, by ultimately rooting him to the same place, conveys Macbeth's deeper fear of the space of no space as he poignantly identifies himself with 'the bat that hath flown/His cloister'd flight' (3.2.40–1). Kurosawa reverses Noh language here for, while the Noh actor's stillness is paradoxically dynamic, Washizu's furious riding is circularly static. Thus, Cobweb Forest is just space-less space, and can offer Washizu only Macbeth's movement in stasis since its material reality is minimized and reduced to immaterial substance.

Kurosawa's minimalist and antithetical representation of time and space is reflected in the fog sequence, which is perhaps the film's most poetically paradoxical set piece. This sequence was clearly inspired by the *suiboku-ga* style of ink monochrome painting, as in Hasegawa Tohaku's antithetical 'Pine Forests', a double six-fold screen depicting *hamamatsu* or beach pines looming blackly in misty whiteness. Significantly, no trees figure in Kurosawa's twelve-shot sequence. All that remains of Tohaku's tableaux in Kurosawa's sequence is the fog through which Washizu and Miki keep riding palely. Hence, Kurosawa's decision to film on Mt. Fuji which Muraki describes as a Hokusai haven of 'mist and fog' (Richie 1973: 122). It is through a haiku like Basho's 'How pleasant-/just once *not* to see/Fuji through mist' (Stryk 1985: 73) that one discerns the formal accuracy of Kurosawa's choice of setting in his recreation of the Shakespearean heath which the Weird Sisters likewise smother in 'fog and filthy air' (1.1.12). By resorting to a foggy texture that functions like 'an opaque veil which hides the surrounding area' (Zambrano 1974: 266), Kurosawa mists the forest to such an extent that the visual effect is 'almost entirely abstract' (Burch 1979: 313). In its mist within mist, Kurosawa's fog sequence functions like a transcendental haiku. Unlike Sampu, whose haiku 'Moving/ deep into mist,/chrystanthemums' (Stryk and Ikemoto 1981: 125) weaves wisps of mist into flowers, Kurosawa mists into nothing the whole sylvan setting.

As Goodwin points out, 'the empty expanses in *Kumonosu-jo* are not a space vacant of meaning' (1994: 184). On the contrary, they imbue *Kumonosu-jo* with the antithetical minimal spirit of the crucial speech where Macbeth comes to the ultimate realization that 'Life's but a walking shadow' (5.5.24). Kurosawa's film translates this shadow into the mist drifting about Washizu – its (im)materiality hinting at his vacuous victory. In this respect, *Kumonosu-jo* seems to owe a thematic debt to Welles's *Macbeth* whose tragic protagonist likewise haunts a realm of fog. Inspired perhaps by the scene where Welles visualizes the obfuscating despair of Macbeth's 'To-morrow, and to-morrow, and to-morrow' speech (5.5.19–28) in terms of 'swirling mists and clouds' (Mullin 1973: 337), Kurosawa reconceives Macbeth as an emissary of mist. Washizu significantly dies in a misty courtyard which recalls that of his Wellesian counterpart. Washizu's arrow-studded death, on the other hand, although '*kabuki*-oriented' (Serper 2000: 21), never becomes 'Verdi's rather than Shakespeare's [...] operatic finale' (Richie 1973: 121) – for it still finds deep resonances in the play. Kurosawa creates here his own version of Birnam Wood, and minimizes it into volleys of arrows whose arboreal origin transforms Washizu's transfixed body into a tottering '*homme-forêt*' (Chauvin 1998: 35). Of equal Shakespearean significance is the forest's misty presence, and especially its swirling white fog that finally claims Washizu's corpse. Washizu's misty end indicates that his is a tale of dark deeds in a white terrain: 'black Hecate's summons' (3.2.41) in 'Pale Hecate's realm' (2.1.52). Malcolm's snowy vision of 'black Macbeth' (4.3.52) finds in both the fog sequence and the final death scene its most minimal expression – for Washizu's fog-enshrouded body dissolves into the whiteness of nothing. Washizu's elemental death evokes, however, no sense of *mono no aware*, the Japanese 'elegaic attitude to suffering' (Collick 1989: 185), with which Kurosawa permeates Hidetora's (Lear's) fate in *Ran*. A much darker film, *Kumonosu-jo* transcends *Ran*'s concern with unbearable human pain and focuses, more nihilistically, on the emptiness of existence. Washizu's very being is significantly distilled to insubstantial sylvan mist.

Wheeling freely: the circles of choice-less choices

As in *Macbeth*, where '[t]he evil of atmospheric effect interpenetrates the evil of individual persons' (Knight 1983: 150), in Kurosawa's film setting and characterization are inextricably linked. Consider, for example, the meeting of Washizu and Miki with the forest's *genius loci*, a figure of misty whiteness crouched in a skeletal hut that is the epitome of Noh stage sparseness. Kurosawa's almost ephemeral hag is, like the forest fog that surrounds her, insubstantial in her substance. Like the three witches she replaces, the forest spirit is an unearthly crone who combines their uncanny gift of soothsaying with their supernatural power to vanish into thin air. Significantly, as Kurosawa himself explains,[8] the face of his forest spirit is made up to resemble the mask worn by the title figure in the Noh demon play *Yamamba* (*Mountain Witch*), where 'natural and supernatural planes of experience' overlap (McDonald 1987: 36). Mask is soul in Noh drama: '[t]he Noh actor, through study of the *omote* ("outside") or dramatic mask, expresses an exterior image of the spirit or essence of character' (Goodwin 1994: 190). As Basho puts it: 'Year by year,/the monkey's mask/reveals the monkey' (Stryk 1985: 25). Similarly, the

Yamamba mask unveils the forest spirit's ambivalence. Like the Weird Sisters, the forest spirit belongs to a category of creatures 'That look not like th' inhabitants o' th' earth,/And yet are on 't' (1.3.41–2). Kurosawa adds an extra layer of local connotations by turning his hag into a cinematic equivalent of the wheel-spinning prophetess of the Noh play *Kurozuka* (*Black Mound*), who 'partakes of both an unearthly being and a real human being' (Yamamoto 1999: 150). True to her ambivalent nature, the forest spirit can only address Miki in a Shakespearean antithesis: 'Your fortune is lesser and greater than General Washizu's' (Kurosawa 1992: 234).[9] Apart from having the forest spirit echo what the first witch tells Banquo, that he is 'Lesser than Macbeth, and greater' (1.3.65), Kurosawa visualizes this paradoxical prophecy through the two wheels that she spins: a large wheel which rotates slowly, representing Miki's gradual but lasting fortune, and a smaller wheel which rotates faster, representing Washizu's meteoric rise and fall.

Wheeling is of the essence here, as it is in the subsequent fog sequence, where Washizu and Miki's circular trajectory is suggestive of the wheel of their own destiny. Crucially, though, Kurosawa's use of circular trajectories should not be interpreted as a distortion of Shakespeare's tragedy of personal responsibility.[10] In fact, a close analysis of this image shows how inadequate such an assessment is, not only in relation to Kurosawa's (re)vision but also in relation to Shakespeare's own tragic vision of human agency in *Macbeth*. Washizu and Miki's circular riding is not simply an extension of the witch's spinning-wheel that symbolizes 'a universe ruled by fate' (Desser 1983: 75). For such circular riding is clearly antithetical: 'breaking out is also breaking in' (Hodgdon 1979/80: 64). Indeed, since Washizu and Miki's journey in *and* out of the mist reveals that they are riding at cross purposes, it implicitly suggests the possibility of diametrically opposed choices, but always within a circular movement. So does the circular path traced by the horseman riding in the courtyard behind the scheming Washizu and Asaji (Lady Macbeth). This is yet another circular trajectory that allows for clockwise and anti-clockwise galloping. Again, when Miki's stallion refuses to be saddled, its movements describe an antithetical circular pattern. Kurosawa's circular trajectories reflect the 'sickening see-saw rhythm' which critics have detected in Shakespeare's play (Knights 1964: 32). Significantly, Macbeth's response to Banquo's antithetical realization that 'The instruments of Darkness tell us truths' (1.3.124), is the similar awareness that such forces can only offer the choice of no choice: 'This supernatural soliciting/Cannot be ill; cannot be good' (1.3.130–1). The choice-less choice is a minimalist variant of the space-less space theme, since the ultimate result in both situations is movement in stasis.

It seems worth stressing that Kurosawa's use of movement and stasis has often been misunderstood, especially in relation to Washizu. McDonald, for example, interprets the conflict between motion and stasis in stark dualistic moral terms: '[i]f the static represents Washizu's evil inclination, the dynamic stands for his reason's challenge to it' (1983: 159). Consequently, MacDonald argues that Washizu's restless pacing while he is plotting Tsuzuki's (Duncan's) murder with Asaji is a sign that 'the forces of light' (1987: 40) are still in control of his conscience. Some critics have gone so far as to argue that Washizu 'has almost nothing to do with inner conflict' (Yamamoto 1999: 152) simply because he is 'one for whom the moral dimension of behaviour [...] seldom crosses the threshold of conceptualisation into verbal poetry' (Blumenthal 1965: 194). But this is to overlook Blumenthal's most crucial point: that Washizu 'thinks in another medium' (1965: 195). Not only does Washizu display Macbeth's moral sensitivity physically but, like Macbeth, he also displays it antithetically through his *giri/ninjo* or 'obligation versus feeling' conflict (Collick 1989: 176). Admittedly, the Noh mask that determines Washizu's features, unlike the unearthly hag's, does not connote visual ambivalence: it is simply the mask of Heida, the warrior spirit. However, as other critics have pointed out, 'the Noh mask varies according to the extent to which each character follows the dictates of their fate' (Collick 1989: 180–1). Washizu is an ambiguous Heida warrior who both accepts and rejects his fate. Like his clockwise and anti-clockwise riding, Washizu's restless pacing reveals a nowhere kind of personality whose space-less space, like its choice-less choice, roots it, as Lady Macbeth would say, to that same 'damned spot' (5.1.34).

Nor is Asaji a less morally ambiguous creature. The Shakumi features of her Noh mask are profoundly paradoxical: 'one half [of the mask] reveals a bright, lively expression, while the other is sad and melancholy' (McDonald 1987: 39). Asaji does not wield 'absolute control [through her being] static, cold, and impassive' (McDonald 1987: 39). Whether motionless or in motion, Asaji retains her essential ambivalence. Sliding her feet without lifting them in typical Noh fashion, and dragging her swishing floral kimono, Asaji embodies Lady Macbeth's advice to her husband: 'look like th' innocent flower,/ But be the serpent under 't' (1.5.64–5). Issa's haiku could not be more antithetically appropriate: 'Never forget:/we walk on hell, gazing at flowers' (Stryk and Ikemoto 1981: 108). As with Washizu, Asaji's poetic medium is her body, and Kurosawa, relying on sounds as minimally sparse as his images, transforms the wooden floor of Japanese architecture into a resonant board for a seductive reptile. But Asaji, true to her Shakumi features, is a Shakespearean Lamia whose silken deadliness conveys more than a tinge of pensive sadness. The snake-like Asaji, unlike Andrzej Wajda's Siberian Ledi Magbet, is certainly no *femme fatale* of passion – but then, like the ghostly Wakasa of Kenji Mizoguchi's *Ugetsu Monogatari*, hers is an elegaic adagio personality. As Bazerman puts it, 'Kurosawa externalizes emotional distress through movement' (1977: 335). Rather than essentially static, Asaji relishes *suri ashi*, or Noh sliding movements, thereby creating her own version of motion in stasis. Nor is Asaji absolved from circularity. At one point she whirls on herself while dancing during Tsuzuki's murder – a circular movement that evokes the forest spirit's wheel of destiny and places her just as unmistakably in the space-less space of Washizu and Miki. In Asaji's case, space-less space manifests itself more bizarrely in the shape of a dark doorway: she disappears into its blackness to return with the drugged potion seconds later. A reminder of the forest spirit's ability to vanish, Asaji's black-hole trajectory indicates that, like Washizu, she is unhinged in time and space.

Either and or: the straight curves of twisted souls

Equally important is that Asaji approaches the doorway of darkness moving diagonally across the room. As with the film's circular motion, both its diagonal and horizontal patterns are intrinsically antithetical. Kurosawa does not simply transform the straight lines and curved forms of the Fujiwara *emakimono*, or illustrated narrative hand-scrolls, into respective 'moral poles of good and evil' (Kinder 1977: 341). Instead, Kurosawa makes them mutate into their diametrically opposed selves, thereby creating a world of angular horizontality as foully fair as Shakespeare's. A typical example of such ambivalence is the sequence where Tsuzuki's army advances in 'a straight horizontal plane and suddenly make[s] a sharp angular turn' near Washizu's castle (Kinder 1977: 342). But the mutation of Tsuzuki's straight horizontal marching into a diagonal of disruption does not simply 'foreshadow [...] his murder' (Kinder 1977: 342), since it hints just as suggestively at his own treachery. Tsuzuki represents a departure from his predecessor because, '[u]nlike Shakespeare's virtuous Duncan, the lord that Washizu murders had gained power by murdering his own lord' (Prince 1991: 144). Similarly, Tsuzuki's hunting expedition turns out to be a military subterfuge. Tsuzuki is essentially another living antithesis whose straight path masks an angular one. So is Asaji, whose approach to the dark door similarly mutates, albeit conversely, from a diagonal into a straight line of equal disruption – since she exits for the drugged drink and returns with it in a straight-line movement, thereby hinting that, even when she moves straight, it is still a crooked path she takes. Asaji's trajectory resembles Macbeth's, whose proverbial straight flight leads him to the 'rooky wood' (3.2.51) of his twisted heart.

There are no fixed lines of movement in *Kumonosu-jo*, since everything is antithetically mutated into its diametric opposite. This is also exemplified by the sequence where Washizu stabs Miki's killer and is seen retreating from the crawling messenger. Kurosawa's camera stays with the dying servant, its medium-long shot perspective diminishing Washizu's figure as it captures him huddling against a looming mural whose labyrinthine design of horizontal lines further accentuates the expansive width of the chamber. Once again, straight lines distort in *Kumonosu-jo*, for they stunt Washizu's growth much like Angus's clothes metaphor belittles Macbeth's stature:

> [...] now does he feel his title
> Hang loose about him, like a giant's robe
> Upon a dwarfish thief.

(5.2.20–2)

Kurosawa's concept of space-less space functions as a reworking of the recurrent image of Macbeth's ill-fitting garments. Equally revealing of such antithetical minimalism is the bird invasion of the council chamber. Kurosawa's sequence is evocative of both Tohaku's pair of screens 'Herons and Crows' and Basho's haiku 'Snow morning-/ one crow/after another' (Stryk 1985: 54),[11] for what comes home to roost are lovely grey–white wood-pigeons and ravens of black repute. Kurosawa creates here a variant of Macbeth's battlements that harbour both Banquo's 'temple-haunting martlet' (1.6.4) and Lady Macbeth's 'hoarse raven' croaking Duncan's 'fatal entrance' (1.5.38–9). Hence the underlying antithesis of the film's Japanese title, which can be glossed as 'the castle of the spider's web'. Just like Cobweb Forest, what Cobweb Castle offers Washizu in spatial terms is more and more about less and less. Far from '[e]verything [being] rigidly either/or' (Richie 1973: 120), everything is concurrently either *and* or in *Kumonosu-jo*.

It is profoundly appropriate that Kurosawa's adaptation of *Macbeth* should rely on the haiku principle of antithetical minimalism, since Shakespeare's play thrives on antithesis and paradox. Significantly, just as Shakespeare dissolves Lady Macbeth into scentless scent – 'all the/perfumes of Arabia will not sweeten this little hand' (5.1.48–9) – so does Kurosawa dissolve Asaji into a doorway of darkness where her time-warping trajectory becomes the visual equivalent of Lady Macbeth's cry 'I feel now/The future in the instant' (1.5.57–8). In trying to become more than something, both women join their husbands in becoming nothing. As Macbeth says: 'I dare do all that may become a man;/Who dares do more, is none' (1.7.46–7). That is also the informing principle of

Kumonosu-jo, whose misty texture is aptly paralleled by a windy sound-track – the equivalent of the weeping gale that rages over Macbeth's castle at the time of Duncan's murder. In *Kumonosu-jo*, however, the moaning wind is almost ever present, reminding us that this a retelling of Macbeth's tale, 'full of sound and fury,/Signifying nothing' (5.5.27–8). Ultimately, what Kurosawa's (and Shakespeare's) vision of the tragic grandeur of the nothingness of being brings hauntingly to mind are Basho's antithetical lines: 'Dying cricket-/how full of/life, his song' (Stryk 1985: 74).

The peculiar quality of Kurosawa's appropriation of Shakespeare's *Macbeth* ultimately rests on his ability to translate familiar responses to the play into unfamiliar conventions. Washizu and Asaji's plight, in other words, is typical of the *huis clos* or the 'no-exit state' of the European theatre of the absurd. *Kumonosu-jo*'s popularity with Western critics and directors may possibly be due to the fact that, despite its medieval Japanese setting and its extensive use of local visual and poetic traditions, it parallels Kott's absurdist interpretation of Shakespeare's tragedy.[12] Significantly, not only does Peter Brook extol *Kumonosu-jo*'s filmic merits[13] but, more crucially, his film adaptation of *King Lear* is much closer to *Kumonosu-jo*'s nihilistic vision of existence than *Ran*, Kurosawa's own version of the same Shakespearean play. Rather than a radical appropriation of the Shakespearean original, *Kumonosu-jo* can therefore best be described as a special homage to a Western tradition that reworks *Macbeth* in modernist terms.

19 Afterword

Barbara Hodgdon

It has become the fashion to see the lady (or gentleman) appear as the Epilogue, now called an 'Afterword', and to speak on behalf of a collection's critical performances. Although it is not an entirely 'new' (could one call it 'retro'?) phenomenon, that a theatrical convention has travelled into critical territory seems, in this case, especially apt. For many of the theatrical and cinematic refashionings of Shakespeare considered in *World-wide Shakespeares* either derive from or engage with the resonant doubleness characteristic of a present-day climate where theatrical and critical cultures intersect, weaving together not only to make new performances of old plays but also to 're-member and dis-member' old plays as new ones (Döring p. 21). Put another way, the 'dramatic field' not only abuts the 'lit-crit' field but also extends Shakespeare's reach beyond the borders of both: travelling here, there and everywhere, occurring in various sites and citings, deploying a wide range of theatrical–textual strategies, encountering local cultural fields and speaking in many languages, Shakespeare is represented here as a resource for mapping the poetics and politics of cultures. What a case am I in, then, for surely such good performances need no epilogue? Taking my cue from Rosalind (although disclaiming her magical properties), my way is to conjure: first, to pose some questions about the critical vocabularies we mobilize in mapping these fields of (inter)*act*ivity; then, to suggest some areas for further research and analysis.

Adaptation/appropriation

In encompassing various attitudes towards 'adaptation' and 'appropriation', these essays engage with two extremely slippery labels. The terms are evoked to differentiate many state-of-the-art Shakespearean performances, whether literary or theatrical, from what we tend to think of (despite knowing it a fiction) as a (textual) 'original'. However useful – for naming, after all, accords status to what *Dream*'s Theseus calls a 'local habitation' – is there a difference between these two terms that we need to mark, and if so, what, exactly, constitutes that difference? The *OED* treads a thin line between the two. Adaptation (2.a.): 'The process of modifying a thing so as to suit new conditions' cites as one instance 'the alteration of a dramatic composition to suit a different audience'. Appropriation, however, casts a wider net, for three definitions seem applicable to the project of re-envisioning Shakespeare's plays: (1.) 'The making of a thing private property, whether another's or (as now commonly) one's own; taking as one's own or to one's own use'; (2.) 'The assignment of anything to a special purpose'; (4.) 'Special attribution or application'. Given these definitional fields (none of which had late sixteenth-century currency), Shakespeare himself might be labeled 'The Great Adapter' *and* 'The Great Appropriator'.

Obviously it needs no ghost come from the grave to say so, however comforting it may be to discover that present-day critical practice has authorial sanction. Nevertheless, the existence of a 'genuinely Shakespearean' appropriation (Jones, p. 122) seems doubtful; instead, whether we think of early refigurations such as those by Colley Cibber and William Davenant or modern, post-modern or post-postmodern instantiations of Shakespeare, we only can mark how each, as Jonathan Dollimore writes, 'takes the play in a direction it was already going' (1986) and, I might add, in directions it never imagined. In marking the distinction between adaptation and appropriation, might it be useful to distinguish between what Harry Berger, Jr. calls 'imaginary audition' (the work of reading) (1989) and 'material audition' (the work of playing)? For any time a reader encounters a Shakespearean play, she adapts the words on the page: reheard, translated into a private lexicon, authorial property becomes, in Michel Garneau's apt phrase, 'tradapted' (1989) – as it meets the mind's 'I'. Although the same of course holds true for the spectator's eye, the ideas of 'assignment … to a special purpose' and of 'special attribution or application' seem more finely tuned to the unusually mobile range of performances created as Shakespearean dramatic texts, reactivated by time and space travel, encounter local conventions and subjectivities and communal, national and global histories and memories.

Do dead playwrights have rights?

Voiced by an irate critic, this question points to the tensions and struggles between 400-year-old dramaturgy and late twentieth- or early twenty-first-century spectators, many of whom not only want to see a textual (or literary) Shakespeare up there on the stage but also have been trained to look for that text 'in' the present performance and who miss it when it's not there. A recent *New Yorker* cartoon image shows a stage set for a drawing-room scene where a number of actors are holding up placards, some with dialogue, others with stage directions or cues. Watching, one spectator says to another: 'They've remained remarkably faithful to the text' (Downes 1999: 101). And while it certainly is the case that mainstream reviewers as well as academic critics have become more open to and excited by Shakespeare's recent adventures in the arts marketplace and in the export/import business of negotiating with intercultural conventions and social formations, the resulting performances still tend to be measured against a textual 'original' which we acknowledge as unstable, just as shape-shifting in print forms as are subsequent performances. Even the notion of a play's 'afterlife' (yet another 'a-' term), insofar as it points to what happens *after* the text, silently, even nostalgically, privileges print over performance. Indeed, even if dead playwrights do not have *copy*rights, the persuasive as well as pervasive 'idea of the play' accords them some rights (and rites) of memory. But what, exactly, are these? Long ago, Peter Brook wrote:

> When I hear a director speaking glibly of serving the author, of letting a play speak for itself, my suspicions are aroused, because this is the hardest job of all. If you just let a play speak, it may not make a sound. If what you want is for the play to be heard, then you must conjure its sound from it.
>
> (1972, 43)

Offering a global cross-section of such 'soundings', these essays consistently and pro-ductively blur distinctions between textual and theatrical performances, shape-shifting Shakespeare (once again) through collaborative strategies of 'co-authorial reconstitu-tion' (Sokolova p. 64). Here, too, writing back from performance (Rutter 2001: xii–xiii) re-performs the 'form and pressure' of Shakespeare's 'body of the time' in terms of pre-millennial and millennial cultures.

Forms and pressures

In taking a slice through this history, *World-wide Shakespeares* offers an ethnography of representational strategies, mapping local socio-cultural contexts and hierarchies of socio-political difference and using particular plays and performances as occasions to expose and interpret local anxieties, politics and histories. What areas, broached here, raise issues that invite further discussion? What plays appear, at certain moments in history, to speak to the forms and pressures of the times? Here, *Merchant of Venice*, the subject of four essays and mentioned in two others, haunts not just a European or Western post-Holocaust cultural imaginary (Jones and Schülting) but also becomes a vehicle for examining 'Crypto-Jewish experience as part of the New Mexican *mestizaje*' (Klein and Shapiro p. 35) and for resonating with the forced evictions and massacres in New Zealand's Maori culture (Houlahan).   When Arnold Wesker faults David Thacker's production of *Merchant* for hiding the historical record of the play's trans-mission and views his own as a more significant critique of Shakespeare's play because it speaks from within the position of the Jew as alien, it is tempting to ask: 'And Shakespeare's play does not?' Of whose appropriation – or adaptation – do we speak? Whose history, whose subjectivity, whose meanings?

If the realtor's mantra – location, location, location – resounds throughout these essays, redrawing Shakespeare's cultural coordinates, how might we undertake a more precise measurement of the continuities and discontinuities among, as well as the recip-rocal impact of, local performance conventions and traditions? Moreover, what relations pertain or, to invoke ideology, 'should' pertain between or among a specific perform-ance, new historicist or cultural materialist readings (especially but not exclusively those focused expressly on early modern contexts) and present-day events and histories? What limits and limitations are involved in such projects? Is there a point at which a performance speaks 'too much' history – or becomes 'too political' and so apparently dislodges or loses entirely (textual) historicity (Bristol and McLuskie 2001)? And as we trace the transformational processes the full complement of critical and theatrical practitioners bring to bear on what they read and witness, perhaps the least theorized arena involves how audiences transform what they hear and see, how spectators refashion a performance to serve individual as well as communal needs. What discursive frameworks – the paratextual documentation appearing in programmes, posters, market-ing ephemera and reviews – manipulate reception? What role do the layerings of memory play in such projects? What gets remembered; what forgotten?

Despite whatever longings we may sustain to speak with the dead (Greenblatt 1988), we are never 'in' Shakespeare's world but in our own, collaborating with him over time and from a distance. Again, Peter Brook: 'It is not the Shakespearean method that interests us. It is the Shakespearean ambition. The ambition to question people and society in action, in relation to human existence. Quintessence and dust' (1987, 55). In addressing that ambition, *World-wide Shakespeares* not only assumes an eminently Shakespearean gaze but also takes an eminently modernist stance. For the Shakespeares described and analysed here produce more and more performance from less and less text. Once associated primarily with cinema or avant-garde theatre, minimalist *textual* Shakespeare seems, in this first decade of a new century, to have become a widespread phenomenon.

In closing, a brief (theatrical) history. A decade ago, Katie Mitchell's *Henry VI: The Battle for the Throne* (RSC 1994) staged a kind of double project, a response to the situations in Bosnia and Rwanda and an ethnography of England's own genocidal civil war (Hodgdon 1999, 16–17). During Summer 2003, Nicholas Hytner's *Henry V* at London's National Theatre restaged front-page images documenting two events: the Vietnam War (the iconic photograph of an officer turning to shoot a prisoner in the head) and the ongoing war in Iraq (hooded prisoners kneeling before heavily armed captors). In Summer 2004, Theatre Complicité's *Measure for Measure* at the same venue made present and local Lucio's phrase from the first brothel scene, 'the sanctimonious pirate, that went to sea with the Ten Commandments, but scrap'd one out of the table' by accompanying it with a video image of George W. Bush. By mid-summer, however, it was not Shakespeare who was addressing the current crisis; it was, instead, Euripides' *Iphigenia at Aulis* and Sophocles' *Lysistrata*, together with a host of new-made satires, documentaries and histories, their titles and materials struck, as the phrase goes, from today's headlines. What will be the plays that will rise up to be remembered, dismembered and re-envisioned – adapted, appropriated, given an afterlife – and to give local habitations and names to our current historical moment, when 'terror' has become both a global and local catchword? What's to come is still unsure, but whatever we may find as we attend to once and future performances, they will probably tell us, as those to which *World-wide Shakespeare*'s contributors pay attention do, how, with Shakespeare in our minds and hands, we imagined ourselves at one particular time.

Notes

1 Defining local Shakespeares

1 This reference is to Foakes (1984).
2 This reference is to Bevington (2001).
3 See, for example, Bristol and McLuskie (2001), Worthen (1997), Bennett (1996) and Grady (1991).
4 Bhabha's essay, 'Of Mimicry and Man: The Ambivalence of Colonial Discourse' (Bhabha 1989), was first published in 1983. In 1988 Bhabha shifted his attention to the notion of 'Thirdspace', which is, however, still firmly dualistic, or at best, dialectic, even when Bhabha insists that it is not: 'It is in this space that we will find those words with which we can speak of Ourselves and Others. And by exploring this hybridity, this 'Thirdspace', we may elude the politics of polarity and emerge as the Others of Ourselves' (Bhabha 1995: 209). Bhabha's association of 'Thirdspace' and marginality in a later essay similarly reinforces traditional binary oppositions between 'centre' and 'periphery' (Bhabha 1992: 56).
5 See, among others, Anthony Davies' *Filming Shakespeare's Plays* (1988), which laid the grounds for later explorations of the relationship between film and stage. More recently, see Peter Donaldson's *Shakespearean Films/Shakespearean Directors* (1990) and Kathy Howlett's *Framing Shakespeare on Film* (2000).
6 I borrow this term from Chakrabarty (2000).
7 See, for example, Willson (2000), Zhang (1996), Williams (1990), Johnson (1996), Joughin (1997), Hortmann (1998), Bristol (1990), Ryuta *et al.* (2001), Li (2003), Trivedi and Bartholomeusz (2005), Shurbanov and Sokolova (2001), and Stříbrný (2000).

2 *A Branch of the Blue Nile:* Derek Walcott and the tropic of Shakespeare

1 For a comprehensive and stimulating discussion of *The Tempest* and its travels through postcolonial writing such as Lamming's, see Hulme and Sherman (2000).
2 Walcott, born in 1930, is just three years younger than Lamming and has dedicated his life's work to the search for a viable artistic idiom for the new world; see Chamberlin (1993) and Döring (2002).
3 For details about historical and biographical contexts, see King (2000: 424–5).
4 For previous discussions, which have influenced my reading, see Breslow (1989) and Klein (2000).
5 By questioning assumptions about the cultural translatability of English drama, Walcott's play addresses pitfalls in globalizing the Shakespeare canon which result from the colonial economy that established this canon in the first place; see Felperin (1990) and Viswanathan (1990).

3 Political *Pericles*

1 Joe Banno and Cam McGee graciously accorded me several private interviews to discuss the production, and Jeanne Addison Roberts called it to my attention. I was able to

see a video of the production courtesy of the Washington Area Performing Arts Video Archive.

2 All quotations from *Pericles* are from my Arden three edition (Gossett 2004).

3 McGee (private communication). The Washington production used the Folger Library General Reader's edition, edited by Louis B. Wright and Virginia A. LaMar (1968), except for this addition and further additions to the brothel scene. The additional passages came from the Oxford/Norton Shakespeare. The Oxford 'reconstruction' is based largely on George Wilkins's novella, *The Painful Adventures of Pericles Prince of Tyre* (1608), whose contested relation to the play is discussed in the Introduction to my edition.

4 In April, 2004, I saw a performance of *Henry IV Part Two* at the somewhat more mainstream Washington Shakespeare Theater. The production struck me as avoiding contemporary parallels, and a friend assured me that in Washington now overtly 'partisan' productions are avoided.

5 See my edition, pp. 87–8, and Boddy (1976) and Murphy (1984) for details.

6 Banno (private communication).

7 My evaluation is based on the video recording. It is possible that the scene had more resonance in live performance.

4 Shylock as crypto-Jew: A new Mexican adaptation of *The Merchant of Venice*

We wish to thank Ramón Flores for permitting us to copy materials from the archives of *La Compañía*, especially the first and final drafts of *The Merchant of Sante Fe* and videotapes of the production and the first *tertulia*. We are also grateful to Richard Edwards for permitting us to copy his collection of documents, notes and clippings pertaining to the production. Both Flores and Edwards shared their recollections with us in a series of interviews in Albuquerque in June 1996. Barry Gaines, Lynn Butler, Susan Seligman, Stanley Hordes, Cathy Herz and David Jones supplied additional material in interviews during the same period.

1 The Bible mentions a place called Sepharad (Obadiah 1:20), a term which medieval Jewish commentators used to refer to Spain and which has given Iberian Jews and their descendants the label *Sephardim*. Jews first appeared in the Iberian Peninsula in Roman times in settlements along the Mediterranean coast and remained in Spain during the Visigoth period and after the Islamic, or Moorish, invasions beginning in the eighth century. Flourishing Jewish communities developed in Andalusian cities such as Cordova, Seville and Granada, as well as in Christian areas such as Catalon, Aragon and Castile. Jews remained in Iberia during the *Reconquista*, the long period of Christian reconquest culminating in fall of Granada in 1492.

2 Most *conversos* probably tried to absorb their new religion, but some probably hoped to retain some form of Jewish practice, belief or identity, and some occupied a precarious middle ground between the two faiths (Gitlitz 1996: 73–96). Scholars disagree about the numbers in each category. Out of these mass conversions of 1391 emerged the phenomenon of the crypto-Jew, the Jew who retained vestigial Jewish practices or who inwardly identified as Jewish. Large-scale conversion continued for the next hundred years. Some families included both Jews and *conversos*, and the Jewish community tried to bring the latter back into the fold. Many New Christians found themselves suspected of judaizing, i.e. secretly adhering to Jewish beliefs and/or practices. Prejudice among Old Christians against all New Christians, whether or not they were crypto-Jews, was fairly widespread and eligibility for certain privileges required demonstration of pure Christian lineage or 'purity of blood' (*limpieza de sangre*). In 1478, to ferret out *judaizantes* from the ranks of New Christians, Ferdinand and Isabella persuaded Pope Sixtus IV to establish the Spanish Inquisition. The Holy Office, as it was also called, began to hold hearings in 1481 under the leadership of Torquemada, himself a *converso*. Such hearings usually resulted in an *auto-da-fé*, or demonstration of faith, in which *judaizantes* would be brought to repentance and so 'reconciled' to the Faith, or if that were not possible, 'released', i.e. turned over to the secular authorities to be burnt at the stake, in some but not all cases after strangulation by garroting. The coming of the Holy Office evidently encouraged some *conversos* to emigrate and others to try to make their Christianity seem beyond reproach.

3 Although precise numbers of those who fled or stayed behind are debated, historians believe that many Jews did convert, more or less sincerely. Others fled to Portugal, where in 1497 they, along with Portugal's own Jewish population, were baptized *en masse* by royal edict. In 1536, the Portuguese Inquisition was established and remained independent even while Portugal was annexed by Spain, from 1580 to 1636. Over a period of almost two-hundred years, many Spanish and Portuguese Jews and *conversos* fled to such places as Southern France, Italy, North Africa, Holland and the Ottoman Empire, where Judaism could be practised safely. Refugees from Portugal became so numerous that as a Portuguese Jesuit remarked, 'In popular parlance, among most of the European nations, "Portuguese" is confused with "Jew"' (Bodian 1997: 13).

4 In the sixteenth century, the Inquisition also found its way to the Americas. Although slightly more tolerant than its Spanish progenitor, the Mexican Inquisition followed the same procedures. *Judaizantes* were denounced, incarcerated, tortured, tried and convicted throughout the sixteenth century. Some had risen quite high in the colonial administration, such as Luis de Carvajal, Governor of the province of New Leon, who was permitted by royal decree to bring over colonists without asking for proof that they were Old Christians. Caravel died in prison in 1590, but prosecutions of his extended family continued for some decades, 'until all but those members of the family who had not escaped to Peru or elsewhere were completely destroyed' (Greenleaf 1969: 171; Liebman 1970: 159–62).

5 Negotiating intercultural spaces: *Much Ado About Nothing* and *Romeo and Juliet* on the Chinese stage

1 For a general study of Shakespearean performance in China see Li (2003), Zhang (1996), Tatlow (1995) and Yu (1990).

2 This production is discussed in greater depth in Li (2003).

3 Jiang and I discussed this production on 20 and 28 February 2001. All citations from Jiang were taken from these two conversations unless otherwise noted.

4 Li Yu, a playwright and drama theorist (1611–c.1679), pointed out that 'too many unnecessary threads [i.e. trivial plots] are the worst possible thing for a play. The reason why *Jingchai ji* (*The Story of the Wooden Hairpin*), *Liu Zhiyuan* (name of the protagonist), *Bai yue ting* (*The Pavilion for Worshiping the Moon*) and *Sha gou ji* (*The Story of Killing a Dog*) are still so popular nowadays is simply because there is only one plot throughout from beginning to end, without any trivial episodes in them. Even if a small child sees such plays, he can understand them easily and learn how to recite them quickly' (Zhongguo Xiqu Yanjiuyuan 1982: 14).

5 See, for example, Sinead Cusak's Beatrice in Terry Hands' 1982 Royal Shakespeare Company production of *Much Ado About Nothing*, described by Penny Gay as 'young, capable of both anger and hurt, but at ease with her sexuality and her body: this was an image that the young women of the 1980s could identify with' (1994: 170).

6 The translation is based on the script that I collected from the Anhui Huangmeixi Company.

7 All quotations from Shakespeare are from Evans (1968).

8 Performers were all Theatre Studies students and most leading actors were finalists. As much as the other two theatre academies on the mainland (Central Academy of Drama in Beijing and Shanghai Theatre Academy), the Drama School in the APA makes a great contribution to the performing arts for public audiences in Hong Kong, and all their performances are staged in professional theatres. Supervised by members of staff, stage crews are all students from the School of Technical Arts. Staging Shakespeare is also a tradition in spoken drama curriculum in China since the 1950s when Soviet practitioners established the education system. For a detailed discussion, see Li (2003).

9 The Chinese concept of 'the giant' is based on Engels's definition of the Renaissance. In his 'Introduction' to *Dialectics of Nature* Engels wrote: 'It [Renaissance] was the greatest progressive revolution that mankind has so far experienced, a time which called for giants and produced giants – giants in power of thought, passion, and character, in universality and learning' (Haldane 1960: 2–3).

10 Huang Zuolin was one of the leading directors in spoken drama in China. His operatic adaptation *Blood-stained Hands* from *Macbeth* made a great contribution to the tradition of Shakespearean performance in China. For further details, see Li (2003).
11 The Shanghai Theatre Academy has trained Tibetan and Mongolian actors since the late 1970s. Apart from the Tibetan *Romeo and Juliet*, they produced a Mongol *Othello* (1986) and *A Midsummer Night's Dream* (1986).

6 'It is the bloody business which informs thus…'. Local politics and performative praxis: *Macbeth* in India

1 See my section on India in Trivedi (2002) for a longer discussion on the adaptive tradition and on the subversive transposition of 'Hindustan' for 'England' in the sexual cartography mapped by Dromio of Syracuse on the globe-like kitchen wench in a Hindi translation (1882) of *The Comedy of Errors*.
2 For a detailed account of the performance of Shakespeare in India, see my introduction to Trivedi and Bartholomeusz (2005).
3 For a detailed discussion of *Barnam Vana* see my 'Folk Shakespeare: The Performance of Shakespeare in Traditional Indian Theatre forms' and for *Gombe Macbeth*, see Laxmi Chandrashekar's '"A sea change into something rich and strange": Ekbal Ahmed's *Macbeth* and *Hamlet*' in Trivedi and Bartholomeusz (2005).
4 H.S. Shiva Prakash is a prolific Kannada playwright and poet who has published over twenty plays and fifteen collections of poetry, including translations and adaptations. His first experiment with Shakespeare was a play, *Shakespeare Swapna Nowke* (Shakespeare's Dreamboat) in 1991, a quizzical look at Shakespeare's art through his life and context.
5 Jainism is a puritanical religious sect founded in the sixth century BC. Asceticism and an emphasis on extreme non-violence are its defining features. Agriculture, for example, is frowned on since cultivation involves the killing of insects. An animistic belief that the universe functions through an interaction of living souls (*jivas*) and that souls inhabit not just human, animal or plant matter, but also stones, water, etc., is the basis of their pacifism.
6 The play *Maranayakana Drishtanta* has often been interpreted as an environmentalist play protesting the indiscriminate destruction of forests in South India. One such production was Krishnamurty Kavatar's with the group Abhinayataranga in Mangalore in 1995.
7 Kattimani's first such workshop was at Bellary Central Jail in 1997. He moved to work at Mysore prison when Bellary did not allow the prisoners to present the show outside the jail.
8 Ironically, this DIG of Police used the rehabilitation programme to get publicity for himself, which helped him to get elected to the state assembly after his retirement. Subsequent officers, who could not exploit the programme for its political mileage, had no use for it and no regular theatre therapy programme has been established.
9 Lokendra Arambam is the director of the Forum for Laboratory Theatres of Manipur, a progressive group committed to experimental work. His most well known is *Nhaumm Chaka Moireng Ngamva*, a play which focuses on tribal rivalries and revenge. For a detailed account of contemporary theatre in Manipur see *Seagull Theatre Quarterly*, special number on Manipuri Theatre, vol. 14/15, Sept. 1997.
10 For a discussion of the challenge of reading intercultural adaptations, see my 'Reading Other Shakespeares', in Trivedi (2003).

7 Relocating and dislocating Shakespeare in Robert Sturua's *Twelfth Night* and Alexander Morfov's *The Tempest*

1 The same programme was used for the later productions with additions due to changes in the cast.
2 Georgi Alexi-Meskhishvili is Sturua's collaborator of many years and scenographer of international repute. Besides Georgia, he has worked in London, Dusseldorf, Moscow and Buenos Aires and has taught in Georgia and the USA.

3   Ghia Kancheli is a world-famous composer of film, theatre and symphony music. Most of his life he has worked in his native Georgia and throughout the Soviet Union. His appearance in the West, has been described by Michael Walsh of *Time* magazine 'as possibly the most important event from the time of Shostakovich to the present day' (Quoted in the theatre programme, Sofia 2001–2). In 2000 he won the Sony Award for a best-selling composer.
4   Maria's part was performed by Reni Vrangova.
5   This is a piece of information which I have not been able to check independently. My discussion is based on newspaper publications, most notably: Dimiter Tsolov's (2001) and Krasimira Vasileva's (2001).
6   All quotations are from Kermode (1954).
7   In conversation with Boika Sokolova, May 2002.
8   Krustyu Lafazanov, Petur Popyordanov and Teodor Elmazov.

8 'I am not bound to please thee with my answers': *The Merchant of Venice* on the post-war German stage

1   In the following years, some German theatres organized stage readings and public discussions of *Der Müll, die Stadt und der Tod*. For further details on the controversy about Fassbinder's play, see Bodek (1991), Delekat (1998), Hadomi and Horch (1996), Ohland and Jung (1998) and Pankow (1998).
2   On the 'Historikerstreit', see Augstein (1995), Wippermann (1997), Peter (1995) and Kosiek (1988).
3   On Kortner's career as an actor in the Weimar Republic, see Brand (1981).
4   *I would my daughter were dead at my foot and the jewels in her ear: Improvisations on Shakespeare's Shylock.*
5   'Antonio ist traurig' ('Antonio is Sad'), 'Bassanio braucht Geld' ('Bassanio needs money'), 'Alter Gobbo trifft Jungen Gobbo/Lanzelot' ('Old Gobbo meets Young Gobbo'), etc.
6   The so-called 'Kristallnacht' was the night of 9–10 November 1938, when the Nazis organized a pogrom throughout Germany, burning synagogues, destroying and pillaging Jewish shops and houses, and transporting tens of thousands of Jews to the concentration camps in Dachau, Buchenwald and Sachsenhausen.
7   This is reflected in Fassbinder's *Der Müll*, where the fear of the rich Jew is motivated by the fact that he *could* speak about Auschwitz and his parents' death, as the Nazi Hans von Gluck bemoans: 'The Jew is to blame because he puts the blame on us, because he is there. If he had stayed where he came from or if they had gassed him, I could sleep better today. They forgot to gas him' (Fassbinder 1998: 75). However, Fassbinder's Jew does not figure as a witness; he hardly mentions the Shoah at all but leaves the field to Hans von Gluck, Müller, Roma B.'s father and others without questioning their version of the story.
8   'Muselmann' or 'living corpses', is the name given to those victims in the concentration camps in whom everything but the mere physical functions of survival have died.
9   However, this does not apply to Dieter Dorn's *Kaufmann von Venedig* at the Residenztheater in Munich (2001), probably one of the most important productions of *The Merchant of Venice* in recent years. Dorn avoided any explicit references to the Shoah. For Hortmann, Dorn's production was a 'trans-Holocaust' (rather than 'post-Holocaust') *Merchant*, concentrating on the hope for a more peaceful future as represented by the younger generation (Hortmann 2003: 223).

9 Katherina 'humanized': Abusing the Shrew on the Prague stage

1   Rather than using the more common abbreviation, *The Shrew*, which implicitly assumes the presence of a shrewish character in the play, I refer to Shakespeare's play as *Taming*, since the taming of Katherina is always indisputably present. Similarly, I avoid calling Katherina 'Kate' since 'Kate' silently endorses Petruchio's abusive practices.
2   Diana Henderson stresses that Western Europe and North America produce film versions of *Taming* at times of intense backlash against feminism (1997: 150). Emily Detmer argues that,

to perceive the play as a comedy, 'readers and viewers … must minimize the violence, and, at the same time, justify its use' (1997: 274). Shirley Garner points out that, in this context, the audience must accept 'the premise…that a shrewish woman is less than human…[and] so may be treated as an animal'. Garner asks: 'Could the taming of a "shrew" be considered the proper subject of farce in any but a misogynist culture? How would we feel about a play entitled *The Taming of the Jew* or *The Taming of the Black?* I think we would be embarrassed by anti-Semitism or racism in a way that many of us are not by misogyny' (1988: 109–10).

3   This and following translations from Czech are mine.

4   The results of the study showed, for instance, that one in six people have experienced domestic violence, and that 61% have witnessed it; 47% were uncertain whether they would respond to neighbours screaming and crying or whether they would ignore them, and 29% thought that domestic violence should be tolerated and resolved within the family (Dolanský 2001b). In some areas nearly half of the population (46%) did not know the meaning of the term 'domestic violence' (A.V.O. and T.O.F. 2001: 1). The research further pointed out that there is very little in place in terms of a network for victims of domestic violence (L.D.S. 2001: 1).

5   For an overview of the debate, see, for example, Thompson (2003: 17–24, 42–9). All subsequent references from *The Taming of the Shrew* are from this edition.

6   To understand the class-based differences in domination of women as reflected in Shakespeare's *Taming*, I find Detmer's 'Civilizing Subordination' particularly useful. Using early modern domestic manuals, which document a shift in the perception of the proper response of a husband towards an unruly wife from beatings and other violent acts of forced subordination perceived as common or lower class practices to a 'modern', more psychological, form of domination worthy of gentlemen, Detmer argues that Petruchio participates in the newly evolving 'tradition that accepts coercive bonding and oppression as long as they are free of physical violence' (1997: 274, 289).

7   In this specific form of domestic abuse the victim, much like a hostage isolated from others and afraid for her/his safety, responds positively to any show of kindness from the captor/abuser, and 'finds [that] the key to survival [is] to actively develop strategies for staying alive… . [since] alternating coercive threats and kindness sets up situations where victims actively look for ways to please rather than upset their captors' (Detmer 1997: 284, 287).

8   'Ona je má, můj nábytek, mé zboží,/můj dům, můj dvůr, má stodola, mé pole,/můj kůň, můj vůl, můj dobytek, mé všechno!'

9   'to on se pořád o tebe jen stará,/riskuje život na moři i souši,/zná noční bouře, třeskutý mráz snáší,/Když ty si hovíš v bezpečí a v teple.'

10   'Jen do ní, Káčo!/Hortensio: Nedej se, vdovičko!'

10 *Shooting the Hero*: The cinematic career of Henry V from Laurence Olivier to Philip Purser

1   In the film version, Fluellen's statement at the end of the scene, namely that they will resume the interrupted discussion later, is cut (3.2). It suggests that the conflict with the French unites the representatives of Britain. With Macmorris, Fluellen would seem to argue that war 'is no time to discourse' (3.2.106).

2   Asked later for the secret of his success in the cinematic role of Henry the Fifth, Olivier would reply: 'I don't know – I'm England, that's all' (Spoto 1991: 96).

3   Spoto recalls how Alexander Korda, in an attempt to please Churchill, used *Lady Hamilton* to drive home the parallel between Napoleon and Hitler *vs.* Nelson and Churchill (1991: 133).

4   All references are to Craik 1995.

5   Emphasis on this controversial issue may be found in recent academic writing on Olivier's film. Peter Drexler (1995: 132) shows how these two films reveal 'similarities in the handling of symbolic codes', suggesting, for example, that the patriotism of Olivier's film is best measured in comparative terms against the contemporary output of the German film industry. See also Anthony Davies (2000: 167–8).

11 Lamentable tragedy or black comedy?: Friedrich Dürrenmatt's adaptation of *Titus Andronicus*

1 Dürrenmatt's adaptation has been briefly discussed in Kolin (1995: 505–8) and in Cohn (1976: 29–37); see also Mehlin (1972: 73–98). As I refer throughout this essay to the sixteenth-century tragedy as 'Shakespeare's *Titus Andronicus*', a word concerning the play's authorship seems in order. Brian Vickers (2002: 148–243) has recently advanced forceful reasons to believe that George Peele wrote the play's long opening scene and, possibly, three further scenes, 2.1, 2.2 and 4.1. Vickers' case seems convincing, and he may well be correct. Even if Peele contributed to *Titus Andronicus*, however, the greatest part of the play is still by Shakespeare; for the sake of convenience, I will therefore refer to the play as his.

2 For Dürrenmatt's adaptation of *King John*, see Reber (1976: 80–9). For Dürrenmatt's projected adaptation of *Troilus and Cressida*, see Bloch (1972: 67–72).

3 'Er erzählte ..., dass er seine Stücke am liebsten in Dialekt geschrieben hätte' (Weber and von Planta 1994: 78). See also Dürrenmatt (1980c: 120–4).

4 *Titus Andronicus* 'stellt den Versuch dar, das berüchtigte, chaotische Jugendwerk Shakespeares für die deutsche Bühne spielbar zu machen, ohne die Shakespearschen Grausamkeiten und Grotesken zu vertuschen' (Dürrenmatt 1980b: 158). Unless otherwise stated, the translations are mine.

5 Schauspielhaus Düsseldorf, 12 December 1970.

6 I quote from Bate's 1995 edition throughout this chapter.

7 Note that Bate's Arden three edition breaks with editorial tradition by printing as one continuous scene what previous editors had divided into 1.1 and 2.1.

8 I refer to and quote from Dürrenmatt (1980a).

9 'Die Tragödie setzt Schuld, Not, Mass, Übersicht, Verantwortung voraus. In der Wurstelei unseres Jahrhunderts, in diesem Kehraus der weissen Rasse, gibt es keine Verantwortlichen mehr. Alle können nichts dafür und haben es nicht gewollt. Es geht wirklich ohne jeden. ... Uns kommt nur noch die Komödie bei' (Dürrenmatt 1966: 122).

10 Whereas Edward Ravenscroft's adaptation in the late seventeenth century emphasized and enlarged the Moor's character, Dürrenmatt thus does the opposite.

11 'Noch/Ein Nierchen, Leber, Hirn, ein Rippenstück' (193). This kind of black humour is of course also present in Shakespeare's play, as exemplified by Titus' puns on hands: 'Come hither, Aaron. I'll deceive them both:/Lend me thy hand and I will give thee mine' (3.1.187–8); 'Speak, Lavinia, what accursed hand/Hath made thee handless in thy father's sight?' (3.1.67–8); 'O handle not the theme, to talk of hands,/Lest we remember still that we have none' (3.2.29–30).

12 By contrast, a Stratford production of 1923 still dissolved in audience laughter (see Cohn 1976: 35).

13 Here and elsewhere, it is easy to perceive the influence the work of Bertolt Brecht exerted on the Swiss dramatist.

14 Recently, the specific question of dormant Swiss bank accounts Nazi victims sparked an international debate leading to a full-scale investigation into the economic facts of the Holocaust by the Swiss Independent Commission of Experts, known as the 'Bergier Commission', from 1997 to 2002. Its findings were published in Bergier Commission (2002). See also Wylie (2003: 300–31).

15 See, for instance, Dürrenmatt (1969: 62–73).

16 'Die Schweiz wagte jedoch nachträglich nicht mehr zu sich selber zu stehen, sie empfand die Notlage als schändlich, in der sie sich während des Krieges befand, und dichtete sich dann vom Menschlichen ins Heldische oder ins Teuflische um. Die Wahrheit ist, daß wir keine Wahl hatten. Wir haben sicher im Krieg viele Fehler gemacht, aber im wesentlichen war unsere Politik menschlich. Man kann von den Politikern nicht das Heldische fordern. Wir haben kein Recht, auf unsere damaligen Politiker Steine zu werfen. Sie haben ihr politisches Ziel erreicht, nämlich die Schweiz aus dem Kriege herausgehalten. Sie haben es mit moralisch oft ungenügenden und sogar bedenklichen Mitteln getan. ... In einer unwürdigen

Zeit ist keine rein würdige Haltung möglich. Nachträglich zu verlangen, unsere Politiker hätten Helden sein sollen, geht nicht an' (Dürrenmatt 1996: 252–3).

17 'An den Patriotismus glauben nur jene, die von ihm profitieren, die Mächtigen, und die Gerechtigkeit dient dazu, deren Macht zu legitimieren' (Dürrenmatt, 1980a: 210).

12 Subjection and redemption in Pasolini's *Othello*

1 Pasolini's films, including *Nuvole*, were recently shown in London at the French Institute (12–24 March 2004), in collaboration with the Italian Institute (London) and the Fondazione Pier Paolo Pasolini (Rome).

2 See, for example, Neill (1989), Parker (1994: 84–100), Petcher (1996), Adelman (1997) and Callaghan (2000: 75–96).

3 'I maestri son fatti per essere mangiati in salsa piccante.' All translations from Italian primary and secondary sources are mine.

4 This poem was included in *Poesia in Forma di Rosa* (1961–4); see Chiarcossi and Siti (1999: 721–35).

5 Line references are to Honigmann (1997).

6 'Ah,/uccellaccia nera, che ti fingi bianca.'

7 'tu/dormi,/dove e come non so, *verso di Shakespeare*, ritornato/per istinto stagionale/da terre che non hanno nulla/a che fare con noi.'

8 'Tutto ciò che ho saputo, per grazia/o per volontà, smetta di essere sapienza. … E, per un po' di scienza della storia che mi dà esperienza/… mi prendo tutta l'innocenza della vita futura!'

9 'Otello, apri l'occhi!'; 'È stato Jago a dà a Cassio quel fazzoletto'; 'Cassio non parlava de Desdemona! Parlava de Bianca! A disgrazziato pure a te! Magara tocchi Desdemona te facciamo vede noi!'

10 'Povera bambina,/è morta per amor/povera bambina/è morta per amor./La gente che qui passa/le getterà un bel fior.'

11 'Sì, mio signore … (*lo schiaffo ricevuto ha aumentato il suo rispetto e il suo amore*) però che schiaffo m'avete date! E il primo schiaffo che piglio! Se volete darmene un altro … (*ha un ambiguo sorriso di sottomissione*).'

12 'Burattinaio: Forse … sei tu che vuoi ammazzar[la]./Otello: Come? Me piace ammazzare? E perchè?/Burattinaio: Forse … perchè a Desdemona piace essere ammazzata./Otello: Ah! È così? (*ha una faccia sconvolta dal terrore e dalla meraviglia*).'

13 'Marrano, tu insidi le nostre ragazze … '

14 'Egli insidia l'onore delle nostre donne, signor Governatore! Scandalo! Scandalo!'

15 I am grateful to Douglas Lanier, who has pointed out how films which use the motif of players rehearsing or re-enacting *Othello* have a long history in the Continental European and in the Anglo-American traditions. The first film was a Danish two-reeler, *Desdemona [For Åbent Tæppe*], directed by August Blom (1910), and it was followed by: *A Modern Othello, aka The Shadow of Night, The Lash of Jealousy, and The Mad Lover* [*Een Moderne Othello*], a full-length Pathe film scripted by Leonce Perret and produced by Harry Rapf in 1917; *Carnival*, directed by Harley Knowles in 1921 (from the play by Alexander Matheson Lang and H.C.M. Haringe); *Carnival: Venetian Nights*, a sound remake of the Knowles film directed by Herbert Wilcox in 1931; *Men are not Gods*, directed by Alex Korda in 1937; *The Strangler*, directed by Harold Huth in 1940; and *A Double Life*, directed by George Cukor in 1947.

16 'un sogno dentro ad un sogno'

17 For more details on the four posters and on the role of a further painting by Velasquez, 'Venus and Cupid', which is posted, as an unlikely pin-up, to the garbage collector's van, see Pistoia (1990) and Iafrate (1990).

18 Alberto Marchesini reports that 'la critica è propensa ad associare la scoperta di Velasquez alla lettura di Foucault' (critics tend to relate [Pasolini's] discovery of Velasquez to his reading of Foucault; 1994: 15n). Marchesini may be wrong, because Pasolini visited El Prado in 1964, when, as his poem 'Patmos' reveals, he was fascinated by Velasquez's paintings.

Francesco Galluzzi, on the other, hand, is right when he establishes a connection which my essay explores in detail. 'Tutta la critica', he explains, 'ha rilevato la dipendenza di questa scelta pasoliniana dall'analisi del dipinto condotto da Michel Foucault in *Les Mots et les Choses*, ... dove *Las Meninas* viene definito "una sorta di rappresentazione della rappresentazione classica" (critics have established the origin of Pasolini's choice in Michel Foucault's analysis of the painting in *Les Mots et les Choses*, ... where *Las Meninas* is referred to as 'a sort of representation of classical representation'). See Galluzzi (1994: 64).

19 'A questo pubblico che prende parte alla vicenda se ne affianca un altro mutevole e irraggiungibile: noi che guardiamo il cortometraggio. Noi coincidiamo con il pubblico del teatrino durante la rappresentazione dell' *Otello*, e di conseguenza gli ammiccamenti di Jago sono rivolti contemporaneamente a due pubblici diversi. ... Lo sguardo di Jago, che è perfettamente consapevole della nostra complicità, partecipa della stessa natura vincolante del pittore all'interno del quadro, della cui traiettoria siamo prigionieri.'

20 'Il potere mercifica il corpo, riducendolo a "cosa" e mai, come durante il nazi-fascismo, questa cosa è stata anche visiva, concreta, fisica. Il potere oggi, secondo me, manipola più profondamente le coscienze.'

21 'E coinvolto anch'esso/nel mondo della nostra ricchezza,/e pur guardando fuori del quadro ne è dentro!'

22 'Velasquez è in prigione perché ha un corpo.'

23 'La società chiusa, squallida degli spettatori, in cui sussiste l'obbligo di agire secondo un ruolo prestabilito da altri ... è un vero inferno, il cui braccio armato è la scempiaggine del pubblico-massa che reagisce solo in base alla schematizzazione di ciò che vede, esteriormente, accadere. Il pubblico entra nell'opera e lo fa a pezzi ed è solo questo che può fare nella sua somma inconsapevolezza, nel suo abbruttimento sociale, nell'accecamento che nasce dal non comprendere ciò che si consuma, e da cui si pretende, in quanto paganti, la soddisfazione delle proprie aspettative, borghesemente "etiche".'

24 Only a year before *Nuvole*, Pasolini directed *Hawks and Sparrows* (1966), a clear homage to Roberto Rossellini's *Francesco Giullare di Dio* (1950).

25 'serio e dolce, un vecchio, paziente filosofo'

26 'Lo specchio di Velasquez e il sogno pasoliniano, nel comune tradimento della mimesi, intrecciano al motivo della visione, quello più inquietante dell'elusione, quel non detto che rappresenta la cifra più autentica dell'esistenza dei burattini.'

27 'Oh, straziante, meravigliosa bellezza del creato.'

28 'Le ciliege del peccato'

29 'Una sola finestrella ... , piccola come una feritoia'

13 'Meaning by Shakespeare' south of the border

1 'At first he thought that everyone else was like him, but the look of surprise from a colleague with whom he started to discuss such trifle made him realize his mistake...' (my translation). With love to Mónica, Sarah, Dina and Mayté. My gratitude to Sonia, another Sonia, and Bernice.

2 For instance, Denis Salter's view that 'the Shakespearean text will have to go on being enacted elsewhere – but not (and not ever again?) in postcolonial space' (1996: 129) is debatable. As an English-speaking post-colonial subject who assumes that he *must* deal with Shakespeare exclusively in his original language, Salter may justifiably feel that his linguistic and artistic practices are constrained. But he altogether rejects the possiblity of employing what, with or 'without his language', remains a valuable vehicle for locally significant, transformative initiatives, although he acknowledges that 'Québécois actors do have a greater degree of freedom, partly because they can perform Shakespeare in their own language' (1996: 125).

3 Throughout, my uses of 'tactic' refer to de Certeau (1984), and those of 'transformation' and 'interpolation' to Ashcroft (2001).

4 'Cannibalization' refers to de Campos (2000a).

5   A thought-provoking discussion of our problematic relationship with the USA may be found in Monsiváis (2003).
6   Their products, however, cannot help being rightly perceived as anxiously catering to 'global' taste by means of pleasing mimicry, shock or exoticism, as suggested by the international success of Mexican films such as *Como agua para chocolate* (1992, dir. Alfonso Arau) or *Amores perros* (2000, dir. Alejandro González Iñárritu), and the enlistment of their makers in the ranks of the Hollywood industry.
7   It should be noted that the word 'glocalization' probably originated from a Japanese term meaning 'a global outlook adapted to local conditions', became usual in business jargon throughout the 1980s, and eventually was 'one of the marketing buzzwords of the beginning of the nineties' (see Robertson 1995: 28).
8   My reference is to the original text in Portuguese; the present translation is found in Larsen (2001: 78–9).
9   Many cases take forms corresponding to either 'tradaptation' (Brisset 1996) or 'transcreation' (de Campos 2000b; Ribeiro Pires Vieira 1999). For a stimulating array of recent views on Shakespeare translation, all involving issues of locality, see Hoenselaars (2004).
10   Mexican productions of Shakespeare then were generally consistent with Dennis Kennedy's descriptions of the contemporary trends of Shakespeare staging in Europe (see 1996: 137–45; and 2001b: 152–302).
11   Or actually towards Broadway. That is, many affluent Mexicans prefer to attend a show in New York once or twice a year to seeing a Mexican production.
12   As I have elsewhere pointed out, the adoption of a Spaniard's version amounts to a blind denial of local linguistic and literary history (see Modenessi 2001: 155–7; 2004: 243–8).
13   The most common Spanish last names end in '-ez', signifying 'the son or daughter of such or such *father*'.
14   For example, Germán Castillo in his adaptation *Los señores Macbeth* ('Lord and Lady Macbeth', 1977).
15   See, for example, *Richard II* (1994, dir. Enrique Singer), an unmemorably flat *Hamlet* (1997, dir. Martín Acosta), and a superb *As You Like It* (2002, dir. Mauricio García Lozano).
16   *Love's Labour's Lost* by José Caballero (2000); see Modenessi (2004). Other examples include *Macbeth* by Jesusa (2002) and *Titus Andronicus* by Ana Francis Mor (2003).
17   *Hamlet P'urhepecha* (1990, dir. Juan Carlos Arvide; see Modenessi 2001); *Los señores de la noche* ('Lord and Lady of the Night', 1992), an adaptation of *Macbeth* directed by José Luis Cruz; and *La noche que raptaron a Epifania* ('The night Epifania was abducted', 2001) a free version of *Twelfth Night* by Gerardo Mancebo, directed by Ana Francis Mor.
18   *A la manera de Shakespeare* (performed in English as *Perchance to Dream*, 1990) written and directed by Susana Wein; and *Morir, dormir, soñar* ('To die, to sleep, to dream', 1994) by David Olguín, directed by Lorena Maza.
19   Jesusa usually takes a year or more to prepare a major project. This time the strain proved too much for several members of the cast, who dropped out near the final stages of production.
20   Jesusa and Pimentel modernized Enriqueta González Padilla's translation, which was published by the National University of Mexico in 1991, although they regrettably failed to do away with its cumbersome usage of Iberian Spanish (Modenessi 2001. 155–7).
21   A treble pun suggesting that her production would have been as much a 'mise' (*puesta*) as a 'bet' (*apuesta*) 'en scène', but ended up being an '*un-mise-en-scène*' (*a-puesta*, where the use of 'a' as prefix indicates 'absence of').

14 Dreams of England

1   A key innovation in this respect, established by Madame Lucia Elizabeth Vestris in 1840 at Covent Garden (and which would remain in place until challenged by Harley Granville Barker in 1914), was the cross-casting of Oberon. As Williams observes, this 'addressed the patriarchal Victorian culture in complex, fascinating ways'; with Queen Victoria enthroned at the head of a trading empire that was gradually extending its claims over India and Africa,

it offered a provocative, alluring nexus of power and desire, 'an eroticized woman theatre manager stepped into the role of a male ruler ... simultaneously as appealing and disturbing to men as a dominatrix', who was also 'the adorable, diminutive enchantress in a child's fairy world, Lolita as well as angel' (Williams 1997: 96–7).

2   In 1981, the same year that the Time Life/BBC Television Shakespeare version featured Hugh Quarshie as Philostrate, Ron Daniels's RSC production cast Mike Gwilym as Theseus and Oberon, playing the latter as a figure from the *Arabian Nights*, and a black actor, Joseph Marcell, as Puck; stressing integration and reconciliation, Daniels averred that (in opposition to the Prime Minister's 'no-alternative' conviction politics, and in particular her administration's divisive racial policies) the play promoted 'the movement of our lives ... towards being whole and not toward being exclusive or fearful or dogmatic' (Williams 1997: 244). The show memorably used tiny puppets as fairies, including a miniature black double of Puck; the final image was of Oberon shaking its hand. This was progressive, integrationist politics of an fairly overt kind, and became a strong feature of English *Dream* performance during the next two decades, as represented, in different ways, by Robert Lepage's notorious Royal National Theatre production of 1992, which entertained complex – and contradictory – perspectives on the construction of sexuality and race by constructing a space inhabited by 'an American Bottom, an Asian Hippolyta ... [and] an African Oberon' (Hodgdon 1998: 183–4); Jatinder Verma's Tara Arts twentieth anniversary production of 1997, which utilized Burmese, African and Indian performers, performance styles drawn from Indian classical dance, kabuki, West African storytelling, and raga, and interpolated snatches of 'Binglish' (Bangladeshi English); and Christine Edzard's 2001 film *The Children's Midsummer Night's Dream*.

3   The 2002 season was notable for its determination both to promote opportunities for non-white performers and to challenge the RSC's status as a bastion of white high culture. The *Royal Shakespeare Company Review* for 2002 emphasizes the visual evidence of black performers strategically placed in key roles: Nonso Anozie in the lead in the RSC Academy's *King Lear*, Chuk Iwuji in *Julius Caesar*, Shelley Conn and Sasha Behar in *The Island Princess* and *Eastward Ho!*, Claire Benedict in *The Malcontent*, and Ray Fearon and Kananu Kirimi in Adrian Noble's Bollywood-extravaganza-style *Pericles*; the volume also documents the Tricycle Theatre/Yorkshire Playhouse co-production *Brixton Stories*.

15 The cultural logic of 'correcting' *The Merchant of Venice*

My thanks to Palgrave Macmillan for permission to include work published earlier in my book, *Shakespeare's Culture in Modern Performance* (2003).

1   See also Dessen's discussion of 'rescripting' and *rewrighting* in Dessen (2002).
2   *The Merchant of Venice. The Oxford Shakespeare* (Halio 1993). All further references to the play are to Halio (1993).
3   Royal Shakespeare Theatre Prompt Book, *The Merchant of Venice*, 1993 (The Shakespeare Centre Library).
4   All references to the play are from Wesker (1990).
5   Birmingham Repertory Theatre Programme, *The Merchant* (12 October – 4 November 1978), Birmingham Central Library collection.
6   See Wesker (1997: 381); Everitt (1978); Chaillet (1978); Seaton (1978).
7   However, Michael Scott praises 'two brave attempts' by Wesker and Charles Marowitz (*Variations on The Merchant of Venice*, 1977) to confront the play's problems but suggests: 'we may need to demythologize Shylock and allow Shakespeare's blatant image to stand in the context of the Elizabethan's possible conception of the play. Theatrical cosiness and pandering to conscience would be dissipated in the offensive image of the Shakespearean original' (Scott 1989: 58–9).
8   Homi K. Bhabha identifies 'third space' as exceeding forms of knowledge locked into binary oppositions (1995); see also Soja (1996), who understands space as simultaneously real and symbolic.

16 Dancing with art: Robert Lepage's *Elsinore*

1 Joseph Grigely offers a strong expression of Shakespeare's drama as experienced cultural history in Grigely 1995, where he includes texts as varied as comic books and Thomas Bowdler's 1807 abridged edition of the plays as equally legitimate expressions of Shakespeare's work (89–199).
2 Lepage explains an idea of theatre as process in conversation with Alison McAlpine (Delgado and Heritage 1996: 135).
3 Lepage productions previously staged at the National were *Tectonic Plates* (1990), *Needles and Opium* (1992), *A Midsummer Night's Dream* (1992–3) and *The Seven Streams of the River Ota* (1996). *Coriolan* played at the Nottingham Playhouse in 1993, but did not transfer to London.
4 This is the figure cited by Hannon and McNeil (1996), Glaister (1996) and Spencer (1996a). Brian McMaster, Chief Executive of the Edinburgh International Festival, refused to speculate on cancellation costs (Anon. 1996).
5 Hamlet's first encounter with Rosencrantz and Guildenstern (2.2.243–378), for example, happened before Polonius showed his love letter to the King and Queen (2.2.86–159), rather than after his 'mad' scene with Polonius (2.2.171–211); Ophelia's narrative of Hamlet's visit to her closet was set in counterpoint to Hamlet's 'nunnery' speeches (2.1, 3.1); Gertrude's monologue describing the death of Ophelia (4.7.166–83) was interspersed with snatches of the maid's songs (4.5); and Hamlet's accounts of the pirate attack and his recomposition of the commission to England were conflated (4.6, 5.2). All line numbers are keyed to Spencer (1980).
6 See Furness (1877). The emendation can be found, for example, in Deighton (1891), and survives in slightly modified form in the annotation on 'Location' provided by *The Riverside Shakespeare*: 'Elsinore. A guard-platform of the castle' (Evans 1997).
7 The version performed by Darling at BAM opened, for example, with an anguished Hamlet sitting in a chair listening to (or reliving?) the Ghost's tale of murder, immediately followed by the 'To be or not to be' soliloquy, and the idea for 'The Mousetrap' was moved to Scene 4 from its placement at Scene 6 in the London staging. The effect of such alterations was to focus attention on Claudius, the murder, and Hamlet's revenge.
8 'What draws me to Hamlet is his inability to forge a link between the acts he must undertake and his own thoughts … [I]sn't it the absence of blind passion that prevents him doing what he has to do? Some might say that this isn't the most important paradox of Hamlet's nature; but for me it is the only one, because it's the one I share' (Lepage 1997).

17 Hekepia? The *Mana* of the Maori *Merchant*

1 'Authority, prestige, influence' (Orsman 1997: 465).
2 Earlier versions of this essay were generously heard and discussed by audiences in Auckland and at the 2002 MLA Convention in New York. Financial assistance was provided by the MLA, the Leave Committee of the University of Waikato and the Faculty of Arts and Social Sciences, University of Waikato. The essay could not have been completed without the support and encouragement of Sonia Massai, Margaret Jane Kidnie, Susan Zimmerman, Valerie Wayne, Michael Neill and Catherine Silverstone.
3 The 'reality' Curnow is describing here was that captured by a generation of post-1945 New Zealand poets. My citing it here, by analogy, serves to apply his claim to the rich specificity not just of Selwyn's film but indeed of all the local Shakespeares this collection celebrates. Curnow's later, post-modern poetic practice evokes a 'local' terrain which, like many of the Shakespeares analysed here, is contingent and strategic rather than rigidly essentialized.
4 The film screened in Hawaii in November 2002, where it won a people's choice award, at the Shakespeare Association of America meeting in Victoria, British Columbia in 2003 and at a symposium on translation in the Pacific at the University of California, Irvine, January 2004 (Neill 2004: 10).

5 The film was launched in Hamilton because Jones was from the main *iwi* or tribe in that area, Tainui. The film then toured New Zealand, being welcomed in turn by the local *iwi* of each specific area. Only after this tribal tour of New Zealand was the film launched overseas at the Hawaiian festival Valerie Wayne records (2003).

6 Jones gives the main characters and locations Maori names: 'Weniti' for Venice, 'Pohia' for Portia and so on. Here, I use the more familiar Shakespeare names.

7 The first European definitively to visit New Zealand and record proof of his visit was the Dutch sailor Abel Tasman in 1642, after whom of course Tasmania is named and after whose native province of Zeeland New Zealand takes its name. The story of the progressive revelation of New Zealand to Europeans and of European cultures to the Maori is ably told in Anne Salmond's *Two Worlds* (1991).

8 In July of 2004, Turia was re-elected to Parliament, as the first member of a new Maori Party.

9 Quote from video record of the forum, 9 July 2000, staged during *Dislocating Shakespeare: Limits, Crossings, Discoveries: the 6th Biennial Conference of the Australia and New Zealand Shakespeare Association.* My thanks to Professor Michael Neill for making available a copy of this video.

18 The Haiku *Macbeth*: Shakespearean antithetical minimalism in Kurosawa's *Kumonosu-jo*

1 See Buxton Forman (1948: 144) 'To John Hamilton Reynolds. Sunday 3 May 1818' (Letter 64).

2 Kurosawa, interviewed by Tony Rayns (1981: 173).

3 For quotations from Basho, see Stryk (1985). For all other haiku quoted, see Stryk and Ikemoto (1981).

4 See Muir 1970: xxxi.

5 Zeami Motokiyo (1363–1443) is the most influential of Noh theorists. See also Rimer and Yamazaki (1984: 75–6).

6 Kurosawa, interviewed by Tadao Sato, and quoted in Manvell (1979: 104).

7 References to *Macbeth* are from Muir 1970.

8 Quoted in Manvell (1979: 103).

9 See Hisae Niki's translation of the script of *Throne of Blood* in Kurosawa (1992).

10 For such views, see Mesnil (1973: 48), Richie (1973: 115, 117) and Prince (1991: 144).

11 I am indebted to Treat Paine and Soper for this link between Basho and Tohaku (1974: 98).

12 See '*Macbeth*, or Death-Infected' in Kott (1964: 89–100).

13 Despite his reservations about Kurosawa's omission of Shakespeare's text, Brook calls *Kumonosu-jo* 'a great masterpiece, perhaps the only true masterpiece inspired by Shakespeare.' Quoted in Kinder (1977: 339).

Bibliography

Abu-Lughod, Janet (1991) 'Going Beyond Global Babble', in A.D. King (ed.) *Culture, Globalization and the World-System*, Basingstoke: Macmillan, 131–7.

Adelman, Janet (1997) 'Iago's Alter Ego: Race as Projection in *Othello*', in *Shakespeare Quarterly*, 48, 125–44.

Agamben, Giorgio (1999) *Remnants of Auschwitz: The Witness and the Archive*, New York: Zone Books.

Aire, Sally (1978) '*The Merchant*', in *Plays and Players*, 26 December, 28.

Anon. (1978) 'Shylock im Souterrain', in *Die Welt*, 23 November.

Anon. (1978) 'Untitled', in *Punch*, 25 October.

Anon. (1996) 'A Riveting End to the Festival's Showpiece', in *The Daily Express*, 15 August.

Anon. (1998) 'Convicts Show Zest for Life in Stage Play', in *The Indian Express*, 18 June.

A. P.: čv (2001) 'Násilí na lidech i zvířatech spolu souvisí' [Abuse of animals and of people is related], in *Mladá Fronta Dnes (Young Front Today)*, 4 July, 10.

Armitstead, Claire (1994) 'The Trial of Shylock', in *The Guardian*, 13 April.

Ashcroft, Bill (2001) *Post-Colonial Transformation*, London and New York: Routledge.

Augé, Marc (1995) *Non-Places: Introduction to an Anthropology of Supermodernity*, trans. J. Howe, London: Verso.

Augstein, Rudolf (ed.) (1995) *"Historikerstreit": die Dokumentation der Kontroverse um die Einzigartigkeit der nationalsozialistischen Judenvernichtung*, Munich: Piper.

A.V.O and T.O.F. (2001) 'Domácí násilí většina lidí na Vysočině vůbec nezná' [Domestic abuse unknown to majority in Vysočina region], in *Mladá Fronta Dnes [Young Front Today]*, 14 November, 1.

Bachelard, G. (1994) *The Poetics of Space*, trans. M. Jolas, Boston: Beacon Press.

Bakhtin, M. (1979) *Problemy Poetiki Dostoyevskogo*, 4th edn, Moscow: Nauka.

Banno, Joe (1998) *Pericles*: 'Program Notes', The Washington Shakespeare Company.

Barber, J. (1997) 'Review of *A Midsummer Night's Dream*', in *The Daily Telegraph*, 9 May.

Bastin, Georges L. (1998) 'Adaptation', in Mona Baker (ed.) *The Routledge Encyclopedia of Translation Studies*, London: Routledge, 5–8.

Bate, Jonathan (ed.) (1995) *Titus Andronicus*, The Arden Shakespeare, third series, London: Routledge.

—— (2003) 'In the Script Factory', in *The Times Literary Supplement*, 18 April, 3–4.

Bazerman, C. (1977) 'Time in Play and Film: *Macbeth* and *Throne of Blood*', in *Literature/Film Quarterly*, 5.4: 333–7.

Bean, John C. (1980) 'Comic Structure and the Humanizing of Kate in *The Taming of the Shrew*', in Carolyn Ruth Swift Lenz, Gayle Greene and Carol Thomas Neely (eds) *The Woman's Part: Feminist Criticism of Shakespeare*, Urbana: University of Illinois Press, 1980: 65–78.

Bělíková, Markéta (2000) 'Násilí partnera nelze omlouvat' [Abuse of partner should be inexcusable], in *Mladá Fronta Dnes [Young Front Today]*, 18 December, 3.

Benjamin, Walter (1968) 'The Task of the Translator', trans. J. Hynd and A.M. Valk, in *Delos*, 2: 76–99.

Bennett, S. (1996) *Performing Nostalgia: Shifting Shakespeare and the Contemporary Past*, London: Routledge.

Berger, Jr., Harry (1989) *Imaginary Audition: Shakespeare on Stage and Page*, Berkeley: University of California Press.

Bergier Commission (2002) *Switzerland, National Socialism, and the Second World War*, Zürich: Pendo Editions.

Bevington, David (ed.) (2001) *Troilus and Cressida*, The Arden Shakespeare, third series, London: Thomson Learning.

Bhabha, Homi (1989) 'Of Mimicry and Man: The Ambivalence of Colonial Discourse', in Philip Rice and Patricia Waugh (eds) *Modern Literary Theory: A Reader*, London: Arnold, 234–41.

—— (1992) 'Postcolonial Authority and Postmodern Guilt', in L. Grossberg, C. Nelson and P.A. Treichler (eds) *Cultural Studies*, New York and London: Routledge, 56–68.

—— (1994) *The Location of Culture*, London and New York: Routledge.

—— (1995) 'Cultural Diversity and Cultural Differences', in Bill Ashcroft, Gareth Griffiths and Helen Tiffin (eds) *The Post-Colonial Studies Reader*, London and New York: Routledge, 206–9.

Billington, Michael (1996) 'Visual Feast Goes Emotionally Cold', in *The Guardian*, n.d. (This article was located in the Ex Machina archives).

—— (2002) 'Review of *A Midsummer Night's Dream*', in *The Guardian*, 21 February.

Bloch, Peter André (1972) 'Dürrenmatt's Plan zur Bearbeitung von Shakespeares *Troilus and Cressida*', in *Deutsche Shakespeare-Gesellschaft West: Jahrbuch*, 67–72.

Blumenthal, J. (1965) '*Macbeth* into *Throne of Blood*', in *Sight and Sound*, 34.4: 190–5.

Boddy, G.W. (1976) 'Players of Interludes in North Yorkshire in the Early Seventeenth Century', in *North Yorkshire County Record Office Publications Journal*, 3: 95–130.

Bodek, Janusz (1991) *Die Fassbinder-Kontroversen. Entstehung und Wirkung eines literarischen Textes*, Frankfurt a.M.: Peter Lang.

Bodian, M. (1997) *Hebrews of the Portuguese Nation*, Bloomington: University of Indiana Press.

Bonino, Guido Davico (1973) *Pier Paolo Pasolini: Il Teatro*, Milano: Garzanti.

Boose, Lynda E. (1992) 'Scolding Brides and Bridling Scolds: Taming the Woman's Unruly Member', in *Shakespeare Quarterly*, 42: 179–213.

—— (1994) 'The Taming of the Shrew, Good Husbandry, and Enclosure', in Russ McDonald (ed.) *Shakespeare Reread: The Texts in New Contexts*, Ithaca, NY: Cornell University Press, 193–225.

Borgna, Gianni (1995) *Pier Paolo Pasolini: Un Poeta D'Opposizione*, Milano: Skira.

Bourdieu, Pierre (1979) *Distinction: A Social Critique of the Judgement of Taste*, trans. Richard Nice, London: Routledge.

—— (1993) *The Field of Cultural Production: Essays on Art and Literature*, ed. by R. Johnson, Cambridge: Polity Press.

—— (1995) *The Rules of Art: Genesis and Structure of the Literary Field*, trans. Susan Emanuel, Stanford: Stanford University Press.

Brand, Matthias (1981) *Fritz Kortner in der Weimarer Republik: Annäherungsversuche an die Entwicklung eines jüdischen Schauspielers in Deutschland*, Rheinfelden: Schäuble Verlag.

Brathwaite, Edward Kamau (1984) *A History of the Voice: The Development of Nation Language in Anglophone Caribbean Poetry*, London, Port of Spain: New Beacon Books.

Breslow, Stephen P. (1989) 'Trinidadian Heteroglossia: A Bakhtinian View of Derek Walcott's Play *A Branch of the Blue Nile*', *World Literature Today* 63: 36–9.

Brisset, Annie (1996) *A Sociocritique of Translation: Theatre and Alterity in Quebec, 1968–1988*, trans. R. Gill and R. Gannon, Toronto, Buffalo and London: Toronto University Press.

Bristol, Michael (1990) *Shakespeare's America, America's Shakespeare*, London: Routledge.

—— (1996) *Big-Time Shakespeare*, London: Routledge.

Bristol, Michael and Kathleen McLuskie, with Christopher Holmes (eds) (2001) *Shakespeare and Modern Theatre: The Performance of Modernity*, London and New York: Routledge.

Brook, Peter (1957) 'An Open Letter to William Shakespeare, or As I Don't Like It', in *The Sunday Times*, 1 September, reprinted in (1987) *The Shifting Point: Theatre, Film, Opera 1946–1987*, New York: Harper & Row.

—— (1972) *The Empty Space*, Harmondsworth: Penguin.

—— (1987) *The Shifting Point: Theatre, Film, Opera 1946–1987*, New York: Harper & Row.

Bulman, James C. (ed.) (1996) *Shakespeare, Theory and Performance*, London and New York: Routledge.

Burch, N. (1979) *To the Distant Observer: Form and Meaning in the Japanese Cinema*, A. Michelson (rev. and ed.), London: Scolar.

Burt, Richard (1998) *Unspeakable ShaXXXspeares: Queer Theory and American Kiddie Culture*, New York: St. Martin's Press.

—— (2003) 'Shakespeare, "Glo-cali-zation", Race, and the Small Screens of Post-Popular Culture', in Richard Burt and Lynda E. Boose (eds) *Shakespeare the Movie II: Popularizing the Plays on Film, TV, Video, and DVD*, London and New York: Routledge, 14–36.

Butler, Judith (1997) *Excitable Speech: A Politics of the Performative*, New York and London: Routledge.

Butler, L. (1993) 'Co-author's Statement', Program for *The Merchant of Sante Fe*.

Butler, L. and R. Flores (1993) *The Merchant of Sante Fe*, unpublished script.

Buxton Forman, M. (ed.) (1948) *The Letters of John Keats*, London: Oxford University Press.

Callaghan, Dympna (1996) 'Representing Cleopatra in the Post-Colonial Moment', in Nigel Wood (ed.) *Antony and Cleopatra: Theory in Practice*, Buckingham: Open University Press, 40–65.

—— (2000) *Shakespeare Without Women: Representing Gender and Race on the Renaissance Stage*, London and New York: Routledge.

Carlson, Susan (1998) 'The Suffrage Shrew: The Shakespeare Festival, "A Man's Play", and New Woman', in Jonathan Bate, Jill L. Levenson and D. Mehl (eds) *Shakespeare and the Twentieth Century: the Selected Proceedings of the International Shakespeare Association World Congress, Los Angeles, 1996*, Newark: University of Delaware Press, 85–102.

Cartelli, Thomas (1999) *Repositioning Shakespeare: National Formations, Postcolonial Appropriations*, London and New York: Routledge.

Cartwright, Garth (1997) 'Silent Grief in Tribal *Macbeth*', in *The Guardian*, 22 August.

Cavendish, D. (2002) 'Review of *A Midsummer Night's Dream*', in *The Daily Telegraph*, 7 June.

Chaillet, Ned (1978) '*The Merchant*: Birmingham Rep', in *The Times*, 18 October.

Chakrabarty, Dipesh (2000) *Provincialising Europe: Postcolonial Thought and Historical Difference*, Princeton: Princeton University Press.

Chamberlin, Edward J. (1993) *Come Back To Me My Language: Poetry and the West Indies*, Urbana: University of Illinois Press.

Chambers, Colin (1978) 'Brum Rushes In', in *The Morning Star*, 20 October.

—— (2004) *Inside the Royal Shakespeare Company: Creativity and the Institution*, London and New York: Routledge.

Chauvin, S. (1998) 'Le labyrinthe et les nuées: les espaces aberrants de Kurosawa', in P. Dorval (ed.) *Shakespeare et le Cinéma*, Paris: Société Française Shakespeare, 31–5.

Chedgzoy, Kate (1995) *Shakespeare's Queer Children*, Manchester: Manchester University Press.

Chiarcossi, G. and W. Siti (eds) (1999) *Pier Palo Pasolini: Bestemmia II*, 2nd edn, Milano: Garzanti.

Christensen, Ann C. (1997) 'Petruchio's House in Postwar Suburbia: Reinventing the Domestic Woman (Again)', in *Post Script*, 17: 28–42.

Čírtek, Pavel (1997) ‚Ožeňe, která by měla být zkrocená' [A woman to be tamed], in *Právo*, 2 October, 12.

Cohn, Ruby (1976) *Modern Shakespeare Offshoots*, Princeton: Princeton University Press.

Collick, J. (1989) *Shakespeare, Cinema and Society*, Manchester: Manchester University Press.

Cook, Judith (1990) *Women in Shakespeare*, London: Virgin Books.

Costa, Maddy, with Richard Eyre and Jude Kelly (2004) 'Saint Nick', in *The Guardian*, 22 March, 2–5.

Cottrell, John (1975) *Laurence Olivier*, Englewood Cliffs, NJ: Prentice-Hall.
Coveney, M. (1978) 'Theatre', in *The Financial Times*, 14 October.
—— (1996) 'First Person Singular', in *The Observer*, n.d. (this article was located in the Ex Machina archives).
—— (2002) 'Review of *A Midsummer Night's Dream*', in *The Daily Mail*, 21 February.
Craik, T.W. (ed.) (1995) *King Henry V*, The Arden Shakespeare, third series, London and New York, Routledge.
Č.T.K. (2000) 'Oběti násilí postrádají pomoc' [Victims of Abuse Lack Resources], in *Mladá Fronta Dnes [Young Front Today]*, 6 December, 2.
—— (2001) 'Nová rada vlády bude dohlížet na práva žen: Projekt předpokládá vyškolení asi 300 úředníků' [New commission will oversee rights of women: The Project's goal to train 300 office workers], in *Lidové Noviny [The News of the People]*, 10 October, 2.
Curnow, Allen (1960) *The Penguin Book of New Zealand Verse*, Harmondsworth: Penguin.
Curtis, Nick (1997) 'Not Boldness but Sheer Arrogance', in *The Evening Standard*, 6 January.
Daileader, C.R. (2000) 'Casting Black Actors: Beyond Othellophilia', in C.M.S. Alexander and S. Wells (eds) *Shakespeare and Race*, Cambridge: Cambridge University Press, 177–202.
D.A.M. (2001) 'Domácího násilí neustále přibývá' [Domestic abuse always on the rise], in *Mladá Fronta Dnes [Young Front Today]*, 25 September, 1.
Davies, Anthony (1988) *Filming Shakespeare's Plays: The Adaptations of Laurence Olivier, Orson Welles, Peter Brook and Akira Kurosawa*, Cambridge: Cambridge University Press.
——(2000) 'The Shakespeare Films of Laurence Olivier', in Russell Jackson (ed.) *The Cambridge Companion to Shakespeare on Film*, Cambridge: Cambridge University Press, 163–82.
Davies, Anthony and Stanley Wells (eds) (1994) *Shakespeare and the Moving Image: The Plays on Film and Television*, Cambridge: Cambridge University Press.
de Alva, J.J.K. (1995) 'The Postcolonization of the (Latin) American Experience. A Reconsideration of "Colonialism", "Postcolonialism" and "Mestizaje"', in G. Prakash (ed.) *After Colonialism, Imperial Histories and Postcolonial Displacements*, Princeton: Princeton University Press, 241–75.
de Campos, Haroldo (2000a) 'De la razón antropofágica: diálogo y diferencia en la cultura brasileña', in *De la razón antropofágica y otros ensayos*, trans. R. Mata, Mexico: Siglo XXI, 1–23.
—— (2000b) 'De la traducción como creación y como crítica', in *De la razón antropofágica y otros ensayos*, trans. R. Mata, Mexico: Siglo XXI, 185–204.
de Certeau, Michel (1984) *The Practice of Everyday Life*, trans. S.F. Randall, Berkeley: University of California Press.
Decheva, Violeta (2001) 'Sturua's Theatre', in *Kultura*, 4 May, 3.
Deer, Harriet A. (1991) 'Untyping Stereotypes: *The Taming of the Shrew*', in Sara Munson Deats and Lagretta Tallent Lenker (eds) *The Aching Hearth: Family Violence in Life and Literature*, New York: Plenum Press, 63–78.
Deighton, K. (ed.) (1891) *Hamlet, Prince of Denmark*, London: Macmillan.
Delekat, Thomas (1998) 'Ein Theater probt den Skandal. Wieder wird über das Drama "Der Müll, die Stadt und der Tod" gestritten: War sein Autor Fassbinder ein Antisemit?', in *Die Welt*, 2 September. [Available online at <http://www.welt.de/daten/1998/09/02/0902s377761.htx?print=1> (accessed 4 May 2004)].
Delgado, Maria M. and Paul Heritage (eds) (1996) *In Contact with the Gods? Directors Talk Theatre*, Manchester: Manchester University Press, 129–57.
Desmet, C. and R. Sawyer (eds) (1999) *Shakespeare and Appropriation*, London and New York: Routledge.
Dessen, Alan C. (1990) 'Adjusting Shakespeare in 1989', in *Shakespeare Quarterly*, 41: 356–8.
—— (1994) 'The Image and the Script: Shakespeare on Stage in 1993', in *Shakespeare Bulletin*, 12: 5–8.
—— (2002) *Rescripting Shakespeare: The Text, the Director, and Modern Productions*, Cambridge: Cambridge University Press.
Desser, D. (1983) *The Samurai Films of Akira Kurosawa*, Ann Arbor: UMI Research Press.

Detmer, Emily (1997) 'Civilizing Subordination: Domestic Violence and *The Taming of The Shrew*', in *Shakespeare Quarterly*, 48: 273–94.

D.Í.K. (2001) ‚Domácí násilí se vetšinou nesoudí' [Domestic Abuse most likely not to reach court], in *Mladá Fronta Dnes [Young Front Today]*, 11 October, 3.

Dlouhý, Michal (2000–1) 'Personal Interview', Petruchio: *Zkrocení Zlé Ženy*, CD94; Petruchio: *Zkrocení Zlé Ženy*, Letní Shakespearovské Slavnosti.

Dobrev, Chavdar (2000) 'Shakespeare's *The Tempest* at the National Theatre', *Bulgarski pisatel*, 17: 10–11.

Dobson, M. (2003) 'Shakespeare Performances in England, 2002', in *Shakespeare Survey*, 56: 256–86.

Dočekal, Michal (2001) 'Personal Interview', *Zkrocení Zlé Ženy*, *Kupec Benátský*, 23–27 July.

Dolan, Frances (1996) *The Taming of the Shrew: Texts and Contexts*, Boston and New York: Bedford Books of St. Martin's Press.

Dolanský, Lukáš (2001a) ‚Nejsme Připraveni' [We are not ready], in *Mladá Fronta Dnes [Young Front Today]*, 23 May, 3.

—— (2001b) ‚Svědci si obvykle ničho nevšímají' [Witnesses tend to ignore abuse], in *Mladá Fronta Dnes [Young Front Today]*, 23 May.

Dollimore, Jonathan (1986) 'Middleton and Barker: Creative Vandalism', Introduction to the programme for Howard Barker's rewriting of Thomas Middleton's *Women Beware Women*, London.

Donaldson, Peter S. (1990) *Shakespearean Films/Shakespearean Directors*, London: Unwin-Hyman.

Donnelly, Pat (1995) 'It's all Lepage – from Hamlet to Gravedigger', *The Toronto Star*, 11 November.

Döring, Tobias (2002) *Caribbean–English Passages: Intertextuality in a Postcolonial Tradition*, London and New York: Routledge.

Downes, Nick (1999) 'Cartoon Image', in *The New Yorker*, 1 November, 101.

Drexler, Peter. (1995) 'Laurence Olivier's *Henry V* and Veit Harlan's *Der grosse König*: Two Versions of the National Hero on Film', in Peter Drexler and Lawrence Guntner (eds) *Negotiations with Hal: Multi-Media Perceptions of (Shakespeare's) Henry the Fifth*, Braunschweig: Technische Universität Braunschweig, 127–32.

Durgnat, Raymond (1970) *A Mirror for England: British Movies from Austerity to Affluence*, London: Faber & Faber.

Dürrenmatt, Friedrich (1966) *Theater-Schriften und Reden*, Zürich: Arche.

—— (1969) *Monstervortrag über Gerechtigkeit und Recht*, Zürich: Arche.

—— (1980a) *'König Johann', 'Titus Andronicus'*, *Werkausgabe in 30 Bänden*, vol. 11, Zürich: Diogenes.

—— (1980b) *Kritik*, *Werkausgabe in 30 Bänden*, vol. 25, Zürich: Diogenes.

—— (1980c) *Literatur und Kunst: Essays und Reden*, *Werkausgabe in 30 Bänden*, vol. 26, Zürich: Diogenes.

—— (1996) *Gespräche, 1960–1991*, 4 vols, Zürich: Diogenes.

Dyer, R. (1997) *White*, London and New York: Routledge.

Edwardes, Jane (1997) 'Elsinore', *Time Out*, 1 January.

Engler, Balz (2000) 'Shakespeare in the Trenches', in C.M.S. Alexander and S. Wells (eds) *Shakespeare and Race*, Cambridge: Cambridge University Press, 101–11.

Enzensberger, Christian (1977) 'Das Schöne im Warentausch: William Shakespeares *Kaufmann von Venedig*', in *Literatur und Interesse*, vol. 2, Munich/Vienna: Carl Hanser Verlag, 15–89.

Erml, Richard (2000) ‚Totálně zkrocená Kateřina' [Completely tamed Katharine], in *Reflex*, 40: 70.

Espiner, M. (2002) 'Review of *A Midsummer Night's Dream*', in *Time Out*, 1 May.

Evans, Gwynne Blakemore (ed.) (1968, rpt 1997) *The Riverside Shakespeare*, Boston: Houghton Mifflin.

Everitt, Anthony (1978) '*The Merchant*', in *The Birmingham Post*, 13 October.

Fang Ping (ed.) (2000) *Xin Shashibiya quan ji* (*New Version of the Complete Works of Shakespeare*), 12 vols, vol. 4, Shijiazhuang: Hebei Jiaoyu Chubanshe.

Fanon, Frantz (1986) *Black Skin, White Masks*, trans. Charles Lam Markmann, London: Pluto.

Fassbinder, Rainer Werner (1976) *Schatten der Engel. Ein Film von Daniel Schmid nach dem Theaterstück 'Der Müll, die Stadt und der Tod' von Rainer Werner Fassbinder*, Munich: Filmverlag der Autoren.

—— (1998) *Der Müll, die Stadt und der Tod. Nur eine Scheibe Brot*, Frankfurt a.M.: Verlag der Autoren.

Felperin, Howard (1990) *The Uses of the Canon: Elizabethan Literature and Contemporary Theory*, Oxford: Clarendon Press.

Ferrero, Adelio (1977) *Il Cinema di Pier Paolo Pasolini*, Venezia: Marsilio.

Flores, R. (1990) 'The Adaptation of the Classics to the Chicano or Hispanic Milieu', paper presented at the Contemporary Black Arts Program Conference on *Cultural Diversity in the American Theater: Moving Toward the Twenty-First Century*, San Diego, 9 November.

—— (1993a) '*The Merchant of Santa Fè*', a concept paper delivered 18 March 1993.

—— (1993b) 'Crypto-Jews in 17th Century New Mexico', videotape of *tertulia* at Albuquerque Museum, 13 February.

Foakes, R.A. (ed.) (1984) *A Midsummer Night's Dream*, The New Cambridge Shakespeare, Cambridge: Cambridge University Press.

Foucault, Michel (1989) *The Order of Things: An Archeology of the Human Sciences*, London: Routledge.

Franckóva, Illona (2000) ‚Dočekalovo Zkrocení sází plně na divákovu vnímavost' [Dočekal's *Taming* bids on viewer's perception], in *Zemské Noviny* [*The News of the Land*], 9 September, 11.

Freedman, Barbara (1996) 'Frame-Up: Feminism, Psychoanalysis, Theatre', in Helene Keysar (ed.) *Feminist Theatre and Theory*, New York: St. Martin's Press, 78–108.

Froude, James Anthony (1909) *The English in the West Indies, or The Bow of Ulysses*, London: Longman.

Frye, Northrop (1976) *The Secular Scripture: A Study of the Structure of Romance*, Cambridge, MA: Harvard University Press.

Furness, H.H. (ed.) (1877) *A New Variorum Edition of Shakespeare: Hamlet*, vol. 1, Philadelphia: J.B. Lippincott.

Gaines, B. (1993) 'Shakespeare and the Jews', paper presented to the Jewish–Catholic Dialogue of Albuquerque, 28 April.

Galluzzi, Francesco (1994) *Pasolini e la Pittura*, Roma: Bulzani.

García Canclini, Néstor (2002) 'Diccionario para consumidores descontentos', *Letras Libres* 4, 37: 22–6.

Garneau, Michel (1989) 'Préface' (par Eugene Lion) to *Coriolan de William Shakespeare*, traduit par Michel Garneau, Montreal, Québec: VLB Éditeur, 7–8.

Garner, Shirley Nelson (1988) '*The Taming of the Shrew*: Inside or Outside the Joke?' in Maurice Charney (ed.) *"Bad" Shakespeare: Revaluations of the Shakespeare Canon*, Rutherford: Farleigh Dickinson University Press, 105–19.

Gay, Penny (1994) *As She Likes It: Shakespeare's Unruly Women*, London and New York: Routledge.

—— (1999) 'Recent Australian Shrews: The "Larrikin Element"', in Marianne Novy (ed.) *Transforming Shakespeare: Contemporary Women's Re-visions in Literature and Performance*, New York: St. Martin's Press, 35–50.

Geduld, Harry M. (1973) *Filmguide to 'Henry V'*, Bloomington, IN, and London: Indiana University Press.

Gerlach, J. (1973) 'Shakespeare, Kurosawa, and *Macbeth*: A Response to J. Blumenthal', in *Literature/Film Quarterly*, 1.4: 352–9.

Gillies, John (1994) *Shakespeare and the Geography of Difference*, Cambridge: Cambridge University Press.

Gitlitz, D. (1996) *Secrecy and Deceit: The Religion of the Crypto-Jews*, Philadelphia: Jewish Publication Society.

Glaister, Dan (1996) 'Fated, not Feted', in *The Guardian*, 15 August.

Goodwin, J. (1994) *Akira Kurosawa and Intertextual Cinema*, Baltimore: The Johns Hopkins University Press.

Gossett, Suzanne (ed.) (2004) *Pericles*, The Arden Shakespeare, third series, London: Thomson Learning.

Grady, Hugh (1991) *The Modernist Shakespeare: Critical Texts in a Material World*, Oxford: Clarendon Press.

Granville-Barker, Harley (1993) *Prefaces to Shakespeare: A Midsummer Night's Dream, The Winter's Tale, Twelfth Night*, London: Nick Hern Books.

Greenblatt, Stephen (1980) *Renaissance Self-Fashioning: From More to Shakespeare*, Chicago and London: University of Chicago Press.

—— (1988) *Shakespearean Negotiations*, Berkeley: University of California Press.

Greenblatt, Stephen, Walter Cohen, Jean E. Howard and Katharine Eisaman Maus (eds) (1997) *The Norton Shakespeare*, New York: Norton.

Greene, Alexis (1998) '*Pericles*', in *InTheater*, 20 November.

Greene, Naomi (1990) *Pier Paolo Pasolini: Cinema as Heresy*, Princeton: Princeton University Press.

Greenleaf, R. (1969) *The Mexican Inquisition of the Sixteenth Century*, Albuquerque: University of New Mexico Press.

Grigely, Joseph (1995) *Textualterity: Art, Theory, and Textual Criticism*, Ann Arbor: University of Michigan Press.

Gross, J. (2002) 'Review of *A Midsummer Night's Dream*', in *The Sunday Telegraph*, 9 June.

Gruzen, T. (1996) 'Secret Jews Believe They Still Have Crosses to Bear', in *The Chicago Tribune*, 28 May.

Guryča, Richard (2001) ‚Domácí násilí ničí tisíce žen‘ [Domestic abuse known to thousands of women], in *Mladá Fronta Dnes* [*Young Front Today*], 3 February, 1.

Hadfield, Andrew (1997) 'Shakespeare's "British" Plays and the Exclusion of Ireland', in Mark Thornton Burnett and Ramona Wray (eds) *Shakespeare and Ireland: History, Politics, Culture*, Houndmills: Macmillan, 47–67.

Hadomi, Leah and Hans Otto Horch (1996) ‘ "In Deutschland mißverständlich über Juden schreiben – das heißt schlecht schreiben": Anmerkungen zur Rezeption von Rainer Werner Fassbinders Skandal-Stück *Der Müll, die Stadt und der Tod* in Deutschland und Israel. Mit einem Epilog über einen postmodernen Rettungsversuch aus den USA', in Hans-Peter Bayerdörfer (ed.) *Theatralia Judaica II. Nach der Shoah. Israelisch-deutsche Theaterbeziehungen seit 1949*, Tübingen: Max Niemeyer Verlag, 115–35.

Haldane, J.B.S. (1960) 'Preface to Friedrich Engels, *Dialectics of Nature*', ed. and trans. by Clemens Dutt, New York: International Publishers.

Halevy, S. (1996) 'Manifestations of Crypto-Judaism in the American Southwest', in *Jewish Folklore and Ethnology Review*, 18: 68–76.

Halio, Jay (ed.) (1993) *The Merchant of Venice*, The Oxford Shakespeare, Oxford: Oxford University Press.

—— (1994) *A Midsummer Night's Dream: Shakespeare in Performance*, Manchester: Manchester University Press.

Hall, Stuart (1991) 'The Local and the Global: Globalization and Ethnicity', in A.D. King (ed.) *Culture, Globalization and the World-System*, Basingstoke: Macmillan, 19–39.

—— (1996) 'When was the Post-Colonial? Thinking at the Limit', in Iain Chambers and Linda Curti (eds) *The Post-colonial Question: Common Skies, Divided Horizons*, New York: Routledge, 242–60.

Hannerz, Ulf (1991) 'Scenarios for Peripheral Cultures', in A.D. King (ed.) *Culture, Globalization and the World-System*, Basingstoke: Macmillan, 107–28.

Hannon, Martin and Robert McNeil (1996) 'Festival Gloom as Theatre Showpiece Cancelled', *The Scotsman*, 14 August.

Hapgood, Robert (1994) 'Kurosawa's Shakespeare Films: *Throne of Blood, The Bad Sleep Well*, and *Ran*', in Anthony Davies and Stanley Wells (eds) *Shakespeare and the Moving Image: The Plays on Film and Television*, Cambridge: Cambridge University Press, 234–49.

—— (1997) 'Popularizing Shakespeare: The Artistry of Franco Zeffirelli', in Richard Burt and Lynda Boose (eds) *Shakespeare, the Movie: Popularizing the Plays on Film, TV, and Video*, London and New York: Routledge, 80–94.

Harvie, Jennifer and Erin Hurley (1999) 'States of Play: Locating Québec in the Performances of Robert Lepage, Ex Machina, and the Cirque du Soleil', in *Theatre Journal*, 51: 299–315.

Hawkes, Terence (1992) 'Shakespeare and the General Strike', in *Meaning by Shakespeare*, London and New York: Routledge, 42–60.

—— (2002) *Shakespeare in the Present*, London and New York: Routledge.

Healy, Margaret (1999) '*Pericles* and the Pox', in Jennifer Richards and James Knowles (eds) *Shakespeare's Late Plays: New Readings*, Edinburgh: Edinburgh University Press, 92–107.

Healy, Thomas (1994) 'Remembering with Advantages: Nation and Ideology in *Henry V*', in Michael Hattaway, Boika Sokolova and Derek Roper (eds) *Shakespeare in the New Europe*, Sheffield: Sheffield Academic Press, 174–93.

Heaney, Peter F. (1998) 'Petruchio's Horse: Equine and Household Management in *The Taming of the Shrew*', in *Early Modern Literary Studies* 4:1, available on line at http://www.shu.ac.uk/emls/04-1/heanshak.html (accessed 2 October 2004).

Hedrick, Donald K. (2003) 'War is Mud: Branagh's *Dirty Harry V* and the Types of Political Ambiguity', in Richard Burt and Lynda Boose (eds) *Shakespeare, the Movie, II: Popularizing the Plays on Film, TV, Video, and DVD*, London and New York: Routledge, 213–30.

Heinrichs, Benjamin (1988) 'Das Messer im Koffer. "Der Kaufmann von Venedig": Peter Zadeks verblüffende Shakespeare-Inszenierung', in *Die ZEIT*, 16 December.

Henderson, Diana (1997) 'A Shrew for the Times', in Richard Burt and Lynda Boose (eds) *Shakespeare, the Movie: Popularizing the Plays on Film, TV, and Video*, London and New York: Routledge, 148–68.

Hendricks, Margo and Patricia Parker (eds) (1994) *Women, "Race", and Writing in the Early Modern Period*, London: Routledge.

Hensel, Georg (1978) 'Shakespeare, Jazz und Judenhaß: George Tabori's Shylock-Improvisationen', in *Frankfurter Allgemeine Zeitung*, 23 November.

Herodotus (1910) *The History of Herodotus*, trans. George Rawlinson, vol. 1, London: Dent.

Hodgdon, Barbara (1979/80) 'Of Time and the Arrow: A Reading of Kurosawa's *Throne of Blood*', in *University of Dayton Review*, 14.1: 63–70.

—— (1991) *The End Crowns All: Closure and Contradiction in Shakespeare's History*, Princeton, NJ: Princeton University Press.

—— (1996) 'Looking for Mr. Shakespeare After the Revolution: Robert Lepage's Intercultural *Dream* Machine' in J.C. Bulman (ed.) *Shakespeare, Theory and Performance*, London and New York: Routledge, 68–91.

—— (1998) *The Shakespeare Trade: Performances and Appropriations*, Philadelphia: University of Pennsylvania Press.

—— (1999) 'Making it New: Katie Mitchell Refashions Shakespeare-History', in Marianne Novy (ed.) *Transforming Shakespeare: Contemporary Women's Re-Visions in Literature and Performance*, New York: St. Martin's Press, 13–33.

Hoeniger, F.D. (ed.) (1963) *Pericles*, The Arden Shakespeare, second series, London: Methuen.

Hoenselaars, Ton (ed.) (2004) *Shakespeare and the Language of Translation*, London: Thomson Learning.

Holden, Anthony (1988) *Olivier*, London: Weidenfeld & Nicolson.

Holland, Peter (1994) 'Shakespeare Performances in England, 1992–1993', in *Shakespeare Survey*, 47: 181–207.

—— (1997) *English Shakespeares: Shakespeare on the English Stage in the 1990s*, Cambridge: Cambridge University Press.

Honigmann, E.A.J. (ed.) (1997) *Othello*, The Arden Shakespeare, second series, London: Thomson Learning.

Hopkins, Gerald Manley (1974) in W.H. Gardner (ed.) *Poems and Prose*, Harmondsworth: Penguin.

Hordes, S. (1993) 'The Sephardic Legacy in the Southwest: Crypto-Jews of New Mexico,' in *Jewish Folklore and Ethnology Review*, 15: 137–8.

Hortmann, Wilhelm (1998) *Shakespeare on the German Stage: The Twentieth Century*, Cambridge: Cambridge University Press.

—— (2003) 'Wo, bitte, geht's nach Belmont? Über ein Dilemma von Inszenierungen des *Kaufmanns von Venedig* nach dem Holocaust', in *Shakespeare Jahrbuch*, 139: 217–25.

Houlahan, Mark (2002) 'Shakespeare in the Settlers' House', in *Journal of New Zealand Literature*, 20: 112–25.

Howlett, Kathy M. (2000) *Framing Shakespeare on Film*, Athens, OH: Ohio University Press.

Hrdinová, Radmila (2000) 'Shakespearovský duel za zvuku bubnů' [Shakespearean duel to the sound of Drums], in *Právo* [*The Right*], 7 April, 12.

Hristova-Radoeva, Vessela (2001) 'Whiteness as a Parable: Georgi Alexi-Meskhishvili's Scenography to *Twelfth Night*', in *Duma*, 19 May, 9.

Huang Zuolin (1983) '*Roumiou yu Youliye: daoyan de hua* [Romeo and Juliet: The Director's Words]', in *Shashibiya yanjiu* (*Shakespeare Studies*), 1: 271–9.

Hulme, Peter and William Sherman (eds) (2000) *'The Tempest' and Its Travels*, London: Reaktion Books.

Hunt, Nigel (1989) 'The Global Voyage of Robert Lepage', in *The Drama Review*, 33: 104–18.

Iafrate, Giuseppe (1990) 'Pier Paolo Pasolini: la Terra, la Luna, le Nuvole', in AA.VV. *Le Giovani Generazioni e il Cinema di Pier Paolo Pasolini*, supplement to *La Scena e lo Schermo*, 1-2: 31–5.

Innes, Christopher (1997) 'Beyond Categories (Redefining "Mainstream")', in Peter Paul Schnierer (ed.) *Beyond the Mainstream, Contemporary Drama in English*, vol. 4 [1996], Trier: WVT Wissenschaftlicher Verlag Trier, 55–67.

Jackson, Macdonald (2002) 'All Our Tribe', in *Landfall*, 204: 155–64.

J.A.M. (2001) ‚Studio nato.ilo film o násilí' [Studio created film about domestic abuse], in *Mladá Fronta Dnes* [*Young Front Today*], 25 November, 24.

Jameson, Fredric (1990) 'Modernism and Imperialism', in T. Eagleton, F. Jameson and E.W. Said *Nationalism, Colonialism and Literature*, intr. by S. Deane, Minneapolis: University of Minnesota Press, 43–66.

—— (1998) 'Notes on Globalization as a Philosophical Issue', in Fredric Jameson and Masao Miyoshi (eds) *The Cultures of Globalization*, Durham and London: Duke University Press, 54–77.

Javorková, Anna (2001) 'Personal Interview', *Zkrocení Zlé Ženy*, Letní Shakespearovské Slavnosti, 10 August.

Jeníková, Eva (2000) ‚Shakespeare na Pražském Hradě bude Slovensko-Český, erotický, i němý' [Shakespeare at the Prague Castle will be Slovak-Czech and mute], in *Zemské Noviny* [*The News of the Land*], 15 June.

—— (2000a) ‚Zlá žena zaráží vulgaritami' [Mean woman bewilders by obscenities], in *Zemské Noviny* [*The News of the Land*], 3 July.

Jessen, Norbert (1999) 'Unkontrollierte Mehrdeutigkeiten: Fassbinders "Der Müll, die Stadt und der Tod" in Tel Aviv', in *Die Welt*, 26 April. Available online at <http://www.hagalil.com/archiv/99/04/fassbinder.htm> (accessed 4 May 2004).

Jewell, Keala Jane (1992) *The Poiesis of History: Experimenting with Genre in Post-War Italy*, Ithaca and London: Cornell University Press.

Jiang, David (2004) 'Programme Notes for *Romeo and Juliet*', Hong Kong Academy for Performing Arts, 5 March.

Jiang Weiguo (1994) 'Shashibiya, *huangmeixi, he Wushishengfei* (Shakespeare, *Huangmeixi* & *Looking for Trouble*)', in *Shashibiya yanjiu* (Shakespeare Studies), 4: 379–96.

Johns, I. (2002) 'Review of *A Midsummer Night's Dream*', in *The Times*, 6 June.

Johnson, D. (1996) *Shakespeare and South Africa*, Oxford: Clarendon Press.

Jordan, Constance (1997) *Shakespeare's Monarchies: Ruler and Subject in the Romances*, Ithaca, NY: Cornell University Press.

Joughin, J. J. (ed.) (1997) *Shakespeare and National Culture*, Manchester: Manchester University Press.

Kasimova, Maria (2001) 'Robert Sturua's *As You Will, Or Twelfth Night* – The Divine Theatre', in *Dnevnik*, 27 April.

Kennedy, Dennis (1985) *Granville Barker and the Dream of Theatre*, Cambridge: Cambridge University Press.

—— (ed.) (1993) *Foreign Shakespeare: Contemporary Performance*, Cambridge: Cambridge University Press.

—— (1995) 'Shakespeare and the Global Spectator', *Shakespeare Jahrbuch*, 131: 50–64.

—— (1996) 'Shakespeare without his Language', in J.C. Bulman (ed.) *Shakespeare, Theory, and Performance*, London and New York: Routledge, 133–48.

—— (2001a) 'Shakespeare World Wide', in Stanley Wells and Margareta de Grazia (eds) *The Cambridge Companion to Shakespeare*, Cambridge: Cambridge University Press, 251–65.

—— (2001b) *Looking at Shakespeare: A Visual History of Twentieth-Century Performance*, 2nd edn., Cambridge: Cambridge University Press.

Kennedy, Gwynne (1991) 'Lessons of the "Schoole of Wisedom"', in Carole Levin and Karen Robertson (eds) *Sexuality and Politics in Renaissance Drama*, Lewiston, NY: Edwin Mellen, 113–36.

Kerbr, Jan (2000) ‚Zase krotíme Kateřinu‘ [Taming Katharine Again], in *Mladá Fronta Dnes* [*Young Front Today*], 31 October, 24.

Kermode, Frank (ed.) (1954) *The Tempest*, The Arden Shakespeare, second series, London: Methuen.

Kinder, M. (1977) '*Throne of Blood*: A morality dance', in *Literature/Film Quarterly*, 5.4: 339–45.

King, A.D. (ed.) (1991) *Culture, Globalization and the World-System*, Basingstoke: Macmillan.

King, Bruce (1995) *Derek Walcott and West Indian Drama: 'Not Only a Playwright But a Company'*, *The Trinidad Theatre Workshop, 1959–1993*, Oxford: Clarendon Press.

—— (2000) *Derek Walcott: A Caribbean Life*, Oxford: Oxford University Press.

King, Michael (2003) *The Penguin History of New Zealand*, Auckland: Penguin.

Kingston, Jeremy (1997) 'Thane on Thames', in *The Times*, 22 August.

Klein, Bernhard (2000) 'Die unendliche Vielfalt der Welt: *Antony and Cleopatra*', in William Shakespeare/Frank Günther *Antonius und Kleopatra: Zweisprachige Ausgabe*, Cadolzburg: Ars Vivendi, 352–75.

Klein, Naomi (2001) *No Logo*, London: Flamingo.

Kleist, Heinrich von (1989) *On a Theatre of Marionettes*, trans. G. Wilford, London: Acorn Press.

Knight, G. Wilson (1947) *The Crown of Life: Essays in Interpretation of Shakespeare's Final Plays*, London: Methuen.

—— (1964) *Shakespearian Production, with Especial Reference to the Tragedies*, London: Routledge & Kegan Paul.

—— (1967) 'St George and the Dragon', in *Shakespeare and Religion: Essays of Forty Years*, New York: Simon & Schuster, 91–111.

—— (1989) *The Wheel of Fire; Interpretations of Shakespearian Tragedy*, London: Methuen.

Knights, L.C. (1964) *Explorations: Essays in Criticism*, Harmondsworth, Peregrine.

Knowles, Richard Paul (1997) 'Focus, Faithfulness, Shakespeare, and The Shrew: Directing as Translation as Resistance', in *Essays in Theatre*, 16: 33–52.

—— (1998a) 'From Dream to Machine: Peter Brook, Robert Lepage, and the Contemporary Shakespearean Director as (Post)Modernist', in *Theatre Journal*, 50: 189–206.

—— (1998b) '"The Real of It Would Be Awful": Representing the Real Ophelia in Canada', in *Theatre Survey*, 39: 21–40.

—— (2002) 'Reading Elsinore: The Ghost and the Machine', in *Canadian Theatre Review*, 111: 87–8.

Kolářová, Kateřina (2000) ‚V Komedii uvedou Zkrocení i s epilogem‘ [*Taming* with the epilogue at Komedie] in *Mladá Fronta Dnes* [*Young Front Today*], 14 September, 9.

Kolářová, Lucie (2001) ‚Násilí v rodině je trestným činem‘ [Abuse in family is criminal offence], in *Mladá Fronta Dnes* [*Young Front Today*], 12 April, 10.

Kolin, Philip C. (ed.) (1995) *Titus Andronicus: Critical Essays*, New York and London: Garland.

Korda, Natasha (1996) 'Household Kates: Domesticating Commodities in *The Taming of the Shrew*', in *Shakespeare Quarterly*, 47: 109–31.

Kortner, Fritz (1979) *Aller Tage Abend*, Munich: Kindler.

Kosiek, Rolf (1988) *Historikerstreit und Geschichtsrevision*, Tübingen: Grabert.

Kostova, Vladislava (2001) 'Robert Sturua in Bulgaria', in *Literaturen forum*, 22 May.

Kott, J. (1965 [c. 1964]) *Shakespeare Our Contemporary*, (tr.) B. Taborski, 2nd ed., London: Methuen.

Kozova, Liliana (2001) 'Robert Sturua chose Bulgaria', in *Zemya*, 19 April, 5.

Kučera, Zdeněk (2001) 'Personal Interview', *Zkrocení Zlé Ženy*, Letní Shakespearovské Slavnosti, 28 August.

Kurosawa, A. (1957) Dir. *Kumonosu-jo* (aka *Throne of Blood*). Perf. Toshiro Mifune and Isuzu Yamada, Videocassette. Connoisseur (CR 043).

—— (1992) *Throne of Blood*, (tr.) H. Niki, in *Seven Samurai and Other Screenplays*, London: Faber, 227–66.

Lamming, George (1973) *Water With Berries*, London: Longman.

—— (1984) *The Pleasures of Exile*, London: Alison & Busby.

Lang, Michal (2001) 'Personal Interview', Director, *Zkrocení Zlé Ženy*, CD 94, 27 August.

Lankesh, Gauri (1998) ' "The Play's the Thing" ', in *The Sunday*, 2–8 August.

Larsen, Neil (2001) *Determinations: Essays on Theory, Narrative, and Nation in the Americas*, London and New York: Verso.

Lau, Jörg (1998) 'Die Stadt, der Müll und der Streit', in *Die ZEIT*, 3 September.

Lavender, Andy (2001) *Hamlet in Pieces: Shakespeare Reworked by Peter Brook, Robert Lepage, Robert Wilson*, London: Nick Hern Books.

L.D.S. (2001) ‚Násilí zná z domova každý šestý' [One in six knows abuse from home], in *Mladá Fronta Dnes [Young Front Today]*, 23 May, 1.

Ledebur, Ruth Freifrau von (1982) '*The Merchant of Venice*: Drama – Bühnengeschichte – Theaterrezension', in Rüdiger Ahrens (ed.) *William Shakespeare: Didaktisches Handbuch*, vol. 3, Munich: Fink, 851–83.

Lepage, Robert (1997) 'Director's Note', *Elsinore* programme, Royal National Theatre, London, 4–11 January.

—— (2002) *Elsinore*, based on *Hamlet* by William Shakespeare, produced by Ex Machina, in *Canadian Theatre Review*, 111: 89–99.

Li Ruru (2003) *Shashibiya: Staging Shakespeare in China*, Hong Kong: University of Hong Kong Press.

Lichtenstein, Heiner (ed.) (1986) *Die Fassbinder-Kontroverse oder Das Ende der Schonzeit*, Königstein, Ts.: Athenäum.

Liebman, S. (1970) *The Jews in New Spain: Faith, Flame and the Inquisition*, Coral Gables: University of Miami Press.

Lloyd Evans, G. (1977), 'Review of *A Midsummer Night's Dream*', in *The Stratford-upon-Avon Herald*, 13 May.

Loehlin, James N. (1996) *Henry V*, Shakespeare in Performance, Manchester: Manchester University Press.

Londré, Felicia Hardison (1996) 'Confronting Shakespeare's "Political Incorrectness" in Production: Contemporary American Audiences and the New "Problem Plays" ', in *On-stage Studies*, 19: 67–82.

Loomba, Ania (1989) *Gender, Race, Renaissance Drama*, Manchester: Manchester University Press.

Loomba, Ania and Martin Orkin (eds) (1998) *Post-Colonial Shakespeares*, London and New York: Routledge.

López-Morillas, Julian (1999) *Pericles*: 'Program Notes', American Players Theater, Spring Green, WI.

Macaulay, Alastair (1997) 'All cut up over Hamlet', in *The Financial Times*, 7 January.

MacCarthy, D. (1914), 'Review of *A Midsummer Night's Dream*', in *The New Statesman*, 21 February.

McDonald, K.I. (1983) *Cinema East: A Critical Study of Major Japanese Films*, Rutherford: Fairleigh Dickinson University Press.

—— (1987) 'Noh into film: Kurosawa's *Throne of Blood*', in *Journal of Film and Video*, 39.1: 36–41.

Machalická, Jana (2000) ‚Zkrocení zlé ženy jako uspěchaná fraška' [*Taming of the Shrew* a hurried farce], in *Lidové Noviny* [*The News of the People*], 3 July.

Mackay, A. (1992) 'The Jews in Spain during the Middle Ages', in E. Kedourie (ed.) *Spain and the Jews: the Sephardi Experience and After*, London: Thames & Hudson, 33–50.

Maguire, Laurie E. (1995) 'Cultural Control in *The Taming of the Shrew*', in *Renaissance Drama*, 26: 83–104.

Maley, Willy (1997) ' "This Sceptred Isle": Shakespeare and the British Problem', in John J. Joughin (ed) *Shakespeare and National Culture*, Manchester: Manchester University Press, 83–108.

Manvell, R. (1979) *Shakespeare and the Film*, Cranbury: Barnes.

Mâori Merchant of Venice (The) production website: http://www.Mâorimerchantofvenice.com (accessed 17/05/04). [Video and dvd sales of the film available through this site.]

Marchesini, Alberto (1994) *Citazioni Pittoriche nel Cinema di Pier Paolo Pasolini: Da Accattone a Decameron*, Firenze: La Nuova Italia Editrice.

Massey, Doreen and Pat Jess (1995) 'The Contestation of Place' in Doreen Massey and Pat Jess (eds) *A Place in the World?: Places, Cultures and Globalization*, Oxford: The Open University and Oxford University Press, 133–74.

Matásek, David (2001-2) 'Personal Interview', Petruchio, *Zkrocení Zlé Ženy*; Graziano, *Kupec Benátský*, Komedie.

Maxwell, J.C. (ed.) (1953) *Titus Andronicus*, The Arden Shakespeare, second series, London: Methuen.

Mehlin, Urs (1972) 'Claus Bremer, Renate Voss, *Die jämmerliche Tragödie von Titus Andronicus* – Friedrich Dürrenmatt, *Titus Andronicus* – Hans Hollmann, *Titus Titus* – Ein Vergleich', in *Deutsche Shakespeare-Gesellschaft West: Jahrbuch*, 73–98.

Meng Xianxiang (1994) *Zhongguo shaxue jianshi* (*The Concise History of Shakespeare Studies in China*), Changchun: Dongbei Shifan Daxue Chubanshe.

Mesnil, M. (1973) *Kurosawa*, Paris: Seghers.

Mikulka, Vladimír (2000) 'Trabant, Koubek, Mafiáni a nastudování jednoho Shakespeara' [Trabant, Koubek, the Mafia and the interpretation of one Shakespeare], in *Divadelní Noviny* [*Theater News*] 16: 6–23.

Modenessi, Alfredo Michel (2001) 'Of Shadows and Stones: Revering and Translating "the Word" Shakespeare in Mexico', in *Shakespeare Survey*, 54: 152–64.

—— (2004) ' "A Double Tongue within your Mask": Translating Shakespeare in/to Spanish-speaking Latin America', in T. Hoenselaars (ed.) *Shakespeare and the Language of Translation*, London: Thomson Learning, 240–54.

Moisan, Thomas (1991) '"Knock Me Here Soundly": Comic Misprision and Class Consciousness in Shakespeare', in *Shakespeare Quarterly*, 42: 276–90.

Monsiváis, Carlos (2003) 'Tan cerca, tan lejos: las ilusiones ópticas de la vecindad', in *Letras Libres* 5, 53: 22–5.

Morfov, Alexander (1996–7) *The Tempest*: 'Programme Notes', The Ivan Vazov National Theatre, Sofia.

Mountford, F. (2002) 'Review of *A Midsummer Night's Dream*', in *The Evening Standard*, 6 June.

Muir, K. (ed.) (1970) *Macbeth*, The Arden Shakespeare, second series, London: Methuen.

Mullaney, Steven (1988) *The Place of the Stage: License, Play, and Power in Renaissance England*, Chicago: University of Chicago Press.

Mullin, M. (1973) '*Macbeth* on Film', in *Literature/Film Quarterly*, 1.4: 332–42.

Murphy, John (1984) *Darkness and Devils: Exorcism and King Lear*, Athens, OH: Ohio University Press.

Murri, Serafino (1995) *Pier Paolo Pasolini*, Milano: Il Castoro Cinema.

Musilová, Martina (2000) 'Krotitelé' [Tamers], in *Svět a Divadlo* [*The World and Theater*] 6: 50–3.

Myerson, J. (2002) 'Review of *A Midsummer Night's Dream*', in *The Independent*, 27 February.

Nathan, David (1978) 'Enter Shylock, Ghetto Hero', in *Jewish Chronicle*, 13 October.

Neill, Michael (1989) 'Unproper Beds: Race, Adultery and the Hideous in *Othello*', in *Shakespeare Quarterly*, 40: 383–412.

—— (1994) 'Introduction', in *The Tragedy of Anthony and Cleopatra*, The Oxford Shakespeare, Oxford: Clarendon.

—— (1998) 'Post-Colonial Shakespeare? Writing Away from the Centre', in A. Loomba and M. Orkin (eds) *Post-Colonial Shakespeares*, London and New York: Routledge, 164–85.

—— (2004) 'Maori Shakespeare in California', in *The University of Auckland News*, March, 10–11.

Neulander, J. (1994) 'Crypto-Jews of the Southwest: an Imagined Community,' in *Jewish Folklore and Ethnology Review*, 16: 64–8.

Nightingale, Benedict (1993) 'Shylock Among the City Slickers', *The Times*, 7 June.

—— (1997) 'Missing the point', *The Times*, 6 January.

—— (2002) 'Review of *A Midsummer Night's Dream*', *The Times*, 21 February.

Nikolova, Patricia (2001) *Sega*, 3 May, 13.

O'Connor, G. (1977) 'Review of *A Midsummer Night's Dream*', in *The Financial Times*, 9 May.

Ohland, Angelika and Rainer Jung (1998) 'Im Gespräch: Micha Brumlik. Juden in Deutschland. Eine heikle Beziehung. Zwischen Juden und Nichtjuden gibt es viele Rituale, und viele Abgründe. Nur Normalität ist rar', *Deutsches Allgemeines Sonntagsblatt*, 18 September. Available online at: <http://www.sonntagsblatt.de/artikel/1998/38/38-s2.htm> (accessed 4 May 2004).

Olivier, Laurence (1982) *Confessions of an Actor*, London: Weidenfeld & Nicolson.

—— (1986) *On Acting*, London: Weidenfeld & Nicolson.

Omotoso, Kole (1982) *The Theatrical into Theatre: A study of the drama and theatre of the English-speaking Caribbean*, London, Port of Spain: New Beacon Books.

Orsman, Harry (1997) *The Dictionary of New Zealand English: A Dictionary of New Zealandisms on Historical Principles*, Auckland: Oxford University Press.

Palfrey, Simon (1997) *Late Shakespeare: A New World of Words*, Oxford: Oxford University Press.

Pancheva, Evgenia (1994) 'Nothings, Merchants, Tempests: Trimming Shakespeare for the 1992 Bulgarian Stage', in Michael Hattaway, Boika Sokolova and Derek Roper (eds) *Shakespeare in the New Europe*, Sheffield: Sheffield Academic Press, 247–60.

Pankow, Horst (1998) 'Der Müll, die Deutschen und das Ungefähre. Das Theaterstück von Rainer Werner Fassbinder war 1985 so antisemitisch wie es heute ist', in *Jungle World* (9 September 1998). Availble online at: <http://www.nadir.org/nadir/periodika/ jungle_ world/_98/37/23a.htm> (accessed 4 May 2004).

Parker, Patricia (1994) 'Fantasies of "Race" and "Gender": Africa, *Othello*, and Bringing to Light', in Margo Hendricks and Patricia Parker (eds), *Women, "Race", and Writing in the Early Modern Period*, London: Routledge, 84–100.

Parr, Anthony (ed.) (1995) *Three Renaissance Travel Plays: The Travels of the Three English Brothers, The Sea Voyage, The Antipodes*, Manchester: Manchester University Press.

P.D.K. (2001) ‚Domácí násilí zná nejmén. 16 procent Čechů ‘[Domestic abuse known to at least 16% of Czechs], in *Lidové Noviny* [*The News of the People*], 7 July, 3.

Penfold, Merimeri (2000) *Nga Waiata Aroha a Hekepia: Love Sonnets by Shakespeare*, Auckland: University of Auckland.

Petcher, Edward (1996) '"Have You not Read Some Such Thing?": Sex and Sexual Stories in *Othello*', in *Shakespeare Survey*, 49: 201–16.

Peter, J. (2002a) 'Review of *A Midsummer Night's Dream*', in *The Sunday Times*, 3 March.

—— (2002b) 'Review of *A Midsummer Night's Dream*', in *The Sunday Times*, 16 June.

Peter, Jürgen (1995) *Der Historikerstreit und die Suche nach einer nationalen Identität der achtziger Jahre*, Frankfurt/Main: Lang.

Pistoia, Marco (1990) 'Il Cinema è Sogno: i due Mondi di *Che Cosa sono le Nuvole?*' in AA.VV. *Le Giovani Generazioni e il Cinema di Pier Paolo Pasolini*, supplement to *La Scena e lo Schermo*, 1–2: 81–6.

Pramatarova, Maya (2001) 'Interview with Robert Sturua', *Capital*, 8 April.

Pressley, Nathan (1998) 'Offbeat *Pericles* Offers Vivid, Empty Journey', in *The Washington Times*, 21 May.

Přeučil, Jan (2001) 'Personal Interview', *Zkrocení Zlé Ženy*, Letní Shakespearovské Slavnosti, 29 August.

Prince, S. (1991) *The Warrior's Camera: The Cinema of Akira Kurosawa*, Princeton: Princeton University Press.

Purser, Philip (1990) *Friedrich Harris: Shooting the Hero*, London and New York: Quartet Books.

Ranald, Margaret Loftus (1979) ' "As Marriage Binds, and Blood Breaks": English Marriage and Shakespeare', in *Shakespeare Quarterly*, 30: 68–81.

Rayns, T. (1981) 'Tokyo Stories', in *Sight and Sound*, 50.3: 170–6.

Reber, Trudis Elisabeth (1976) 'Dürrenmatt und Shakespeare: Betrachtungen zu Dürrenmatts *König Johann* (Nach Shakespeare)', in *Friedrich Dürrenmatt: Studien zu seinem Werk*, Heidelberg: Lothar Stiehm Verlag, 80–9.

Reed, O. (1993) '*Merchant's* a Play to Die For', in *The Albuquerque Tribune*, 1 October, 8.

Reyes, C. (1993) 'Unfocused 'Merchant': A Poor History Lesson', in *The Albuquerque Journal*, 7 October, E4.

Ribeiro Pires Vieira, Else (1999) 'Liberating Calibans: Reading of Antropofagia and Haroldo de Campos' Poetics of Transcreation', in H. Trivedi and S. Bassnett (eds) *Post-colonial Translation: Theory and Practice*, London and New York: Routledge, 95–113.

Rich, Frank (1991) '*Pericles* Hints at Shakespearean Things to Come', in *The New York Times*, 25 November.

Richie, D. (1973) *The Films of Akira Kurosawa*, Berkeley: University of California Press.

—— (1994) 'The Influence of Traditional Aesthetics on the Japanese film', in L.C. Ehrlich and D. Desser (eds) *Cinematic Landscapes: Observations on the Visual Arts and Cinema of China and Japan*, Austin: University of Texas Press, 155–63.

Rimer, J.T. and M. Yamazaki (tr.) (1984) *On the Art of the No Drama: The Major Treatises of Zeami*, Princeton: Princeton University Press.

'RNC' (1977) 'Review of *A Midsummer Night's Dream*', in *Berrows Worcester Journal*, 12 May.

Roberts, Jeanne Addison (1983) 'Horses and Hermaphrodites: Metamorphoses in *The Taming of the Shrew*', in *Shakespeare Quarterly*, 34: 159–71.

Robertson, Roland (1995) 'Glocalization: Time–Space and Homogeneity–Heterogeneity', in M. Featherstone, S. Lash, and R. Robertson (eds) *Global Modernities*, London: Sage, 25–44.

Rodríguez, Jesusa and Luz Aurora Pimentel (1996) *El rey Lear: una (a)puesta en escena*, Mexico: Ediciones El Hábito.

Rose, Lloyd (2000) 'Washington, Bard to the Bone', in *The Washington Post*, 23 April.

Rosenberg, Marvin (1961) *The Masks of Othello*, Newark and London: University of Delaware Press and Associated University Presses.

Roth, C. (1932) *The History of the Marranos*, Philadelphia: Jewish Publication Society.

Rothschild, Thomas (1997) 'Die Wunde versteht das Messer: Juden auf Taboris Bühne', in J. Strümpel (ed.), *George Tabori, Text und Kritik*, 133: 4–10.

RSC Education (1993) *The Merchant of Venice*, Production Pack.

Rutter, Carol Chillington (2001) *Enter the Body: Women and Representation on Shakespeare's Stage*, London and New York: Routledge.

Ryan, P.M. (1994) *P.M.Ryan's Dictionary of Modern Maori*, Auckland: Heinemann Education.

Rychlý, Michal (2001–2) 'Personal Interview', *Zkrocení Zlé Ženy*, Producer, Letní Shakespearovské Slavnosti; Director, Agentura SCHOK.

Ryuta, M., I. Carruthers and J. Gillies (2001) *Performing Shakespeare in Japan*, Cambridge: Cambridge University Press.

Sachar, H. (1985) *Diaspora: An Inquiry into the Contemporary Jewish World*, New York: Harper and Row.

Sahlins, Marshall D. (2000) *Culture in Practice: Selected Essays*, New York: Zone Books.

Said, Edward W. (1983) *The World, the Text, and the Critic*, Cambridge, MA: Harvard University Press.

Salmond, Anne (1991) *Two Worlds: First Meetings between Maori and Europeans 1642–1772*, Auckland: Viking.

Salter, Denis (1996) 'Acting Shakespeare in Postcolonial Space', in J.C. Bulman (ed.) *Shakespeare, Theory, and Performance*, London and New York: Routledge, 113–32.

Santillanes, M. (1993) 'Flagging Culture Pride Endangers Future Hispanic Heritage', in *The Albuquerque Journal*, 10 July, A11.

Schenk, Otto (dir.) (1968–9) *Der Kaufmann von Venedig*, TV film, Germany.

Schoch, R. (1998) *Shakespeare's Victorian Stage: Performing History in the Theatre of Charles Kean*, Cambridge: Cambridge University Press.

Schödel, Helmut (1978) 'Der dreizehnfache Shylock', in *Die ZEIT*, 1 December.

Schülting, Sabine (2000) '*The Merchant of Venice:* Shylock geht – und immer kehrt er wieder', in *Interpretationen von Shakespeares Dramen*, Stuttgart: Reclam.

Schütze, Peter (1994) *Fritz Kortner*, Reinbek: Rowohlt.

Schwartz, B.D. (1992) *Pier Paolo Pasolini: Requiem*, New York: Pantheon.

Schwarz, Roberto (1999) *Seqüências brasileiras*, São Paulo: Companhia de Letras.

Scott, Dick (1975) *Ask that Mountain: the Story of Parihaka*, Auckland: Heinemann.

Scott, Michael (1989) *Shakespeare and the Modern Dramatist*, Basingstoke: Macmillan.

Scuro, Daniel (1995) '*Titus Andronicus:* A Crimson-Flushed Stage!', in P.C. Kolin (ed.) *Titus Andronicus: Critical Essays*, New York and London: Garland, 399–410.

Seaton, Ray (1978) 'What Shylock Meant To Say', in *The Express & Star*, 12 October.

Selwyn, Don C. (dir.) (2001) *Te Tangata Whai-Rawa o Weniti* [*The Maori Merchant of Venice*], He Taonga Films/Te Mangai Paho.

Serper, Z. (2000) 'The Bloodied Sacred Pine Tree: A Dialectical Depiction of Death in Kurosawa's *Throne of Blood* and *Ran*', in *Journal of Film and Video*, 52.2: 13–27.

Shurbanov, Alexander and Boika Sokolova (2001) *Painting Shakespeare Red: An East-European Appropriation*, New York and London: Associated University Presses.

Shuttleworth, Ian (1996) 'Playing Games with Hamlet', in *The Financial Times*, 21 November.

S.I.B. (2001) ‚Pojem ‚domácí násilí' má být v zákon' [The term 'domestic abuse' to appear in law], in *Lidové Noviny* [*The News of the Land*], 28 October, 11.

Siberry, Michael (1998) 'Petruchio in *The Taming of the Shrew*' (45–59), in Robert Smallwood (ed.) *Players of Shakespeare 4: Further Essays in Shakespearean Performance by Players with the Royal Shakespeare Company*, Cambridge: Cambridge University Press, 45–59.

Simon, John (1998) 'Parlous *Pericles*', in *New York*, 23 November.

Siti, Walter and Franco Zabagli (2001) *Pier Paolo Pasolini: Per il Cinema*, vol. I, Milano: Mondadori.

Sitta, Martin (2001) 'Personal Interviews', *Zkrocení Zlé Ženy*, Letní Shakespearovské Slavnosti, 15–28 August.

Skeele, David (1998) *Thwarting the Wayward Seas*, Newark: University of Delaware Press.

—— (ed.) (2000) *Pericles: Critical Essays*, New York and London: Garland.

Soja, E.W. (1996) *Thirdspace*, Oxford: Blackwell.

Sommers, Michael (1998) 'Stiff Production Lacks any Sense of Magic', in *Star-Ledger*, 12 November.

Soprová, Jana (1997) ‚Jak se krotí dáblice: Shakespearova hra pro Antifeministy' [How to tame a devil: Shakespeare's play for anti-feminists], *Večerník Praha* [*Evening Prague*], 1 December.

Špalková, Petra (2001–2) 'Personal Interviews', *Zkrocení Zlé Ženy* CD94, 31 August 2001; 13 June 2002.

Spencer, Charles (1996a) 'To Be or not to Be at Edinburgh Festival Depends on a Broken Rivet', in *The Daily Telegraph*, 15 August.

—— (1996b) 'When the Machinery Stops the Show', in *The Daily Telegraph*, 15 August.

—— (2002) 'Review of *A Midsummer Night's Dream*', in *The Daily Telegraph*, 23 February.

Spencer, T.J.B. (ed.) (1980) *Hamlet*, The New Penguin Shakespeare, London: Penguin.

Spoto, Donald (1991) *Laurence Olivier: A Biography*, London: Harper Collins.

Šrámková, Vítězslava (1997) ‚Kruté hry spolu lidé hrají' [People's cruel games], in *Týdeník Rozhlas* [*Radio Weekly*], no. 44, 27 October–2 November, 15.

Stallybrass, Peter (1999) 'Editing as Cultural Formation: The Sexing of Shakespeare's *Sonnets*', in Stephen Orgel and Sean Keilen (eds) *Shakespeare's Poems*, New York: Garland, 133–45.

Stanley-Baker, J. (1995) *Japanese Art*, London: Thames & Hudson.

Starzecka, D.C. (ed.) (1996) *Maori Art and Culture*, Auckland: David Bateman, in association with the British Museum Press.

Steinberg, D. (1993) '"Merchant of Sante Fe" adapts Shakespeare play for N.M.', in *The Albuquerque Journal*, 5 October, 12.

Štréblová, Alena (2002) 'Personal Interview', *Zkrocení Zlé Ženy*, Katherina, Komedie.

Stříbrný, Zdeněk (2000) *Shakespeare and Eastern Europe*, Oxford: Oxford University Press.

Strnisko, Vladimír (2001) 'Personal Interview', *Zkrocení Zlé Ženy*, Letní Shakespearovské Slavnosti, 9 August.

Stryk, L. (tr.) (1985) *On Love and Barley: Haiku of Basho*, Harmondsworth: Penguin.

Stryk, L. and T. Ikemoto (tr.) (1981) *The Penguin Book of Zen Poetry*, Harmondsworth: Penguin.

Sturua, Robert (2001–2) *Twelfth Night*: 'Programme Notes', Ivan Vazov National Theatre, Sofia.

Sutherland, John, and Cedric Watts (2000) *'Henry V, War Criminal?' and Other Shakespeare Puzzles*, Oxford: Oxford University Press.

Suzuki, D.T. (1973) *Zen and Japanese Culture*, Princeton: Princeton University Press.

S.V.E. (2001) ‚Násilníci napadají nejen svoje družky a manželky, ale i matky' [Abusers attack not only wives and partners, but also mothers], in *Mladá Fronta Dnes*, 21 February, 7.

Šverdík, Michal (2001) ‚Oběti domácího násilí maří trest' [Victims of domestic abuse thwart justice], in *Mladá Fronta Dnes [Young Front Today]* 12 December, 1.

Tabori, George (1979) *Ich wollte meine Tochter läge tot zu meinen Füßen und hätte die Juwelen in den Ohren: Improvisationen über Shakespeares Shylock. Dokumentation einer Theaterarbeit*, ed. by Andrea Welker and Tina Berger, Munich: Carl Hanser Verlag.

Tatlow, Antony (1995) '*Macbeth* and *Kunju* Opera', in *Shakespeare in Comparison*, Hong Kong: Hong Kong University Press, 169–201.

Taylor, Gary (1999) 'Afterword: The Incredibly Shrinking Bard', in C. Desmet and R. Sawyer (eds.) *Shakespeare and Appropriation*, London and New York: Routledge, 197–205.

Taylor, P. (2002) 'Review of *A Midsummer Night's Dream*', in *The Independent*, 7 June.

Thaxter, J. (2002) 'Review of *A Midsummer Night's Dream*', in *What's On*, 1 May.

Thompson, Ann (ed.) (2003) *The Taming of the Shrew*, The New Cambridge Shakespeare, Cambridge: Cambridge University Press.

Thornber, Robert (1978) 'Merchant', in *The Guardian*, 15 October.

Tichý, Zdeněk (1997) ‚Krotit Špalkovou se vyplácí' [Taming of Špalková worth the effort], in *Mladá Fronta Dnes [Young Front Today]*, 10 October, 19.

Tobias, H. (1990) *A History of the Jews in New Mexico*, Albuquerque: University of New Mexico.

Treat Paine, R. and A. Soper (1974) *The Art and Architecture of Japan*, Harmondsworth: Penguin.

Trim, Peter (2000) *Black Kings Red Queens*, Waikanae: Reikorangi Books.

Trivedi, Harish and Susan Bassnett (eds) (1999) *Post-colonial Translation: Theory and Practice*, London: Routledge.

Trivedi, Poonam (2002) 'Shakespeare on the Stages of Asia', in Stanley Wells and Sarah Stanton (eds) *The Cambridge Companion to Shakespeare on Stage*, Cambridge: Cambridge University Press, 259–83.

—— (2003) 'Reading Other Shakespeares', in Pascale Aebischer, Edward J. Esche and Nigel Wheale (eds) *Remaking Shakespeare: Performance Across Media, Genres and Cultures*, Basingstoke: Palgrave, 56–73.

Trivedi, Poonam and Dennis Bartholomeusz (eds) (2005) *India's Shakespeare: Translation, Interpretation and Performance*, Newark: University of Delware Press.

Tsolov, Dimiter (2001) 'An Autumnal Theatre View', in *Bulgarski pisatel*, 7 November, 10.

Urbanová, Alena (1997) ‚Rozverné hravé krocení zlé Ženy v Činoherním Klubu' [High-spirited and playful *Taming of the Shrew* in Klub], in *Denní Telegraf [The Daily Telegraph]*, no. 234, 6 October, 13.

Vasileva, Krasimira (2001) 'An Old-fashioned Legend for a Lot of Money', in *Literaturen forum*, 22 May, 2001.

Vickers, Brian (2002) *Shakespeare, Co-Author*, Oxford: Oxford University Press.

Viswanathan, Gauri (1990) *Masks of Conquest: Literary Study and British Colonial Rule in India*, London: Faber.

'VJD' (1977) 'Review of *A Midsummer Night's Dream*', in *The Evesham Journal & Four Shires Advertiser*, 12 May.

Vlastník, Jiří (2000), Česko-Slovenské krocení zlé ženy' [Czech-Slovak taming of a mean woman], in *Kladenský Deník* [*The Daily of Kadno*], 25 May.

Walcott, Derek (1986) *Three Plays: The Last Carnival; Beef, No Chicken; A Branch of the Blue Nile*, New York: Farrar, Straus & Giroux.

—— (1993a) *The Antilles: Fragments of Epic Memory*, London: Faber.

—— (1993b) 'Meanings (1970)', in Robert Hamner (ed.) *Critical Perspectives on Derek Walcott*, Washington: Three Continents Press, 45–50.

Walkley, A.B. (1914) 'Review of *A Midsummer Night's Dream*', in *The Times*, 7 February.

Walser, Martin (1998) *Erfahrungen beim Verfassen einer Sonntagsrede. Rede zum Friedenspreis des Deutschen Buchhandels 1998*, Frankfurt/Main: Suhrkamp.

Ward, David (1994) 'A Genial Analytic Mind: "Film" and "Cinema" in Pier Paolo Pasolini's Film Theory', in P. Rumble and B. Testa (eds) *Pier Paolo Pasolini: Contemporary Perpectives*, Toronto: University of Toronto Press, 127–51.

—— (1999) 'Pier Paolo Pasolini and the Events of May 1968: The "Manifesto per un Nuovo Teatro"', in Z.G. Barański (ed.) *Pasolini Old and New: Surveys and Studies*, Dublin: Four Courts Press, 321–44.

Ward, Stuart (1978) 'The Interview: Wesker', in *Polygon*, October.

Wardle, I. (1977) 'Review of *A Midsummer Night's Dream*', in *The Daily Telegraph*, 9 May.

Wayne, Valerie (2004) 'Review of *Te Tangata Whai-Rawa o Weniti*', in *The Contemporary Pacific*, 16: 425–9.

Weber, Ulrich and Anna von Planta (1994) *Friedrich Dürrenmatt: Schriftsteller und Maler*, Zürich: Diogenes.

Weiß, Wolfgang (1995) ' "Spielt das Stück nicht mehr": Über die Schwierigkeiten im Umgang mit einer Komödie', in William Shakespeare, *Der Kaufmann von Venedig*, bilingual edition, transl. by Frank Günther, Munich: dtv, 260–79.

Welch, David (1983) *Propaganda and the German Cinema, 1933–1945*, Oxford: Clarendon Press.

Wells, Stanley and Gary Taylor (1986) *The Complete Works*, Oxford: Clarendon Press.

Wesker, Arnold (1990) *The Journalists; The Wedding Feast; Shylock*, Penguin Plays, vol. 4, London: Penguin.

—— (1993) 'A Nasty Piece of Work', in *The Sunday Times*, 6 June.

—— (1997) *The Birth of Shylock and the Death of Zero Mostel: Diary of a Play 1973 to 1980*, London: Quartet Books.

Williams, G.J. (1997) *Our Moonlight Revels: A Midsummer Night's Dream in the Theatre*, Iowa City: University of Iowa Press.

Williams, S. (1990) *Shakespeare on the German Stage, 1586–1914*, vol. 1, Cambridge: Cambridge University Press.

Willson, R.F. (2000) *Shakespeare in Hollywood, 1929-1956*, Madison, NJ: Fairleigh Dickinson University Press.

Wippermann, Wolfgang (1997) *Wessen Schuld? Vom Historikerstreit zur Goldhagen-Kontroverse*, Berlin: Elefanten Press.

Witznitzer, A. (1962) 'Crypto-Jews in Mexico during the Sixteenth Century', *Publications of the American Jewish Historical Society*, 51, reprinted in M. Cohen (ed.) (1971), *The Jewish Experience in Latin America: Selected Studies from the Publications of the American Jewish Historical Society*, New York: Ktav Publishing House, 88–132.

Worthen, W.B. (1997) *Shakespeare and the Authority of Performance*, Cambridge: Cambridge University Press.

Wylie, Neville (2003) *Britain, Switzerland and the Second World War*, Oxford: Oxford University Press.

Yachnin, Paul (2001) ' "To Kill a King": The Modern Politics of Bardicide', in Michael Bristol and Kathleen McLuskie with Christopher Holmes (eds) *Shakespeare and Modern Theatre: The Performance of Modernity*, London and New York: Routledge, 36–54.

Yamamoto, H. (1999) 'The Originality of Kurosawa's *Throne of Blood*', in T. Anzai, I. Soji, H. Klein and P. Milward (eds) *Shakespeare in Japan*, Lewiston: Edwin Mellen, 148–58.

Yu Weijie (1990) 'Topicality and Typicality: The Acceptance of Shakespeare in China', in Erika Fischer-Lichte, Josephine Riley and Michael Gissenwehrer (eds) *The Dramatic Touch of Difference: Theatre, Own and Foreign*, Tübingen: Narr, 161–7.

Zadek, Peter (dir.) (1988) *Der Kaufmann von Venedig*, Video, Wiener Burgtheater.

Zambrano, A.L. (1974) '*Throne of Blood:* Kurosawa's *Macbeth*', in *Literature/Film Quarterly*, 2.3: 262–74.

Zhang Xiaoyang (1996) 'Shakespeare on the Chinese Stage', in *Shakespeare in China: A Comparative Study of Two Traditions and Cultures*, Newark and London: University of Delaware Press and Associated University Presses, 130–72.

Zhongguo Xiqu Yanjiuyuan [The National Institute of Traditional Chinese Drama] (ed.) (1982) '*Xian qing ou ji* [Occasional Notes at Leisure Time]', in *Zhongguo gudian xiqu lunzhu jicheng* [*Collection of Works on Chinese Classical Dramatic Theory*], 10 vols, vol. 7, Beijing: Zhongguo Xiju Chubanshe.

Zídek, Petr (2001) ‚Diskriminováni jsou muži' [Men's discrimination], in *Lidové Noviny* [*The News of the People*], 10 October, 3.

Zimmerman, R. (1993) 'Play Gives Shakespeare a Crypto-Jewish Twist', in *The Link*, 22: 8 September, 12.

Index

Related titles from Routledge

Accents on Shakespeare Series

General Editor: Terence Hawkes

Books in the *Accents on Shakespeare* series provide short, powerful, 'cutting-edge' accounts of and comments on new developments in the field of Shakespeare studies. In addition to titles aimed at modular undergraduate courses, it also features a number of spirited and committed research-based books.

The *Accents on Shakespeare* series features contributions from leading figures and the books include:

Shakespeare and Appropriation
Edited by Christy Desmet and Robert Sawyer

Shakespeare Without Women
Dympna Callaghan

Philosophical Shakespeares
Edited by John J. Joughin

Shakespeare and Modernity
Early Modern to Millennium
Edited by Hugh Grady

Marxist Shakespeares
Edited by Jean E. Howard and Scott Cutler Shershow

Shakespeare in Psychoanalysis
Philip Armstrong

Shakespeare and Modern Theatre
The Performance of Modernity
Edited by Michael Bristol and Kathleen McLuskie

Shakespeare and Feminist Performance
Ideology on Stage
Sarah Werner

Shame in Shakespeare
Ewan Fernie

The Sound of Shakespeare
Wes Folkerth

Shakespeare in the Present
Terence Hawkes

Making Shakespeare
Tiffany Stern

Available at all good bookshops

For a full series listing, ordering details and further information please visit:
www.routledge.com